# ciao italia
# family classics

# Also by Mary Ann Esposito

Ciao Italia Five-Ingredient Favorites

Ciao Italia Slow and Easy

Ciao Italia Pronto!

Ciao Italia in Tuscany

Ciao Italia in Umbria

Ciao Italia: Bringing Italy Home

Ciao Italia

Nella Cucina

Celebrations Italian Style

What You Knead

Mangia Pasta!

more than
200 treasured recipes
from three generations
of italian cooks

ᘒᘒᘒ

# ciao italia
# family classics

## Mary Ann Esposito

### PHOTOGRAPHS BY JOHN HESSION

St. Martin's Press
New York

CIAO ITALIA FAMILY CLASSICS. Copyright © 2011 by Mary Ann Esposito. All rights reserved. Printed in China. For information, address St. Martin's Press, 175 Fifth Avenue, New York, N.Y. 10010.

www.stmartins.com

*Photographs by John Hession*

*Design by Kathryn Parise*

*Production Manager: Adriana Coada*

ISBN 978-0-312-57121-4

First Edition: October 2011

10  9  8  7  6  5  4  3  2  1

For Nonna Anna Cerullo Galasso, Nonna Maria

Assunta Ferro Saporito, and my mother,

Louisa Florence Galasso Saporito.

Three wise women whose reverence for the foods

of Italy lives on in these pages.

# contents

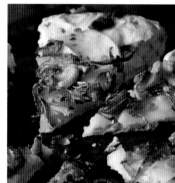

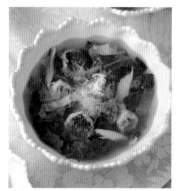

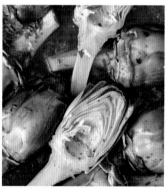

You may have the universe if I may have Italy.

—Giuseppe Verdi's *Attila*

# introduction

everything I know about the traditions of real Italian cooking came not from any stint in culinary school but from three wise, clever, and strong-minded women with humble beginnings: my two southern Italian grandmothers (nonnas), Maria Assunta Saporito, born in Caltanissetta, Sicily, and Anna Cerullo Galasso, born in the little town of Bellizzi, near Naples, and my mother, Louise Florence Saporito, who was a second generation Italian American and the only one of the three who had a formal education. You could say that they lived by their wits and common sense and that was what made them wise. They have all passed on and even though there is no one left in my family to talk to about all the foods that I grew up with and that forever identify me as Italian American, I am left with a deep and persistent need to carry on where they left off.

Each of these women found a way to make cooking a profession. This was, of course, in addition to what was expected of them as housewives of their generation. Nonna Saporito, tall, feisty, and opinionated, became a butcher and had her own butcher shop in Fairport, New York. As a girl, I would spend my school vacations with her, helping her with customer orders. I still have her handmade cleaver with the chestnut wooden handle that she wielded with the grace of a symphony conductor and the force of an ace baseball pitcher when she was cutting meat and chicken.

Nonna Galasso, short, spiritual, and deliberate, ran a boarding house after my grandfather Carmen, a tailor, was tragically killed in an accident. Left with eight children, she cooked her way to prosperity, such as it was. Having the only bathtub in town, she offered patrons a meal and a bath for twenty-five cents. People stood in line outside her door for hours.

My mother, petite, determined, outspoken, generous to a fault, and with fire-red hair, had all the pressing household duties of most women of her generation as well as providing for my father, seven children, and Nonna Galasso, for whom she became the sole caregiver. In her mid-fifties she decided to become a dietician, validating her goal of becoming someone who had a career outside the home.

Growing up in a small town in western New York, it was difficult not to be drawn into a solely southern Italian lifestyle surrounded not only by family members speaking in Neapolitan dialect but also by many of their friends from the old country who lived nearby in a clustered Little Italy where the air was permeated with the smells of simmering tomato sauce and homemade bread. Nonna Galasso's friends spent hours in our kitchen discussing the merits of everything from boiling cardoons to where to buy the best squid. So determined were they to hang on to their traditions that no trek was too great for finding such things as the best fresh eggs, even if it meant walking a mile to purchase them from "the chicken man" so that they could make *maccarun* (macaroni).

Looking back, my favorite day of the week was Sunday because the preparations for dinner started early Saturday morning with bread being made by my mother at her thick maple butcher-block baking center that commanded almost battleship space in the kitchen. Along with bread she would make something sweet for Sunday morning breakfast like fluffy cinnamon rolls, dense with raisins, lots of cinnamon, and the silkiest and most luscious-tasting lemon confectioners' glaze that gave them a truly professional pastry shop look. And she wouldn't stop there because a towering, airy sponge cake was a must for Sunday dessert. The smells coming from that kitchen were so good, they were almost hypnotic, and the anticipation would build all day Saturday for Sunday's meal. Memories like these have stayed with me my whole life and many of them have been preserved in the eleven cookbooks that I have written over the course of twenty years on the subject of regional Italian food. So what is left to say? *Plenty.*

I like to think of this book as a continuing journey into the world of Italian cooking and culinary traditions, past, present, and future. Past because it contains many favorite recipes from home that I want to pass on not only to my family but also to anyone who is passionate about good homemade food. Present because after more than twenty years as the host of *Ciao Italia* on PBS, it has been my goal to keep our loyal viewers informed about changing food trends and how classic Italian ingredients are being adapted for use in today's kitchen. Truthfully, I am both a traditionalist and a minimalist when it comes to cooking. I like the best ingredients to shine on their own, and I am very much against any adulteration or tinkering with any of Italy's core products. Future because as I continue my culinary travels through the regions of Italy, armed with the knowledge my nonnas and mother instilled in me, I have felt right at home cooking in Italian kitchens alongside many chefs and home cooks, who like me want to preserve the essence of Italian home cooking, which is and always will be the quality and integrity of the ingredients simply prepared by the gentle hands of a cook in tune with seasonal foods. That message became the motto of the Slow Food movement that started in Bra in 1986 in the Piedmont region and is now spreading worldwide. I continue to learn that food trends will always come and go, but the crux of what constitutes Italian food is forever rooted in the traditions of the past.

And the past can teach us much about the future of our food supply. When I travel the back roads of Italy with its gorgeous vistas of vineyards, vegetable gardens, and fruit orchards, I hope that this form of artisan farming will survive in a world where many family-run farms are disappearing not only in Italy but here as well. And as I get older, I am grateful that I was exposed at an early age to home gardening at the backdoor so to speak, where Nonna Galasso had her little patch of mint, beans, and tomatoes.

Home cooking is disappearing, too, at an even faster pace as busy lives dictated by relentless schedules swallow us up like a vast black hole. Fears about nutrition have gripped our attention with concerns about the safety of the foods we consume, where they come from, and the pesticides and chemicals they have been exposed to. These are legitimate worries and a great argument for becoming informed about our food supply, getting back into the kitchen, and bringing families back to the table.

In my grandmothers' day putting a meal on the table was arduous work because everything was done from scratch. No immersion blenders, food processors, or bread machines speeded the process. And yet today with all the cooking gadgets at our disposal, and the myriad of choices in the supermarket, making a meal seems for many of us too time-consuming, too daunting, and just too bothersome.

How do we bring back family meals? First we must realize the importance of eating together. This is a quintessentially Italian concept. It's not primarily about the food, it's what the food can lead us to—conversation, togetherness, reassurance, and relaxation. Anyone who has ever shared a meal in an Italian home can attest to long happy hours at the table. Second we need to teach children about good food, where it comes from, and how to make healthy choices that will continue into their adult lives. That means taking the time to involve them in the cooking process. I have to say that as a kid, I hated being in the kitchen trimming beans, making pasta, and washing dishes, but all those chores connected me in an intimate way not only to the food but also to the people who prepared it, and it led me to where I am today. Third, and this is a tough one, we need to try to have as many meals as possible together. Even if you can only have one or two sit-down meals during the week, it is a start.

I recognize that people's lives are complicated; everyone is working, maybe two jobs, schedules conflict, sports interfere. Somewhere along the way someone instituted the thirty-minute time limit for getting dinner on the table and many bought into it, as if more time spent on making and enjoying a meal was actually a nuisance. Ironically statistics tell us that the average adult watches close to four hours of television a day! Wouldn't that time be better spent in the kitchen? The bottom line is that you have to eat so why not eat wisely by cooking well. The recipes in this book can help you do that.

When we cook, we are empowered because we are in control of how our foods are selected and prepared. What is that kind of power worth to you? How could you measure its worth in terms of your and your family's health? Could you set aside one weekend day and devote it to cooking several healthy meals for the week? You could feel a lot less stressed knowing that at the end of a workday you can open the refrigerator and dinner will be waiting for you!

The recipes in this book represent traditional everyday foods that I regard as culinary royalty, always admired, imitated, respected, and passed down through generations. Three wise women were the guiding inspiration for this book as well as my love for all things Italian. If I can inspire you to prepare and cook the way they did, then wisdom is passed on and the past is preserved for the future.

# italian pantry basics

If I could walk into Nonna Saporito's pantry or Nonna Galasso's fruit cellar today, I would find the genius behind their everyday cooking, which was based on having key staple ingredients available at all times. My pantry is a lot like theirs, albeit with a few more indulgent ingredients like *aceto balsamico tradizionale* (artisan-made traditional balsamic vinegar) and dried porcini mushrooms, but in general, what they cooked with, I cook with today and so should you if you want to re-create the flavors of Italian cooking. The list below will get you started but is by no means a complete list; you can always add other ingredients that you use frequently.

**Anchovies.** Anchovies packed in olive oil and anchovy paste can make a pound of pasta sing as well as provide a depth of added flavor to vegetables and sauces.

**Arborio, Carnaroli, or Vialone Nano.** These short-grain, starchy northern Italy rice varieties are necessary for making creamy risottos, rice balls *(arancine)*, and other traditional Italian dishes.

**Beans.** Keep either canned or dried cannellini, fava, chickpea, and lupini beans in your pantry; these are essential in soups and for antipasti and salads.

**Capers.** Usually packed in salt or brine, capers are the unopened flower buds of a plant that grows in the Mediterranean; they add pungency to sauces for fish, meat, and vegetables.

**Cornmeal.** You will need good-quality stone-ground cornmeal for making polenta and for use in breads, cookies, and cakes. Regular yellow or white cornmeal is fine, too, but does not have the same texture as the stone-ground.

**Dried fruits.** Figs, dates, raisins, and candied fruit peels such as orange and lemon are frequently used in baking. Dried citron is also a favorite in many Italian confections such as Neapolitan rice pie.

**Flour.** Keep several kinds on hand like all-purpose, unbleached flour for making fresh pasta, and bread, pastry, cake, caputo, and semolina flour. If you use a lot of flour, keep it in the refrigerator to prevent it from attracting bugs.

**Garlic.** Use only fresh, heavy, tight-papered heads and keep them in a cool, dark, airy place. Do not buy prepared jarred garlic; the flavor is nothing like fresh and will kill the taste of what you are preparing.

**Grains.** Use barley, farro, and wheat berries for soups, stews, and casseroles as well as fillers for vegetables.

**Herbs.** Dried oregano is the only herb I use in its dried state because of its more pronounced flavor. Other herbs that I always use fresh include flat-leaf parsley, basil, thyme, mint, marjoram, rosemary, and sage.

**Lentils.** These tiny lens-shaped dried legumes are used in Italian soups, served as an accompaniment to sausage, and are served on their own.

**Marinated vegetables.** Jarred and marinated vegetables such as olives in brine, red sweet bell peppers, and artichoke hearts all add interest to antipasti and can be used in main dishes and salads.

**Mushrooms.** Wild, dried porcini are used for sauces, in soups and stews, and with braised meats and polenta. When reconstituted they have a meaty texture and woodsy flavor.

**Nuts.** Almonds, pine nuts, hazelnuts, and walnuts are the nuts most frequently used in Italian baked goods, stuffings, and breads. Like flour, once they are opened, store them in the refrigerator.

**Olive oil.** The cornerstone of Italian cooking, olive oil is used for everything from light sautéeing to mixing into salads to drizzling over meats, vegetables, and fish. There are many regional types. They range from thick green to pale gold in color, and from spicy and dense to fruity and light in flavor. Be sure to read the labels; extra virgin means the first, cold pressing and less than 1 percent oleic acid. Store olive oil in a cool, dark place. Don't keep it longer than a year, after which it may become rancid.

**Onions.** Common yellow onions, as well as red onions and small onions called *cippoline,* are essential to most Italian cooking. Store them like garlic.

**Pasta.** Dried pastas made from semolina, a hard wheat durum flour, range in types from small cuts for soup like ditalini or orzo to short cuts like rigatoni and penne to longer cuts like spaghetti and pappardelle.

**Sardines.** Small canned fish packed in olive oil are used to make sauces or as a flavor base for many dishes.

**Tomato paste.** Add to soups, stews, and sauces. Hot red pepper paste is great when you want to add a little heat to a dish.

**Tomatoes.** Stock canned plum San Marzano tomatoes for making sauces or adding to stews and soups.

**Tuna.** Use good-quality tuna packed in olive oil for tossing with pasta or as part of an antipasto.

**Vinegars.** Use white, red wine, and commercially made balsamic vinegars for salads, deglazing pans, and boosting flavor. Traditional balsamic vinegar *(aceto balsamico tradizionale)* is made in Modena and aged in wooden barrels. It is very concentrated and should be used as a condiment, never in cooking. It is usually drizzled over Parmigiano-Reggiano cheese slivers or served over fresh strawberries and figs. Its flavor is intense, its color dark, and its consistency that of syrup.

**Yeast.** For pizza and bread, include Fleischmann's pizza crust yeast, active dry yeast, and rapid rise yeast in your pantry. Yeast should be stored in the refrigerator.

## WHERE'S MY CHEESE?

Let's face it: artisan-made imported Italian cheeses are expensive. But the good thing is that you only need a little bit to enjoy on its own or make the dish you are preparing truly sing. What I want to stress to you is that imitation cheese has no place in any of the recipes in this book. And there are many imitations out there, so beware! My best advice is to always buy Italian cheeses cut from the wheel. That is your guarantee that you are getting an authentic product because the markings on the rinds will identify them. If you buy grated cheese, or cheese with no markings, you might be paying top dollar for imitation cheese.

There are many regional Italian cheeses available, but the two most popular aged cheeses found in American kitchens are Parmigiano-Reggiano and pecorino. There are also fresh cheeses like mozzarella and ricotta that are used frequently in many of the recipes in this book. You will find more detailed descriptions of pecorino cheese on page 8 and Parmigiano-Reggiano on page 10.

Here are some others that I like to use, but by no means are these all of them! The last time I checked there were well over four hundred types of Italian cheese. Thirty-nine of those cheeses have been given DOP status according to the 2010 GAIN (Global Agricultural Information Network) report. Some of the cheeses listed here have been granted DOP status by the European Union. DOP means *Denominazione Origine Protetta* and indicates food products with particular characteristics that are made in a particular geographic location with specific ingredients and time-tested methods. The EU guarantees their authenticity against competing imitations sold as Italian products. Not every cheese receives this designation.

**Asiago.** A straw-yellow color, asiago is a semihard cow's milk cheese from the Veneto region. It has a dark glossy blackish coating and is similar to Swiss cheese with many tiny holes. It has a nutty flavor. There are two types: Pressato, which is fresh and mild in flavor with a whitish color, and mature Asiago d'Allevo, which is yellow and has a grainy texture. This is a great table cheese as well as when used in cooking. This cheese is called *mezzano* at six months of aging, *vecchio* at one year, and *stravecchio* after two years.

**Burrata.** A type of mozzarella made in Puglia that is filled with cream and bits of mozzarella that is very soft and delicate. It is best eaten on its own with some crusty bread.

**Fontina.** A semisoft white cow's milk cheese with a brownish rind from the Val d'Aosta in northern Italy. It is a great melting cheese. One of its classic uses is for *fonduta* (Italian fondue). It is also a great cheese for making a creamy sauce.

**Gorgonzola dolce.** A cow's milk cheese from Lombardy, Gorgonzola dolce is a blue cheese with a sharp taste that makes it a wonderful eating cheese but also good in fillings and sauces. There is also a drier, crumblier version called Gorgonzola *piccante* or *forte.*

**Montasio.** A cow's milk cheese from Friuli, Montasio is available fresh, semi-aged, and aged. It is made from two milkings and is partially skimmed. It was originally made by monks. When fresh it is soft and delicate tasting. As it ages it becomes sharper in taste. A great cheese to accompany fruit, especially pears.

**Mozzarella di bufala.** From the region of Campania, mozzarella di bufala is made from buffalo milk, while fior di late is made from cow's milk. Both these cheeses belong to the pasta filata family of cheeses. Pasta filata is a term that means "spun paste" because the curds are stretched by hand and formed into a soft, fresh cheese that is very perishable and best eaten as the Italians say *"da giornata"* (the day it is made).

**Pecorino.** A name given to cheese made from sheep's milk, Pecorino comes from the word *pecora* for sheep. It has been produced for centuries as is evidenced by a reference to it by Lucio Columella, an important writer on Roman agriculture, who wrote the fifteenth century treatise *De Re Rustica*:

> The milk is usually curdled with lamb or kid rennet, though one can use wild thistle blossoms, càrtame, or fig sap. The milk bucket, when it is filled, must be kept warm, though it mustn't be set by the fire, as some would, nor must it be set too far from it, and as soon as the

curds form they must be transferred to baskets or molds: Indeed, it's essential that the whey be drained off and separated from the solid matter immediately. It is for this reason that the farmers don't wait for the whey to drain away a drop at a time, but put a weight on the cheese as soon as it has firmed up, thus driving out the rest of the whey. When the cheese is removed from the baskets or molds, it must be placed in a cool dark place lest it spoil, on perfectly clean boards, covered with salt to draw out its acidic fluids.

There are many types of this cheese; some are aged longer than others, some are flavored with peppercorns, hot red pepper, black truffles, or other ingredients. Sheep's milk used to make the cheese is mixed with rennet to help coagulate it and form the famous curds, which are pressed into cylindrical shapes and salted.

Pecorino cheese is made between November and late June. It is available as fresh (*fresco*), semihard (*semi-staginato*), and hard (*staginato*). The longer the cheese ages the saltier and harder it will become. When young it is an excellent table cheese and as it ages it makes an excellent grating cheese.

Depending on where the cheese is made in Italy it will have a place of origin attached to it, such as pecorino Romano (often called Locatelli) from the Lazio region. There are characteristic differences in the regional varieties of this cheese, including breed of sheep, grasses they feed on, and method of production.

**Pecorino Romano.** This cheese is straw-white in color, quite salty, and hard, and is mainly a grating cheese as opposed to being a table cheese. It was the cheese that most Italian immigrants used.

**Pecorino Sardo.** This cheese is made exclusively from a breed of sheep raised on inland mountainsides where they feed on certain herbs.

**Pecorino Toscano.** Milder than Pecorino Romano, Pecorino Toscano is used primarily as a table cheese. The wonderful town of Pienza is famous for its production of pecorino cheese and produces many flavored varieties including those studded with flecks of black truffles and those whose rinds have been coated with wine must.

**Provolone.** This cow's milk cheese is made in the southern and northern regions of Italy. The curds are made from a morning and an evening milking and are kneaded until they are firm and shaped into cylindrical form. Pale yellow in color when young, the cheese darkens with age and becomes sharper in taste. Provolone is also a pasta filata–type cheese.

**Ricotta.** The name ricotta means recooked, and the cheese is made by reheating the whey that is drained off from the curds during the cheese-making process. As the cheese forms it is scooped into plastic baskets and allowed to drain. It is used as a filling for everything from pasta to tarts.

**Scamorza.** This cheese is a drier type of cow's milk mozzarella that is often smoked (*scamorza affumicata*). It is often formed into animal shapes.

## PARMIGIANO-REGGIANO

If I could be offered only one cheese in a lifetime, it would have to be Parmigiano-Reggiano, or what Americans call "parmesan." The creation of this cheese is the pride of the region of Emilia Romagna; it is the king of the table. Making this exquisite cow's milk cheese by hand goes back more than eight centuries and the process has not changed much in all that time, and to witness the actual "birth" of this region's most famous product is a rare experience. Each time that I have been privileged to do so, I am in awe of the elements of nature and man working in harmony to create such a unique artisan product.

So it was with great excitement early one morning that I found myself an invited guest to one of the six-hundred cheese houses (*casefici*) in the region to learn about the process. My destination was Baganzolino, a half hour's drive from my hotel in Soragna.

Parmigiano-Reggiano is made every day from raw cow's milk from both an evening and a morning milking. Strict rules surround its production. Only the provinces of Reggio Emilia, Parma, Modena, Bologna (west of the Reno River), and Mantua (east of the Po River) are authorized to make the cheese. Cows must be fed only chemical-free grasses that come from these designated areas. The quality of the raw ingredients along with ideal soil and climatic conditions are the conduits for making Parmigiano-Reggiano. But there is also another element that cannot be overlooked, the ability of human hands to turn these raw materials into this superior cheese.

Once the milk is obtained, it is heated in huge copper cauldrons that look like inverted gigantic church bells. Whey from the previous morning's milking is added along with calf's rennet. This coagulates the milk in about twelve to eighteen minutes and forms the cheese curds. A huge wire whisk is used to break up the curds into pea-size pieces. These tiny pieces are allowed to set, and as they do they form a solid mass, which is brought up from the base of the cauldron with a large wooden paddle. The curds are cut in half to make two cheeses known as *"gemelli"* (twins). They are placed in round wooden molds. A stamped plate with pin dots spelling Parmigiano-Reggiano, and indicating which cheese house made it, and the month and year of production, is placed between the cheese and the mold. This will leave an impression of the words on the rind as it ages, and gives the maker and the buyer an historical record of the cheese's beginning and authenticity. After three days of being in the molds, the cheese is added to a salt brine where it is turned often and aged for twenty-four days. Next comes the aging process, which takes place in the maturing room where the large wheels are stacked on wooden shelves. Wheels age for an average of two years, during which time cheese testers using special hammers tap the entire surface of the cheese to make sure that it makes a uniform sound, or as the cheesemaker puts it, the cheese must make its own fine music, and if it does not, it is rejected. Testers also look for uniform color, pleasant smell, and no gaping holes in the interior. As the cheese ages, amino acids begin to form, which crystalize into tiny white dots visible when the cheese is cut open. These grainy bits give Parmigiano-Reggiano its unique texture. Only when the governing body, the Consorzio del Formaggio Parmigiano Reggiano, gives its approval that the cheese has passed all the criteria, the wheels are stamped with the oval seal that signifies that it is worthy to take its place in the world market-place.

Watching the grand opening of a wheel being cut is almost a spiritual experience. Anticipation builds and silence falls as my eyes are riveted on the cheese tester, who uses a special almond knife to score the eighty-five pound wheels across their diameter and down both sides. The wheel is turned over and the line is completed on the other side. Then a half-inch deep cut is made along the cutting line all around the wheel with a hooked rind cutter. Next a pointed spatula knife is inserted into the center of the top line. Almond-shaped knives are positioned diagonally into opposite corners of the wheel as the cheese tester grasps them and pushes one forward and the other backward to pry the wheel open. After watching this tedious process, I have infinitely more respect for buying a wedge of Parmigiano-Reggiano already cut into wedges in my local supermarket. When the interior texture is revealed, it is rough with peaks and valleys like the surface of jagged stone mountains, and its sunny yellow color and aroma fill one's senses.

Tasting its delicate flavor right in the cheese house was an unforgettable experience, and for those accustomed to purchasing those boxes of what can only be deemed artificial "parmesan" from the supermarket shelves, this comes as true enlightenment.

Parmigiano-Reggiano is a near perfect food, low in fat and sodium, high in calcium, and full of vitamins and other minerals. No wonder it was chosen as the cheese to send into space with Russian cosmonauts. Luckily we need not go that far since it is available in supermarkets and specialty food stores.

## ODE TO OLIVE OIL

"His Holiness would like the olive oil sent to the Vatican." So goes the traditional papal request for extra-virgin olive oil from Umbria. For centuries even popes recognized and appreciated the superiority of the olive oil from trees in this region and paid farmers to plant them on the middle hills, and in the chalky soil of the Umbrian countryside. To this day, Umbrian olive oil still graces the table in the Vatican, and is considered some of the best in Italy. But even before popes recognized its worth, it was held in high regard in biblical times, and its branches became a symbol of peace for the world. The ancient Etruscans, Greeks, and Romans understood olive oil's worthiness for culinary purposes, but its use also extended to oil for their lamps, for rubbing on the body, and for sale as a profitable trading product.

Yet in the American kitchen, the role of olive oil is misunderstood; confusion reigns as to whether to cook with extra-virgin, virgin, or pomace! Should one cook with extra-virgin olive oil or reserve it solely for dressing salads? Can it be used to deep fry foods? Which is the best one to buy? Where should I store it?

I have been cooking with low-acidity extra-virgin olive oil for years and I know what I like: fruity olive oil for salads, and peppery olive oil for sautéing. Selecting olive oil is a lot like selecting a bottle of wine; it can be a daunting task, but if you know what you like, the job becomes easier, and just as there are hundreds of wines to choose from, so, too, the dilemma exists in the multiple choices for olive oil.

Everything is dependent on your palate and whether or not you like fruity, dense, spicy, mild, or peppery as a flavor characteristic. The best way to determine this is to sample different types of olive oils from various regions of Italy. Generally speaking, the further south one travels in Italy, the fruitier, denser, and greener the oil will be, and as one travels north the oil is lighter in color, less dense, and milder. By definition, and by Italian law, extra-virgin olive oil must not contain more that one-percent acidity; the oil must come from the first pressing of the olives, and no heat can be used to extract the oil. Only then is an olive oil characterized as extra-virgin. Other grades have higher amounts of acidity and may come from multiple pressings. In the case of pomace, which is the pulp that remains after several pressings of the olives, any remaining oil is extracted with the use of solvents. This oil is refined and blended with a small percentage of virgin olive oil (higher acidity), and sold at much cheaper prices, but in my estimation, you get what you pay for.

My suggestion is for you to try several extra-virgin olive oils from different regions of Italy. To really taste test olive oil correctly, take a sip and roll it around in your mouth. Do not swallow yet! Taste it at the tip of your tongue, the roof of your mouth, the center of the tongue, and the back of the tongue. Now swallow it for a throat "finish." The different areas of the mouth will produce a variety of tastes, like nutty, peppery, heavy, intense, light, sweet, earthy, grassy, and buttery. If you follow this technique, you will come to appreciate the many properties of olive oil. Find them in Italian grocery stores and on the Internet.

Last, a word about storing olive oil; it is best to keep it in a cool, dark place, not in the refrigerator where temperature extremes can affect its flavor, and only buy enough to use up in a short period of time. Olive oil is best used within a year of its purchase, otherwise it could become rancid. Following these guidelines will ensure that you will be using and enjoying olive oil according to Italian tradition.

However, there are other good oils to try from the Italian pantry shelf, including the following:

**Walnut oil.** Especially popular in the Piedmont and Val d'Aosta regions of Italy where olive trees do not grow, walnut oil is a polyunsaturated fat and a good source of omega-3. It has a high smoke point of 400°F so it is good for frying or baking.

**Peanut oil.** A monounsaturated fat with a medium smoke point of 350°F, use this flavorful oil for light sautéing.

**Sunflower oil.** A polyunsaturated fat with a low-saturated fat level, this oil has a high smoke point of 460°F, making it good for high-heat cooking, like sautéing and frying.

**Canola oil.** Pressed from canola seeds, it is monounsaturated, low in acidity, and good for deep frying.

## A FEW WORDS ABOUT SALT

There seems to be so much confusion about which salt is best for specific cooking needs. First let's be clear about what salt is: a mineral that contains compounds of chlorine and sodium. Salt comes from either the evaporation of briny seawater or from mining underground salt deposits formed eons ago.

Our most common form of salt is called table salt, the one that my mother and grandmothers reached for. Today we have so many choices of salts from flavored salts to pretzel salt and salt for margaritas. On the other hand, we are told to hold the salt and limit our intake to a mere teaspoon a day. That would be hard to do for most people! Too much salt can have adverse effects on our health, like high blood pressure.

There is no question that adding salt to a dish brightens its flavor. How much salt to add is really a personal choice. If you feel the recipes are too skimpy on salt, you can always add more. The salt suggestion is only a guide. When you come right down to it, salt is salt, no matter what clever marketing messages Madison Avenue has thrown at us.

Here are some that I use in the recipes in this book.

**Iodized table salt.** Comes from underground mines and contains anticaking agents, it has a fine grain texture and is combined with iodine, which is necessary for thyroid health. Use this salt in all recipes unless indicated otherwise.

**Kosher salt.** An additive-free coarse-grained salt, it takes its name from the practice of salting kosher meats. It has a flaky texture, is less dense than table salt, and dissolves quicker. If a recipe calls for table salt use roughly two times the amount of Kosher salt because as the salt crystals increase in size so does the amount of space between the grains. So a tablespoon of fine sea salt will contain more salt by weight than a tablespoon of coarse salt because of the size difference of the grains.

**Fine sea salt.** Derived from the natural evaporation of seawater, it has a finer, powdery grind than coarse salt. Both fine and coarse sea salt contain trace minerals, including iron, calcium, and zinc. A tablespoon of fine sea salt will contain more salt by weight than a tablespoon of coarse salt because of the size difference of the grains.

**Coarse sea salt.** A larger, crystallized version of fine sea salt, it is used to grind over meats, fish, breads, and some baked goods to give them a polished gourmet look. A teaspoon of table salt equals one and a half teaspoons of coarse salt.

# Antipasti

Antipasto Salad

Classic Antipasto

Artichoke and Cheese Crostini

Chickpea Fritters

Chickpea Meatballs

Onion Fritters

Roman-Style Rice Balls

Fried Ricotta Cheese

Sicilian Rice Balls

Little Fried Mozzarella Balls

Nonna Galasso's Potato and Onion
    Frittata

Red Pepper Boats

Marinated Salmon Trout
    Locanda dell'Arco

Raw Tuna Antipasto

Carpaccio of Sea Scallops with
    Fennel Slaw

Marinated Shrimp and Cannellini
    Beans

Stuffed Mussels Sicilian Style

Pecorino Cheese and Fava Beans

Fava Bean and Parmigiano-Reggiano
    Cheese Cylinders

Pan-Cooked Scamorza

# keep your fork

**W**henever guests came for dinner, they would hear my mother say, "Keep your fork." For Italians that always meant that the meal was far from over and something else good was coming. For those not familiar with dining like the Italians, the experience became an envious adventure into the ritual of food and its connecting power to all those around the table.

Years ago, the pattern to the meal was very different in Italy than it is becoming today. That's because Italians have always eaten in courses; never would pasta, meat, and vegetables appear all together on one's plate with salad served at the same time. The main meal was served at midday, with something lighter like a soup or pizza served at night. The meal began with antipasto, the opening act for what was to follow, and usually included a selection of locally cured meats like salame or prosciutto, meaty olives, an assortment of colorful marinated vegetables like mushrooms, zucchini, and peppers, and fish marinated *(scapece)* in lemon juice and olive oil, such as squid, octopus, sardines, and anchovies.

Nonna Galasso always started dinner with platters of antipasti whenever we had company or Sunday dinner. Her antipasti consisted of pickled vegetables or *giardiniera,* from the jars of vegetables that were put up the year before. Cauliflower, mushrooms, beans, zucchini, and sweet bell peppers were favorites. When it was affordable, cured meats like capocollo or salame were added. Wine and bread were always on the table.

A *primo piatto* (first course) followed antipasto, usually a soup, pasta, or rice dish, followed by a *secondo* (second course) consisting of meat, fish, or poultry. A salad course was served last, and the meal ended with coffee and fresh fruit.

An Italian meal is never rushed. That would be rude and unthinkable. An hour or more could go by just sitting at the table enjoying antipasto; it allowed people to relax, savor the food, and talk about the events of their day. Today this still goes on in small towns and cities that close their businesses from noon until four, but in large cities like Rome and Florence, businesses are open all day, leaving little time for the leisurely midday meal for many. Sadly, the tradition is fading.

For a younger generation of Italians, antipasti have become more than just something to whet the appetite; they are becoming *the* main course as antipasti bars, similar to tapas bars, take the place of the long leisurely meal, reflecting busy and changing lifestyles.

In this chapter you will find a mix of traditional antipasto garnered from home, like Nonna Galasso's Potato and Onion Frittata (page 36) to some new trendy ones like the unusual Marinated Salmon Trout (page 42) that I fell in love with at Locanda dell'Arco, a lovely country restaurant in the quaint town of Cissone. Or the carpaccio of scallops (page 45) served on a bed of fennel slaw that sent me in search of the chef at Villa Beccaris in Monforte d'Alba.

Eating habits in Italy may be changing, but I believe in the importance of preserving traditions, so "keep your fork" for all the good foods and flavors that come after antipasti!

# Tips for Making Great Antipasti

We eat with our eyes first so how a dish is presented often signals what we choose. Here is a list of helpful hints for creating appealing antipasti.

1) For vegetable-based antipasti, crisp, unblemished, and in season are key.
2) Know your cheeses and buy only imported ones. Choose a selection of fresh and aged ones. Always serve cheese at room temperature.
3) Color is important; keep that in mind when putting together an antipasti menu.
4) Offer both hot and room temperature antipasti.
5) If antipasti are to be passed at a large gathering, choose those that are easy to eat as finger food; crostini are ideal for this.
6) Never serve canned olives; they do not compare in taste to marinated olives, or olives in brine.
7) Choose antipasti to fit a variety of food preferences from meat eaters to vegetarians.
8) Many antipasti can be made ahead and refrigerated; just be sure to bring them to room temperature before serving.
9) Use place cards to identify dishes that are part of an antipasti buffet.
10) Pair the right wines with the antipasti.

# Antipasto Salad

## Insalata di Antipasto

*Looking for a new take on antipasti? Why not serve it salad style with all the proper Italian ingredients mixed together. This is terrific and interesting as lunch, a simple light supper, or to take to your next picnic or tailgate. Vary the ingredients with grilled red bell peppers, eggplant, or zucchini.* **Serves 6 to 8**

Combine the olive oil, vinegar, shallot, oregano, salt, and pepper to taste in a jar. Shake to mix well.

Place all the remaining salad ingredients in a large bowl and toss well to combine. Pour the dressing over the salad and toss really well for 2 or 3 minutes.

Mound the salad on a serving platter and serve tableside with good bread. Pass additional extra-virgin olive oil, red wine vinegar, and salt.

*NOTE: Make the dressing several days ahead. Prep all the remaining ingredients and refrigerate in plastic bags until ready to serve.*

- ⅓ cup extra-virgin olive oil
- 4 tablespoons white balsamic vinegar
- 1 tablespoon minced shallot
- 2 tablespoons minced fresh oregano
- Salt and black pepper
- ½ pound Asiago cheese, cut into thin strips
- ¼ pound sliced mortadella, cut into thin strips
- ¼ pound sliced soppressata, cut into thin strips
- 1 small red onion, thinly sliced into rings
- ½ cup oil-cured olives, such as Gaeta, Cerignola, or Sicilian
- 1 cup shredded radicchio
- 4 marinated artichoke hearts, cut into quarters
- 2 cups arugula, in bite-size pieces

# Classic Antipasto

## Antipasto Classico

*Simple is always best and that is true when it comes to antipasto. Consider thinly sliced prosciutto di Parma (or prosciutti from other regions of Italy), local, dry-cured salame, all sorts of marinated vegetables from artichokes to zucchini, marinated olives, goat cheese, as well as marinated fish including anchovies, sardines, and squid. Keep it simple but authentic.*   *Serves 4 to 6*

**a**rrange the ingredients on a platter. Place on the table for all to enjoy with good bread such as ciabatta or sourdough.

¼ pound thinly sliced prosciutto di Parma or prosciutto di San Daniele

½ pound salame such as soppressata or other imported type

8 marinated artichoke hearts

½ pound olives in brine, such as Gaeta or Cerignola

8 anchovies, packed in olive oil

8 sardines, packed in olive oil

Slices of marinated zucchini and eggplant

½ pound marinated mushrooms

Chips of aged pecorino or Parmigiano-Reggiano cheese

# Artichoke and Cheese Crostini

## Crostini di Carciofi e Formaggio

4 garlic cloves, peeled

2 shallots, peeled and halved

½ pound Parmigiano-Reggiano cheese, grated

1 cup reduced-fat mayonnaise

Two 6-ounce containers mascarpone cheese or one 8-ounce block low-fat cream cheese, at room temperature

Juice of 2 limes

½ teaspoon hot red pepper flakes or hot red pepper paste

Two 12-ounce boxes frozen artichoke hearts, thawed and drained

Olive oil spray

4 day-old baguettes, cut into ½-inch-thick slices and browned in olive oil

*Never dismiss stale bread; clever Italian cooks give it new life as crostini (also called bruschetta). The Italian word* crostini *means "little toasts" because the bread is fried in a little olive oil, or grilled to toast it and then topped with an endless variety of savory spreads like artichoke and cheese. Crostini success depends on the quality of the bread; a country-style loaf with a tight crumb is best, or a baguette is good, too; just don't use spongy, soft bread. This makes enough for a crowd.* **Serves 12**

Preheat the oven to 400°F.

Process the garlic and shallots in a food processor until finely chopped. Add ½ cup of the Parmigiano-Reggiano, the mayonnaise, mascarpone or cream cheese, lime juice, and red pepper flakes. Process until almost smooth, then add the artichoke hearts and pulse until coarsely chopped. Spoon the mixture into a 6-cup gratin dish, lightly greased with olive oil. Sprinkle the top evenly with the remaining Parmigiano-Reggiano cheese.

Bake for 20 minutes, or until bubbly. Serve hot with the toasted baguette slices and let everyone top their own.

*NOTE: Jarred artichoke hearts in water can be used as a substitute for fresh. Be sure to drain them well.*

# Crazy For Crostini

Crostini has recently become all the rage and every restaurant seems to now serve these "little toasts" as an antipasto. Crostini were probably born out of a waste-not-want-not creed that was so ingrained in the *cucina povera* (simple country cooking) tradition. Bread, the common denominator of survival food, was too precious to waste. Crostini must start with good bread like a country baguette; it is usually thinly sliced on the diagonal and the slices are brushed with extra-virgin olive oil before being toasted, usually on a grill or in a frying pan. After toasting, a garlic clove is rubbed over the slices to impart flavor; if the bread is dependable, it will not tear as the garlic is grated across the top. Depending on where you find yourself in Italy, the toppings can be anything from the classic chicken liver crostini in Tuscany to the chopped tomato and basil crostini in Naples.

## Salt + Olive Oil + Vinegar = Antipasti

Many antipasti owe their very existence to salt, olive oil, and vinegar, and quite by accident, Italians have perfected a mind-boggling array of antipasti using these three ingredients. All one has to do is walk through the doors of any restaurant in Italy and see what seems to be mile-long tables of traditional antipasti greeting you as you proceed to your table. On those long tables will be such luscious tastings of marinated vegetables in olive oil and vinegar like eggplant, zucchini, hot peppers, sweet peppers, artichokes, tomatoes, cipolline onions, mushrooms, beans (both fresh and dried), and a dizzying array of olives. But that is just the beginning because salt also plays a huge role when it comes to antipasto because somewhere along the culinary timeline, after fire was discovered, man learned to preserve foods by salting. Salt was so important in ancient times that it was also used as salary to pay the Roman legions and did you know that our word salary is derived from sale (salt)? When we say he or she is not worth their salt, we mean they are not worthy to be paid.

Fish represent one of the oldest salted foods, especially cod, which for Italians is baccalà, that stiff-as-a-board, stinky fish, that when rehydrated with water, formed the basis of many meals. Salt-cured meats like prosciutto, salame locale, and soppressata mixed with spices and stuffed into natural casings are antipasti, too, as well as Italian sausages, salsicce, that again comes from the word for salt. All of these foods reflect the Italian genius of knowing how to preserve them using salt, olive oil, or vinegar.

Olive oil was also well-known in ancient times as a natural preservative, and is still used today to preserve many vegetables because when submerged under oil, known as sott'olio, no air comes in contact with the food that could cause it to spoil. This method was in constant use in my nonna Saporito's kitchen. I still can see the large wooden bucket that she kept in the basement next to my uncle Buzzy's elaborate village model train set. In it she kept raw eggplant that was first steeped in boiling vinegar and then layered in the bucket with salt and covered with oil. She kept the bucket covered and allowed the eggplant to cure for weeks before she used it to make my grandfather's lunches. Whenever I saw Uncle Buzzy going into the cellar with a hunk of bread tucked under his arm, I knew that he was not tweaking train tracks but sneaking Nonna's marinated eggplant and making himself a nice sandwich!

Traditional antipasti based on salt, olive oil, and vinegar have not changed much over the centuries but what is more often presented in Italian American restaurants is all wrong! Placid-looking iceberg lettuce with a scattering of canned California olives, chunks of processed cheese, and domestic cold cuts from the deli are really a far cry from the real thing.

Antipasti represent the purest and best of artisan food products from Italy, many handmade with governing bodies overseeing their production. And luckily for us, many are available here like Parmigiano-Reggiano or prosciutto di Parma from Emilia-Romagna. Wonderful marinated vegetables like mushrooms, peppers, and tomatoes from Calabria and Sicily are also available and many cured pork products like soppressata.

# Chickpea Fritters

## Panelle

2½ cups (8 ounces) chickpea flour

1 teaspoon baking powder

1 teaspoon fine sea salt

1 teaspoon coarsely ground black pepper

3 cups water

3 tablespoons finely chopped flat-leaf parsley or oregano (optional)

4 to 6 cups vegetable oil for frying

*Walking through the streets of the kinetic city of Palermo is an experience for all the senses. Your eyes are drawn at once to a melting pot of architectural styles from Byzantine to Baroque. Beautiful ornate fountains are everywhere, and the hordes of people and dizzying traffic make for fever-pitch activity. Your nose tells you that something good is cooking just around the corner—delicious street food sold from little carts. Buy a soft bun* (pani cu la meuza) *stuffed with beef spleen or iris (bread filled with sheep's milk ricotta cheese) or my favorite,* panelle, *golden brown, fried fritters made from ground chickpeas. Nonna Saporito always made them on December 13, the feast of Saint Lucy, patron saint of eyesight. You will never be able to eat just one. Panelle are easy to make and a great antipasto for a party.* **Makes about 32 panelle**

In a heavy-bottomed 2-quart saucepan, mix the flour, baking powder, salt, and pepper together off the heat. Slowly stir in the water and blend in with a heavy-duty whisk, being careful to avoid lumps from forming. Stir in the parsley or oregano.

Cook the mixture over medium heat, whisking constantly until it thickens and begins to move away from the sides of the pan; this is similar to making polenta. Remove the pan from the heat.

Using a rubber spatula, divide and spread the mixture thinly over four 9-inch round plates, making sure to cover the plate completely to the rim. Set the plates aside to cool for 2 to 3 minutes. Run a butter knife around the outside edge of each plate. Carefully lift the panelle away from the dish. Stack the panelle on top of each other and cut them in half lengthwise, then into quarters. Cut each quarter in half. There should be 32 panelle.

In a deep fryer, heat the vegetable oil to 375°F. Fry the panelle until they are nicely browned. Drain them on brown paper or paper towels and serve immediately. These are best eaten hot.

**Variation:** Another way to form the panelle is to spread the cooked mixture onto an oiled rimless baking sheet or cutting board. Let the mixture cool and then cut it into rectangles. Or fill an empty can with the bottom removed with the mixture and let it cool. Push the mixture out with your hand. Cut the dough into rounds and fry.

NOTE: *To make these ahead of time, form and cut the panelle and freeze them, uncooked, in single layers on a baking sheet. When they are frozen, transfer the panelle to plastic bags and seal well. Defrost as needed and fry.*

Did you know that chickpeas are one of the world's oldest foods? Food historians have dated their use to prehistoric times. Chickpeas are packed with protein and can be served in a variety of ways, from soups to marinated salads.

# Chickpea Meatballs

## Polpettine di Ceci

One 14-ounce can
  chickpeas, rinsed
  and drained

1 small red bell
  pepper, cored,
  seeded, and cut
  into chunks

1 small zucchini, ends
  trimmed and cut
  into chunks

1 small carrot,
  scraped and cut
  into chunks

1 leek, white part
  only, cut into rings

1 garlic clove, peeled

3 tablespoons extra-
  virgin olive oil

3 large eggs

1½ cups dry bread
  crumbs

Canola oil for frying

Fine sea salt

*Mom had her clever ways of disguising foods including these "meatballs" made with chickpeas. Her reasoning was that chickpeas were economical and just as full of protein as other more expensive foods. These are really fabulous on their own or served over a bed of cooked spinach for a filling but inexpensive light supper.* *Serves 6*

Pulse the chickpeas in a food processor and transfer to a bowl. Set aside.

Add the bell pepper, zucchini, carrot, leek, and garlic to the food processor and pulse until the vegetables are minced. Heat the olive oil in a sauté pan and stir in the minced vegetables; cook until softened. Cool about 5 minutes. Transfer the vegetables to the bowl with the chickpeas. Add 1 egg and mix well. With wet hands form the mixture into 1-inch balls. Set aside.

Beat the remaining 2 eggs in a shallow bowl and place the bread crumbs in another shallow bowl.

Coat each ball in the beaten egg, then roll in the bread crumbs and place on a dish. When all the balls are coated, heat 4 cups of oil in a heavy-bottomed, deep pot or in a deep fryer to 375°F.

Fry the balls, a few at a time, until golden brown. Using a slotted spoon, transfer them to paper towels to drain. Sprinkle with salt and serve warm.

# Onion Fritters

## Pastelle

*I always love learning new things from my Italian friends, so when I was in Puglia filming a television program on the famous breads of Altamura, I cooked with my friend Lina Di Gesù who made these wonderful* pastelle *(onion fritters) using an edible wild hyacinth bulb that is available there. Small boiling onions will work well here. Serve these hot.* **Serves 6 to 8**

1 pound small boiling onions, trimmed and peeled

2 large eggs

¼ teaspoon salt

Dash of freshly ground black pepper

½ cup unbleached all-purpose flour

2 tablespoons beer or 2 teaspoons baking powder

Vegetable oil for frying

**b**oil the onions in salted water until they are quite soft when pierced with a fork. Drain them well and set aside to cool.

In a medium bowl, mix the eggs, salt, pepper, and flour together to make a fairly thin batter. Add the beer or baking powder. Mash the onions, add them to the batter, and mix well.

Pour olive oil into a large frying pan to a depth of ¼ to ½ inch. Place over medium-high heat. When the oil is hot, drop the onion batter, a soup spoonful at a time, into the pan, leaving enough room between fritters so they don't stick together as they are cooking. This may mean cooking them in batches. As they brown on one side, turn the fritters over so that both sides are evenly golden brown. When browned, remove from the pan with a slotted spoon and drain well on paper towels.

Sprinkle with coarse sea salt and serve immediately.

# Roman-Style Rice Balls

## Supplí al Telefono

3½ cups homemade or canned low-sodium chicken broth

1 cup Arborio rice

½ cup shredded fresh mozzarella cheese

1 tablespoon finely chopped flat-leaf parsley

½ cup grated Parmigiano-Reggiano cheese

½ cup diced pro-sciutto

4 large eggs

Salt and black pepper

Freshly grated nutmeg

Unbleached all-purpose flour

1 cup bread crumbs

2 cups peanut oil for frying

*Supplí al telefono translates to telephone wires, an endearing name for a classic Roman fried rice ball similar to arancine (page 33) that houses a filling of prosciutto and fresh mozzarella cheese. The rice balls are breaded and fried. Take a bite and oozing strands of delicious cheese (telephone wires) is your reward!*   *Serves 8*

Pour the broth into a soup pot; stir in the rice and bring to a boil. Lower the heat and cook, covered, over medium-low heat until all the liquid is absorbed.

Transfer the rice to a bowl and allow it to come to room temperature. Or make the rice a day ahead and refrigerate it, covered, until ready to use.

Mix the mozzarella, parsley, Parmigiano-Reggiano, and prosciutto in a large bowl. Beat 2 of the eggs and add to the mixture. Blend well. Add salt, pepper, and nutmeg to taste.

With wet hands scoop up a small clump of risotto the size of a golf ball and, with your fingers, form a ball. Poke your finger in the middle to create a hole and push in some of the cheese mixture. Close the ball tightly around the filling, using more rice if need be. Continue making rice balls with the rest of the risotto.

Dredge the balls in flour.

Lightly beat the remaining 2 eggs in a bowl with a fork. Coat the floured balls in the beaten eggs and then coat them evenly in the bread crumbs. Place the balls on a baking sheet.

Refrigerate the balls for 15 minutes.

In a deep fryer or heavy-bottomed deep pot, heat the oil to 375°F. Fry the rice balls a few at a time in oil until golden brown. Using a slotted spoon, transfer them to paper towels to drain. Serve hot.

# Fried Ricotta Cheese

## Ricotta Fritta

*Nonna Galasso loved the fresh ricotta cheese that she bought from the Broadway Market in Buffalo, New York. It was freshly made and firm with a dry, not watery, texture. She pan-fried clumps of it in a little olive oil and sprinkled the top with butcher's coarse black pepper. The taste? Creamy and soothing.*   *Serves 4*

1 pound very firm fresh ricotta cheese

1 teaspoon fine sea salt

¼ teaspoon butcher's black pepper, plus more for sprinkling

6 tablespoons extra-virgin olive oil, plus extra to pass

Eight ½-inch-thick slices country baguette

Place the ricotta cheese in a bowl; add the salt and butcher's pepper and gently fold into the cheese. Set aside.

Heat 3 tablespoons of the olive oil in a medium sauté pan and brown the bread slices on both sides. As they brown transfer them to a platter and set aside.

Heat the remaining 3 tablespoons olive oil in the same pan and, using a ¼-cup measure, drop 8 clumps of the cheese into the pan, spacing them apart. Cook over medium-high heat until the cheese begins to brown along the edges. Using two small spatulas, gently turn them over and brown the other side. As they brown, place each one on top of a bread slice.

Sprinkle a few grains of butcher's pepper over the top of each one and serve two per person. Pass extra-virgin olive oil to drizzle on top.

**Variation:** Roasted red peppers are also delicious served on top of each one.

# Sicilian Rice Balls

## Arancine Siciliane

*Nonna Saporito could do no wrong in her kitchen. She could wield a cleaver like a pro, cut up a chicken lickety-split, and roll out pasta without breaking a sweat. Her signature dish, chicken in wine, is to this day my very favorite and one that I have never been able to duplicate in taste. Never! And when she served it, she also made arancine—fried rice balls. I devoured them. Arancine are traditional Sicilian street food that had its beginnings in many foreign cultures. The rice and saffron from the Arabs, the sheep's milk cheese from the Greeks, ragù from the French, and tomatoes from the Spanish. No wonder they are so good! Do not attempt to make these with regular rice. Make them with Arborio, the short-grain, starchy rice used to make risotto. It has the heft to stand up to deep frying.*   ***Makes about 12 rice balls***

heat the olive oil in a 2-quart saucepan and cook the celery, carrot, and onion until the vegetables soften. Stir in the red pepper flakes. Add the meat and brown it well. Combine the tomatoes with the wine and add to the meat, stirring the ingredients well. Cook over medium-low heat for 45 minutes. The mixture should be thick, not watery. Stir in the peas. Season with salt and pepper to taste. The sauce can be made several days ahead.

Pour the rice into a 2-quart saucepan and add the chicken broth. Stir well and bring to a boil. Lower the heat and allow the rice to cook, covered, until all the liquid has been absorbed.

Strain the saffron threads and add the saffron water to the rice. Stir well. Off the heat stir in the cheese, and 2 of the eggs. Season with salt to taste. Let cool.

**To assemble the rice balls.** Scoop up about 1/2 cup of the rice in the palm of your hand; form small orange-size balls then make an indentation in the center of each ball with your finger. Fill the indentation with a generous tablespoon of the ragù. Close the rice around the filling. Set the balls aside.

Put the flour in a shallow bowl. Beat the remaining 2 eggs with a fork in another shallow bowl. Coat the balls in the flour, then the egg mixture. Roll the balls in bread crumbs to cover completely. See Chef's Secret.

### RAGÙ SAUCE

3 tablespoons extra-virgin olive oil

1/4 cup minced celery

1/4 cup minced carrot

1/4 cup minced onion

1 teaspoon hot red pepper flakes

1 pound ground beef or pork

2 cups crushed plum tomatoes

1/4 cup red wine

Salt and black pepper

1/2 cup peas

### RICE BALLS

1 cup Arborio rice

2 1/2 cups chicken broth

1 teaspoon saffron threads, dissolved in 1/4 cup warm water

1/2 cup grated pecorino cheese

4 large eggs

Unbleached all-purpose flour

2 cups fine dry bread crumbs

4 cups canola or peanut oil for frying

Heat 4 cups of sunflower or canola oil to 375°F in a deep fryer or heavy-bottoned, deep pot.

Fry the arancine in the oil until nicely browned. Drain them on paper towels. Serve them hot with or without tomato sauce on the side.

**Variation:** Make *arancinette*, small olive-size rice balls, for part of an antipasto; instead of ragù filling, use a mixture of diced ham and Italian fontina cheese.

*CHEF'S SECRET: After coating the rice balls in bread crumbs allow them to dry out, uncovered, in the refrigerator for 15 minutes before frying. This will help the bread crumbs stay put when frying.*

# Little Fried Mozzarella Balls

## Bocconcini Fritti

Bocconcini, *which translated means small mouthfuls, are bite-size balls of fresh mozzarella di bufala (buffalo milk cheese). Or they can be fresh mozzarella made from cow's milk and referred to as* fior di latte, *meaning the flower of the milk. In Campania, the making of fresh mozzarella is a true art and the finished product so delicate that something is lost in taste if it is not consumed* (da giornata) *the day it is made.*

*These little gems of cheese ooze buttery goodness, are soft and creamy, and have a slightly tangy taste. With a hunk of country bread, they make an unforgettable lunch. And good as they are on their own, sometimes I like to present them in new ways. They are wonderful marinated in olive oil with fresh thyme, basil, and parsley and served with crusty bread for an antipasto or light lunch. They are absolutely addictive when coated in egg and bread crumbs, fried to a golden brown, and served hot on a puddle of tomato sauce.  Serves 6 as an antipasto*

4 large eggs, slightly beaten

1 teaspoon salt

1½ cups unbleached all-purpose flour

2½ to 3 cups Panko bread crumbs

2 pounds bocconcini, drained

Sunflower oil for frying

12 whole basil leaves

2 cups prepared tomato sauce, warmed

**b**eat the eggs with a fork in a shallow bowl and set aside. Combine the salt and flour in another bowl and set aside. Pour the bread crumbs into a third bowl.

Dry off the bocconcini with paper towels and coat them in flour, then in the beaten egg, and finally in the bread crumbs. Place them on a baking sheet and refrigerate for 15 minutes.

Heat 4 cups of oil to 375°F in a deep fryer or heavy-bottomed, deep pot. Add the bocconcini a few at a time and fry until golden. Drain them on paper towels and keep warm until all the pieces are fried. Add the basil leaves to the oil and fry about 1 minute; drain on paper towels.

Spoon about ⅓ cup of the tomato sauce in the middle of 6 individual salad plates. Place 3 to 4 balls on top of the sauce; add a couple of fried basil leaves for garnish and serve. Or place the bocconcini on a platter, scoop the tomato sauce into a serving bowl, and let everyone help themselves.

*CHEF' SECRET: Jars of marinated bocconcini make a great hostess gift. Add some long strips of lemon peel and a tablespoon of black whole peppercorns to the jar.*

# Nonna Galasso's Potato and Onion Frittata

## Frittata di Patate e Cipolle alla Nonna Galasso

4 medium potatoes
(all purpose, red,
or Yukon Gold),
scrubbed

⅓ cup extra-virgin
olive oil

1 medium yellow
onion, peeled and
diced

5 large eggs

¼ cup minced
flat-leaf parsley

½ cup grated
pecorino cheese

Fine sea salt

Freshly ground black
pepper

*I can conjure up a frittata with potatoes and onions with little effort because this was one dish that was a constant staple at home especially for Saturday lunch or dinner and it was the centerpiece of what to eat during the dank dark days of winter and during Lent. Nonna Galasso made the best in her cast-iron pan but I prefer to use a nonstick pan that allows me to flip the frittata without fear of breaking it.* Serves 6

Microwave or boil the potatoes until tender. Cool, peel, and dice them.

Heat the olive oil in a 12-inch nonstick sauté pan, over medium-high heat. Stir in the onions and cook until soft. Add the potatoes and cook, uncovered, until the potatoes begin to brown slightly. Toss the vegetables now and then as they cook. If the pan seems dry, add more olive oil.

In a separate bowl, beat the eggs with a fork until they are foamy. Beat in the parsley, cheese, and salt and pepper to taste. Pour the mixture evenly over the potatoes and onions. With a wooden spoon or spatula, push any raw egg mixture on the surface to the edge of the pan and lift up the frittata to allow it to run underneath. Cook until the underside is browned and the frittata moves in one piece when the pan is shaken. When the frittata is firm on the bottom, place a dish larger than the diameter of the pan over the top and invert the frittata onto the dish.

If the pan seems dry, add more oil then carefully push the frittata back into the pan to cook the other side; this should take about 3 minutes.

Place a dish over the top of the pan again and invert the frittata onto it. Cut into wedges and serve either hot, room temperature, or even cold.

## Faccia una Frittata

My mother was a fabulous cook; there was nothing she could not make. At age fifty-four she announced to my five brothers, my sister, and I that she was going to get a dietician's degree. She was a great multitasker and her studies consumed what little spare time she had. But she always had dinner on the table, no matter what.

One of her standby dinners when she was pinched for time was frittata. A frittata is a fried egg omelet that can be plain or fancy depending on what you add to it. The word frittata comes from the Italian friggere, to fry. Mom would tell us that her mother (Nonna Galasso) often used the expression: "faccia una frittata" to describe someone who had made a mess of things. I get it.

To make a proper frittata you need to whisk up (or mess up) eggs, at least five of them; that was Mom's rule. Her frittatas were always interesting because she would add leftovers like spinach, or onions or, my favorite, cooked spaghetti. We ate frittatas warm, we ate them cold. We ate them cut into strips and served as antipasto, we ate them cubed and tossed into chicken broth, and we ate them wedged between two slices of bread for our school lunches.

Frittata from my perspective was that ubiquitous food that was invented to make do when cupboards were bare. But where did the tradition for making them really come from? That's like asking who invented pasta. We cannot know for certain but what I do know is that frittata was being made in the days of ancient Rome because a Roman gourmand by the name of Apicius (first century A.D.) left us the following recipe:

> Take 4 eggs, a half pint of milk, a cup of oil, and so mix them that they make one body. Throw a little oil into a thin pan; make it boil, and pour in your preparation. When it is cooked on one side, turn it into a dish, moisten with honey, sprinkle with pepper and serve.

But besides Apicius we can look to the rural landscape of Italy for answers as well. Farming was a way of life for most Italians. On the farm there were chickens (hens) for laying eggs. Rarely did the birds get eaten. This is substantiated by a *charming proverb that goes like this:* meglio un uovo oggi che una gallina domani *(better an egg today than a chicken tomorrow). In other words: eat those chickens and eggs are history!*

*Eggs mixed with bits of whatever was on hand, say some wild herbs, scraps of meat or cheese, bread crumbs, or vegetables, were added to make something filling. Imagine that around the humble fresh egg, the tradition of the frittata grew and today we have very sophisticated variations containing everything from black truffles to exotic mushrooms.*

*Frittata is fun to make as long as you keep to a few rules. 1) Fresh eggs will make the lightest-tasting dish. 2) Use at least 5 eggs. 3) Use a nonstick pan 8 inches in diameter. A larger pan will yield a thinner frittata, a smaller pan, a thicker one. 4) As the eggs begin to cook and set on top, use a flat wooden spatula to push the uncooked portions to the underside of the frittata away from the pan sides and toward the bottom of the pan. 5) When the top is set, place a dish larger than the pan over the top of the pan and turn out the frittata. Slide it back into the pan to finish cooking the underside. A true frittata never gets finished off in the oven or under the broiler. (Remember frittata means to fry. It's a stovetop preparation.) Serve it hot or cold, cut into wedges. And if you stick to these rules you will never* faccia una frittata *(make a mess of things)!*

# Red Pepper Boats

## Peperoni Rossi in Barche

*Sweet red bell peppers are never boring; they can take on so many flavors that when I was asked to create something different for a buffet spread, these red pepper boats came to mind. The play of flavors is an explosion in your mouth that eggs you on to have more than one or two or . . .* **Serves 8**

3 large sweet red bell peppers

½ pound Genoa salame with peppercorns, diced

14 imported black, oil-cured olives, pitted and chopped

3 tablespoons fresh thyme leaves

¼ cup extra-virgin olive oil

Salt and black pepper

⅔ cup grated Asiago cheese

Preheat the oven to 350°F. Oil a 13 × 9-inch baking dish.

Cut away the stem tops of the peppers. Cut the peppers in half lengthwise, then into quarters, and remove the seeds and white membranes. Arrange the quarters, cut side up, in the prepared dish.

In a food processor pulse together the salame, olives, and thyme to create a paste. Transfer the mixture to a bowl. Stir in the olive oil, salt, and pepper. Spread the paste evenly on the pepper quarters.

Bake for 45 minutes, or until the peppers are tender when pierced with a fork. Sprinkle the cheese over the top and continue cooking until the cheese is melted. Serve warm.

*NOTE: Prepare these a day ahead up to the point of baking them. Keep refrigerated and covered.*

# Raw Tuna Antipasto

## Tonno Crudo

*Crudo means raw in Italian and* tonno crudo *is a wonderful way to serve very fresh tuna as part of an antipasto.*   *Serves 6 to 8*

Combine all the ingredients except the thinly sliced lemons, tuna, parsley, and bread in a rectangular glass dish large enough to hold the tuna steaks in a single layer. Add the tuna steaks and coat them in the mixture. Cover and marinate the fish for several hours or overnight, turning the pieces once or twice while they marinate.

To serve as part of an antipasto, arrange a bed of shredded lettuce on a shallow platter and place the tuna slices, overlapping on top of the lettuce. Pour the marinade over the fish and sprinkle with the parsley. Arrange the lemon slices along the platter in an attractive manner.

Serve at room temperature with crusty bread slices.

Juice of 4 lemons

½ cup red wine vinegar

1 small shallot or onion, peeled and thinly sliced

2 celery stalks, thinly sliced

2 tablespoons dried oregano

⅓ cup extra-virgin olive oil

Salt and black pepper

3 tablespoons capers packed, well rinsed

2 lemons, thinly sliced into rounds and halved

2 pounds tuna steak, thinly sliced

⅓ cup minced flat-leaf parsley

Crusty, grilled bread slices for serving

# Carpaccio of Sea Scallops with Fennel Slaw

## Carpaccio di Cappesante e Finocchio

*Sometimes what Italian cooks do with their beautiful raw ingredients just leaves me speechless. And speechless I was when I ate a carpaccio of scallops on a bed of fennel slaw. In a word, it was* elegante! *Carpaccio usually refers to paper-thin slices of raw beef served with good extra-virgin olive oil and herbs, but in this case, it became a clever way to serve scallops. As I savored every bite, I committed the flavors that I was encountering to memory and to my trusty notebook and vowed to make this dish straightaway when I got home. And while our scallops are different from those in Italy, the overriding factor in making this a successful dish is to be sure and use large, dry, and very fresh sea scallops.* **Serves 4**

8 large sea scallops, each sliced into paper-thin rounds

Juice of 1 large lemon

1 teaspoon fine sea salt

⅓ cup fruity extra-virgin olive oil (preferably from Tuscany), plus extra for drizzling

1 shallot, peeled and finely minced

2 tablespoons finely minced flat-leaf parsley

2 tablespoons finely minced tarragon

1 tablespoon white balsamic or rice wine vinegar

1 small fennel bulb, white part only, shaved as for coleslaw

2 tablespoons toasted pine nuts

Place the scallops in a rectangular glass dish large enough to hold them in a single layer, pour the lemon juice over them. Season with salt. Toss gently and allow them to marinate, covered, in the refrigerator for several hours. Turn them once while they are marinating.

In a bowl, combine the olive oil, shallot, parsley, tarragon, and vinegar. Add the shaved fennel and toss again very well. Allow the flavors to develop for 1 hour at room temperature.

To serve, divide and mound the fennel slaw in the center of 4 salad plates. Divide and mound the scallop slices on top of the fennel. Drizzle the top with more olive oil and season with more salt, if desired. Sprinkle the nuts evenly over each dish.

# Marinated Shrimp and Cannellini Beans

## Gamberi e Cannellini Marinati

¾ cup extra-virgin olive oil

Juice and grated zest of one large lemon

1¼ teaspoons fine sea salt

2 tablespoons salt-packed capers, well rinsed

2 tablespoons chopped flat-leaf parsley

½ teaspoon celery salt

2 pounds cooked and shelled medium shrimp (16 to 20 per pound)

One 14-ounce can cannellini beans, rinsed and drained

1 cup cherry tomatoes, halved

2 tablespoons minced shallot or scallions

8 slices of crusty bread, grilled or toasted

*This refreshing shrimp and cannellini bean antipasto can also double as a light lunch or supper. It is perfect for steamy summer weather when turning on the stove would be unthinkable.* **Serves 4**

Combine ¼ cup of the olive oil, the lemon juice, lemon zest, salt, capers, parsley, and celery salt in a bowl. Add the shrimp and toss well. Cover and marinate at room temperature for 1 hour, or prepare the day before and refrigerate.

In a separate bowl, combine the cannellini beans with the remaining olive oil, tomatoes, and shallots or scallions. Cover and allow to stand for 30 minutes.

When ready to serve, combine the cannellini bean mixture with the shrimp mixture and transfer to a shallow platter. Serve with slices of grilled bread.

# Stuffed Mussels Sicilian Style

## Cozze Ripiene alla Siciliana

2½ pounds mussels, scrubbed with a wire brush, beards removed

½ cup extra-virgin olive oil, plus extra for drizzling

1 anchovy, packed in oil, cut into bits

1 cup plain dry bread crumbs

4 garlic cloves, minced

4 large plum tomatoes, skinned, seeded, and diced

Salt and black pepper

1 tablespoon dried oregano

Crusty bread for serving

*It goes without saying that fish and shellfish are mainstays of the Sicilian diet; just a walk through the ancient Vucciria, Ballarò, or Capo outdoor markets near Palermo will confirm this. Mussels (cozze) are particularly delicious and there are hundreds of preparations for them from soups to casseroles to antipasti.* **Serves 4**

Preheat the oven to 350°F. Oil a 13 × 9-inch, or larger, casserole dish and set aside.

Place the mussels in a large sauté pan and cook over medium heat, just until their shells open. Drain, reserving the liquid. Working over a bowl, remove the mussels from their shells. Set the shells aside. Place the mussels in the bowl.

Wipe out the sauté pan and add ¼ cup of the olive oil. Place over medium heat, stir in the anchovy bits, and allow them to dissolve in the oil, then add the bread crumbs and brown them. Transfer the mixture to a plate.

Add the remaining olive oil to the sauté pan, stir in the garlic, and cook until it softens. Stir in the tomatoes, the reserved mussel liquid, and salt and pepper to taste. Cook over medium heat for 5 minutes. Stir in the shelled mussels and half of the bread-crumb mixture. Divide and fill the mussel shells with the mixture and place them in the prepared baking dish.

Divide and sprinkle the remaining bread crumbs over the tops of the mussels and drizzle each one with a little extra-virgin olive oil. Sprinkle the tops with oregano. Bake mussels, uncovered, for 20 minutes.

Serve hot with good crusty bread.

*CAUTION: Do not use any mussels with cracked or open shells and discard any that do not open during cooking.*

# Pecorino Cheese and Fava Beans

## Pecorino e Fave

*Pecorino cheese (sheep's milk cheese) and fresh fava beans are the perfect culinary pair as a simple antipasto with a glass of crisp white wine. The saltiness of the cheese and the nutty texture of the beans are just meant for each other. You'll see.*   *Serves 6 to 8*

**One 1-pound wedge aged pecorino cheese, at room temperature**

**3 pounds shelled fava beans**

**Fine sea salt**

Put the cheese on a cheese board and the fava beans in a bowl. Have a small bowl of salt nearby. Chip off bite-size pieces of the cheese with a cheese knife and eat it with a few fava beans, dipping them first in the salt if you wish. Accompany with a glass of crisp Pinot Grigio.

# Fava Bean and Parmigiano-Reggiano Cheese Cylinders

## Timballini di Fave e Parmigiano Reggiano

*There is an old Italian expression that goes something like this: "Never let the farmer know how good fava beans and cheese are together." Fava beans, both fresh and dried, are a Mediterranean staple and have been for centuries. Mostly boiled and dressed with olive oil and served with salt, they are also sometimes mashed for a spread to top bread, or added to casseroles, soups, and salads. And even though they are associated with humble cooking, they take on gourmet significance when wrapped in easy-to-make Parmigiano-Reggiano cheese cylinders that makes a great presentation.* **Serves 6**

2½ cups grated Parmigiano-Reggiano cheese, plus extra shavings for garnish

4 tablespoons extra-virgin olive oil

2 tablespoons white balsamic vinegar

1 garlic clove, minced

1 large shallot, minced

2 tablespoons minced tarragon

Salt and black pepper

2 pounds fava beans, shelled

2 celery stalks, thinly sliced

**h**eat a nonstick, medium sauté pan over medium heat. Spread ½ cup of the grated cheese in the pan to form a rectangular strip that is 2 inches wide and 6 inches long. Allow the cheese strip to melt. Carefully remove it from the pan, wrap the strip around a glass, and allow it to cool. Make five more and set them aside.

Whisk the olive oil and vinegar together. Add the garlic, shallot, and tarragon, and whisk again. Season with salt and pepper to taste and set aside. (This can be made ahead of time and refrigerated overnight. Bring to room temperature to use.)

Bring a pot of water to a boil and add 1 teaspoon of salt. Add the fava beans and cook them until you can easily slip off the outer skin. Drain and transfer the beans to a bowl. When cool enough to handle, slip off the outer pale green skin to reveal a bright green bean beneath.

Add the fava beans and celery to the olive oil mixture and toss well. Allow to marinate for 30 minutes.

When ready to serve, place one of each of the 6 cheese cylinders on individual salad plates.

Carefully divide and fill the center of each cylinder with some of the fava bean mixture. Top each one with a few shavings of cheese.

Any leftover fava bean mixture can be scattered around each plate. Serve at room temperature.

# Pan-Cooked Scamorza

## Scamorza in Padella

¼ cup extra-virgin olive oil, plus extra if needed

Eight 1-inch-thick slices country-style bread, such as semolina or ciabatta

8 thick slices scamorza

Red wine vinegar

Salt and black pepper

2 tablespoons fresh thyme leaves, minced

*Melted cheese is one of the most satisfying tastes, especially a good scamorza, which is a drier and often smoked version of mozzarella. Cut it and eat it as is, or make this divine antipasto of melted scamorza. I could live on it!*    *Serves 4*

heat the olive oil in a nonstick sauté pan; add the bread slices and brown them on each side, adding more oil as needed. Remove the slices from the pan and place them on a serving dish.

Add the cheese, a few slices at a time, to the same pan and allow them to melt. As they melt, transfer them with a metal spatula and place one on top of each bread slice.

Just before serving, sprinkle the cheese with a little red wine vinegar, season with salt and pepper to taste, and sprinkle with the thyme.

*NOTE: Smoked scamorza has a brownish rind and is called* scamorza affumicata.

charming proverb that goes like this: meglio un uovo oggi che una gallina domani (better an egg today than a chicken tomorrow). In other words: eat those chickens and eggs are history!

Eggs mixed with bits of whatever was on hand, say some wild herbs, scraps of meat or cheese, bread crumbs, or vegetables, were added to make something filling. Imagine that around the humble fresh egg, the tradition of the frittata grew and today we have very sophisticated variations containing everything from black truffles to exotic mushrooms.

Frittata is fun to make as long as you keep to a few rules. 1) Fresh eggs will make the lightest-tasting dish. 2) Use at least 5 eggs. 3) Use a nonstick pan 8 inches in diameter. A larger pan will yield a thinner frittata, a smaller pan, a thicker one. 4) As the eggs begin to cook and set on top, use a flat wooden spatula to push the uncooked portions to the underside of the frittata away from the pan sides and toward the bottom of the pan. 5) When the top is set, place a dish larger than the pan over the top of the pan and turn out the frittata. Slide it back into the pan to finish cooking the underside. A true frittata never gets finished off in the oven or under the broiler. (Remember frittata means to fry. It's a stovetop preparation.) Serve it hot or cold, cut into wedges. And if you stick to these rules you will never faccia una frittata (make a mess of things)!

# Soup

Nonna Galasso's Chicken Soup

Alphabet Soup

Two-Ricotta Cheese Soup

Baked Sardinian Bread
   and Cheese Soup

Barley Soup

Chickpea and Pasta Soup

Pureed Leek, Carrot, and Potato Soup

Chunky Roasted Vegetable Soup

Mrs. B's Swiss Chard Soup with Bread

Fish Broth

Fish Chowder

Sicilian-Style Mussel Soup

Tiny Cheese Soup Dumplings

Shrimp Soup with Orzo and Farro

Meatball Soup

Minestrone

Wedding Soup

Sausage and Barley Soup

# la gallina
· · · · · · · · · · · ·

**W**hen I think about the cavernous kitchen where I grew up, where every day my mother and Nonna Galasso spilled out all the energy they had between them to make meals for me, my six siblings, my dad, and our relatives, I am in awe of what these women could accomplish with what simple ingredients they had. When things were tight, and they often were, their answer to what's for supper was to make soup. And I learned a critical lesson from them about soup even though it was only through my subconscious.

Nonna Galasso spoke very little English, so over time and with repetition, I understood what she meant when she spoke in Neapolitan dialect. I knew the word *gallina* (chicken) very well because she was fond of making chicken soup. I learned that there was a good and a bad way to make it. (And I never paid attention to those details until years later when my own culinary career began.) Good meant personally choosing the right chicken, preferably a hen that had some years and fat on it. That she claimed would give great flavor, more so than some scrawny *giovane* (young) chicken; that would be bad and make weak soup. She would raise her voice in delight when she found just the bird she wanted from the chicken man and proudly say *"una gallina vecchia fa buon brodo."* An old chicken makes good broth.

Once she had the bird, the rest was easy. She threw some carrots, onions studded with whole cloves, parsley, and celery into a pot with it and after simmering away for hours, with a hypnotizing aroma, a good soup was born.

When I make soup, especially chicken soup, I think of what I learned from my nonna Galasso and even though I do not have a "chicken man" to buy from, my local grocery store carries natural grain-fed birds for me to choose from. Like Nonna, I scrutinize the chicken for plumpness, creamy-looking skin and fat, so necessary for that just right flavor. I make sure I use the entire bird and simmer it very slowly so just tiny bubbles are barely visible at the edge of the soup pot. A homemade soup should never boil, just simmer. There is great wisdom in doing that because the flavors are not boiled away into thin air.

Classic soups that I grew up with like minestrone, escarole, meatball (also called wedding soup), chicken and rice, vegetable, and bean are still my favorites to prepare but I also like to experiment with creamy soups *(vellutata)* that neither my mother nor nonna would have known how to make. That would have been in the realm of gourmet cooking and totally unfamiliar to them because their heritage kept them firmly grounded in preparing the peasant dishes of southern Italy, not anything fancy.

Memories of large bubbling pots of Mom and Nonna's homemade soups are a soothing reminder of how easy they really are to make and how much better they are for you without all the sodium and additives of canned soups. For me, nothing in a can could ever come close to the taste of soup made from scratch. That is why in this chapter, I have given you a wide variety of choices. You be the judge.

# Nonna Galasso's Chicken Soup

## Brodo di Pollo alla Nonna Galasso

*There is nothing gimmicky about this chicken soup. It is straightforward in its preparation and ingredients. And as I indicated on page 55, the key to getting that just-like-grandma-used-to-make flavor is to keep the soup at a simmer until the chicken is tender.* **Makes about 2 quarts**

1 plump 3½- to 4-pound chicken, well rinsed in cold water

1 large onion, peeled and studded with 12 whole cloves

2 large carrots, rinsed, scraped, and ends trimmed

2 celery stalks with tops

1 whole bay leaf

Juice of 1 large lemon

2 sprigs flat-leaf parsley, 1 sprig rosemary, and 2 sprigs thyme, tied together with kitchen twine

Salt and black pepper

Place the chicken in a large soup pot and add all the ingredients except the salt and pepper.

Add enough cold water to cover the ingredients by 1 inch and bring to a boil, then lower the heat to a simmer. Cover the pot and allow the soup to cook gently, with hardly a rumble, until the chicken is tender and falling apart, about 2 hours.

Remove the chicken from the broth with a large slotted spoon or strainer and set aside to cool. When cool enough to handle, remove the chicken from the bones and cut into bite-size pieces. Place in a bowl, cover, and refrigerate.

Strain the liquids and vegetables into a large bowl and press on the solids to extract as much broth as possible. Discard the solids.

Cover the bowl and refrigerate.

When ready to serve, skim the accumulated fat off the top of the broth and discard it. Transfer the broth to a soup pot and add the chicken. Bring the soup to a gentle boil, then simmer the soup for 5 minutes.

Ladle into bowls, add a thin slice of lemon, and serve.

**Variations:** Add cooked soup pasta, such as ditalini, orzo, or rice, or make the passatelli (page 73) and add it to boiling soup.

# Alphabet Soup

## Zuppa di Alfabeto

2 onions, peeled and
  quartered

2 leeks, white part
  only, cut into
  quarters

2 large carrots,
  peeled and cut into
  chunks

2 potatoes, peeled
  and quartered

3 celery stalks, cut
  into chunks

5 ripe plum tomatoes,
  cut into chunks

1 large garlic clove,
  peeled

1 small bunch flat-leaf
  parsley

4 sprigs fresh thyme

1 bay leaf

1 teaspoon black
  peppercorns,
  crushed

4 or 5 whole cloves

Fine sea salt

2 tablespoons fresh
  lemon juice

8 cups water

1 cup alphabet
  macaroni

*Who does not recall spelling out his or her name in steaming bowls of alphabet soup as a child? For me it is an enduring memory of good comfort food from home. In this simple but very tasty soup, tiny alphabet pasta is cooked in boiling homemade vegetable broth, which can be made ahead and frozen so it is always on hand. The secret to the flavor of this soup is the long cooking time.* **Makes about 2 quarts**

**P**ut all the ingredients, except the macaroni, in a large soup pot and bring to a boil. Reduce the heat, cover the pot, and simmer for 2 hours.

Place a large colander lined with damp cheesecloth over a large bowl. Strain the broth through the colander, pressing on the vegetables with the back of a wooden spoon to release all the juices. Discard the solids in the colander.

Return the soup to a soup pot and bring to a boil. Add the macaroni and cook until the pasta is al dente. Ladle the soup into bowls and serve hot.

*NOTE: Cubes of fresh mozzarella cheese are delicious stirred into the soup just before serving.*

# Two-Ricotta Cheese Soup

## Zuppa Alle Due Ricotte

*This delicious soup is made from both fresh ricotta and dried and salted ricotta cheese known as ricotta salata. The recipe comes from my pastry chef friend and cooking teacher, Mike McCurdy, who was so infatuated with his first trip to Italy that he signed up for a cooking stint in Florence. He enjoyed this soup in a little Florentine trattoria. Make the soup when zucchini flowers are available in summer and early fall.* **Serves 6**

**h**eat the olive oil in a soup pot and sauté the onion and garlic until they soften. Add the zucchini flowers and stir for another minute or two to combine the ingredients well.

Add the fresh ricotta and the broth. Increase the heat to high and cook for a few minutes more, stirring occasionally.

Add the ricotta salata and the salt, if needed. Go easy on the salt because the ricotta salata may provide enough. Reduce the heat to simmer and cook for 20 minutes. Season with freshly ground pepper.

Transfer the soup to serving bowls and top with a little fresh ricotta in the center if you wish.

2 tablespoons extra-virgin olive oil

1 medium onion, finely chopped

1 garlic clove, finely minced

6 zucchini flowers, finely chopped

2 cups fresh ricotta cheese, lightly whipped

4 cups vegetable broth

¼ pound ricotta salata cheese, crumbled

Pinch of salt, if needed

Freshly ground black pepper

# Baked Sardinian Bread and Cheese Soup

## Zuppa Gallurese

**Small bunch flat-leaf parsley**

**3 or 4 fennel tops**

**2 celery stalks plus tops**

**Freshly grated nutmeg**

**Salt and black pepper**

**2 tablespoons extra-virgin olive oil**

**4 tablespoons (½ stick) unsalted butter, melted**

**2 pounds homemade bread, cut into thin slices**

**½ pound Sardinian pecorino cheese**

**4 cups hot beef broth**

**4 ounces aged pecorino Sardo cheese, grated**

*Zuppa Gallurese, from Gallura, in the northeastern area of Sardinia, is a peasant-style baked "soup" made with humble bread and local cheeses. I had it when I was visiting some friends who live in Cagliari. Originally the soup was cooked in a wood-fired oven. It is so thick that it just does not look like what one would expect soup to look like and you can eat it with a fork. That is why it is known as* suppa cuatta, *or false soup. This is a great way to use up stale bread.* **Serves 6**

Preheat the oven to 350°F.

Make a pesto with the parsley, fennel tops, and celery. Transfer it to a small bowl and stir in the nutmeg, salt, and pepper to taste. Add a little olive oil to obtain a paste-like consistency.

Pour the melted butter into an 11 × 2½-inch casserole dish and place a layer of bread slices in the base of the casserole. Top the bread with a layer of the cheese slices and spread some of the paste mixture over the cheese. Continue making layers until the bread and cheese are used up.

Ladle the broth over the bread slices making sure it is well soaked. Sprinkle the grated cheese over the top.

Bake, covered, for 30 minutes. Uncover and bake 5 minutes longer, or until the broth is absorbed by the bread and the "soup" is fairly dry.

# Barley Soup

## Minestra di Orzo

1 cup pearled barley

2 cups beef broth

3½ tablespoons unsalted butter

¼ pound pancetta, diced

1 carrot, diced

1 celery stalk, diced

2 cups chopped escarole

Whole wheat or pumpernickel bread for serving

*Barley (orzo) is one of the oldest grains in existence. It grows mainly in the regions of the Alto Adige and Friuli and was used in ancient times to make a barley and wheat bread. It is a nutritious ingredient in this soup and was often used as an "extender" in many dishes.* **Serves 4**

Place the barley in a bowl, and soak for at least 1 hour, covered with cold water. Drain and transfer the barley to a 3-quart saucepan. Add the broth. Bring the mixture to a boil, and then lower the heat, cover, and simmer for about 1 hour, or until the barley is tender.

Meanwhile, melt the butter in a sauté pan. Stir in the pancetta and when it begins to render its fat, stir in the carrot and celery. Cook until the pancetta begins to brown, and then transfer everything to the pot with the barley. Stir in the escarole, bring the soup to a boil, and cook an additional 10 minutes.

Serve hot with whole wheat or pumpernickel bread.

# Chickpea and Pasta Soup

## Zuppa di Ceci e Pasta

*Chickpeas and tiny soup macaroni called ditalini, served steaming hot in a bowl with a blanket of grated cheese on top, takes me right back to childhood. This was definitely considered a peasant dish and was a good way to feed the family without breaking the budget—still is!* **Serves 6**

heat the oil in a 2-quart saucepan over medium heat and stir in the salame. Cook until the mixture is fragrant and the salame starts to render its fat. Stir in the celery and continue cooking until the celery softens. Stir in the garlic and red pepper flakes and cook 1 minute longer. Stir in the oregano. Squeeze the tomatoes into the pan and add the chicken broth.

Bring the mixture to a boil, then lower the heat and simmer for 10 minutes. Stir in the ditalini and chickpeas. Cook for a few minutes just until the soup is hot. Add salt and pepper to taste and ladle into soup bowls. Pass the grated cheese to sprinkle on top.

2 tablespoons extra-virgin olive oil

¼ pound diced salame with black peppercorns

½ cup diced celery

2 garlic cloves minced

1 teaspoon hot red pepper flakes or hot red pepper paste

1 teaspoon dried oregano

1 cup canned whole plum tomatoes

3 cups hot chicken broth

2 cups cooked ditalini

1 can chickpeas, well rinsed and drained

Salt and black pepper

Grated pecorino cheese for sprinkling

## Full of Beans

*Dried beans are a cheap source of dietary fiber and protein and can be used in endless recipes for soups, stews, and salads. Unfortunately many people either do not include them in their diet, or if they do, resort to using canned beans that are high in sodium. Like many cooks, I resort to using canned beans when in a pinch, but most of the time I have an ample supply of dried beans in my pantry, especially chickpeas, fava, pinto, cannellini, and borlotti beans. Dried beans will keep for a long time; store them in a cool, dry place in glass jars if possible.*

*Cooking dried beans could not be simpler. Remember that a cup of dried beans, when soaked overnight and then cooked, will double or triple in volume depending on the size and type of bean. To cook them, put the amount called for in the recipe in a large bowl, cover with cold water, and let them soak overnight. This will help to soften the cell wall of the beans and allow them to cook more quickly. When ready to cook, drain off the soaking water, rinse the beans, and transfer them to a pot. Add enough fresh cold water to cover the beans by 1 inch. Bring to a boil, and skim off the foam that accumulates. Lower the heat to a simmer, and cook, covered, until they are tender but not mushy, about 45 to 60 minutes depending on the size and variety. Drain the beans and use as directed in any recipe calling for cooked beans.*

*Here is a simple guide to some of the more common dried beans readily available and how much a 1-pound bag of each would yield after cooking.*

*Black beans—6¼ cups*

*Chickpeas—7½ cups*

*Pinto beans—6¼ cups*

*Red kidney beans—5 cups*

*Cannellini beans—6¼ cups*

# Pureed Leek, Carrot, and Potato Soup

## Passato di Porri e Carote

*A lovely* passato *(pureed soup) is made with simple ingredients already on hand.*
***Serves 4 to 6***

**M**elt 2 tablespoons butter in a small, nonstick sauté pan. Add the bread cubes and brown them. Transfer the croutons to paper towels and set aside.

Melt the remaining butter in a soup pot; add the leeks, carrots, and potatoes and cook until soft but not brown. Add the broth, bring to a boil, lower to a simmer, and cook 30 minutes. Using an immersion blender, puree the soup. If the soup is too thick, stir in just enough milk to thin it down. Serve hot with a sprinkling of parsley and the croutons.

5 tablespoons
    unsalted butter

2 cups small bread
    cubes

2 leeks, dark green
    tops removed and
    discarded, leeks
    well washed and
    diced

2 large carrots,
    peeled and diced

2 medium potatoes,
    peeled and diced

4 cups hot vegetable
    broth

½ cup milk

¼ cup minced
    flat-leaf parsley

# Chunky Roasted Vegetable Soup
## (Zuppa di Verdure Arrostite)

*Mom made her version of a "kitchen sink soup" with vegetables she cleaned out of the refrigerator that had gone limp. And while her soups were always delicious, I introduced her to a new way of getting more flavor by roasting the veggies first. The natural sugars will caramelize as they cook and provide a greater depth of flavor. It's a nice feeling when you can teach your mom something new.* **Serves 8**

**P**reheat the oven to 400°F.

Heat 2 tablespoons of the oil in a large 4-quart soup pot. Add the garlic and leeks and cook over medium-high heat until the leeks are very soft. Turn off the heat.

Combine the salt, pepper, celery seed, and oregano in a large bowl. Add the potatoes, carrots, broccoli, celery, and onion and toss the veggies well in the mixture. Add the remaining 2 tablespoons of the oil to the veggies and coat well.

Transfer the vegetables to a rimmed baking sheet, keeping them in a single layer. Roast them for about 30 minutes, turning them once or twice.

Add the roasted vegetables to the soup pot with the tomato juice and wine. Tie the parsley and thyme together with kitchen twine and add to the pot.

Bring the mixture to a boil, then lower the heat to simmer, and cook for 25 minutes. Remove and discard the parsley and thyme.

Stir in the lemon juice; taste and correct the seasoning adding more salt, if desired. Serve the soup piping hot with crusty bread and accompany with a salad.

---

4 tablespoons extra-virgin olive oil

4 garlic cloves, minced

1 large leek, white part only, well washed and thinly sliced

1½ teaspoons coarse salt

¼ teaspoon coarsely ground black pepper

½ teaspoon celery seed

2 teaspoons dried oregano

3 small red potatoes, cut into chunks

3 large carrots or parsnips, peeled and cut into chunks

2 cups broccoli florets

4 celery stalks, cut into chunks

1 large red onion, peeled and cut into chunks

4 cups tomato juice

½ cup white wine

1 small bunch flat-leaf parsley

2 sprigs fresh thyme

Juice of 1 lemon

Crusty bread

# Mrs. B's Swiss Chard Soup with Bread

## Minestra con Panno Sotto

¼ cup extra-virgin olive oil

1 medium onion, peeled and chopped

2 garlic cloves, peeled and chopped

Three 28-ounce cans whole plum tomatoes

3 sprigs basil

Salt

2 pounds Swiss chard, leaves only, washed and torn into bite-size pieces

1 pound loaf country-style Italian bread, cut into 1-inch slices

½ cup grated pecorino Romano cheese

*Mrs. Belurgi was a friend of my nonna Galasso and a good cook. She kept a garden behind her house, and it was from that plot of land that Mrs. B took her inspiration for what she cooked. Whenever my mother sent me to her house with some goody she had made, Mrs. B would be sure that I got some sort of treat. Her house always smelled welcoming. Her signature dish was something called* minestra con panno sotto *or soup with bread under it. Years later when I was researching family recipes I recalled this dish and asked my mother about it. She rattled it off from memory and said that Mrs. B made this Swiss chard and tomato soup in her home town of Veroli, Italy. Mrs. B would carry the soup in a big cauldron wrapped in a blanket atop her head and march to the farm fields to deliver the soup for the workers' midday meal.* **Serves 8 to 10**

**h**eat the oil in a large soup pot. Stir in the onions and cook them until they are very soft. Add the garlic and cook until it softens. Using clean kitchen scissors, cut the tomatoes right in the can into small pieces. Add them, along with their juice, to the pot. Add the basil and salt to taste. Stir well and bring to a boil. Stir in the Swiss chard, lower the heat, and simmer the soup for 15 minutes. Taste and correct the seasoning if necessary.

Place a layer of the bread slices in a deep rimmed platter or use a Dutch oven. Using a ladle, pour over just enough soup to cover the bread slices. Sprinkle some of the cheese over the top. Continue making layers until all the bread and soup is used.

Scoop into soup bowls to serve.

# Fish Broth

## Brodo di pesce

**1 pound mixed fish and seafood bones and shells**

**½ cup dry white wine**

**2 medium carrots, peeled and cut into chunks**

**1 medium onion, peeled and cut into chunks**

**2 sprigs flat-leaf parsley**

**2 sprigs thyme**

**2 sprigs tarragon**

**Juice of 1 lemon**

**Salt**

*To make a fish broth, save lobster bodies, shrimp shells, and fish bones and freeze them until there is enough to make a respectable broth. Any fish carcass can be used; see what is available from your fishmonger; do not use oily fish like salmon or grouper because the flavor will be too strong. Or use fish heads, readily available in seafood and grocery stores. You will need about a pound total in weight.* **Makes 6 to 7 cups**

Place all the fish parts in a soup pot and add the wine. Bring to a boil, lower the heat, and simmer the ingredients, covered, for 3 to 4 minutes.

Add the carrots and onion. Tie the parsley, thyme, and tarragon together with kitchen twine and add to the pot. Pour in 6 to 7 cups of cold water, or enough to cover the fish parts.

Bring to a boil, lower the heat and simmer, covered, for 45 minutes.

Strain the ingredients through a strainer lined with damp cheesecloth into a large bowl. Discard the solids. Stir the lemon juice into the broth and add salt to taste. The broth is ready to use in recipes calling for fish broth, or can be frozen for future use.

*NOTE: To freeze smaller amounts of the broth for future use, place open, empty sandwich-size ziplock bags in a 2-cup measuring cup and ladle in the broth, leaving 2 inches at the top of the bag for expansion. Zip the bags closed, label, and freeze.*

# Fish Chowder

## Zuppa di Pesce

*Truth be told, I would rather eat fish than meat any day of the week, and since I live in a seacoast town, fresh fish is always available. Growing up we ate cheap cuts of fish like mackerel and squid all combined to make* zuppa di pesce *(fish soup). What I re-member most were those fish heads swimming along in the soup pot, which Nonna said was where all the flavor was. It was a battle to get me to eat it! I have manipulated that old recipe from home to create my own version; sort of a blend of Italy meets New England. In this recipe, haddock is the star and ladling out this delicate fish chow-der always brings me great satisfaction because it can be made in less than thirty minutes, but looks like it took some time. Quality is key so buy the freshest fish. That means it looks plump and does not smell of ammonia.* **Serves 8**

**h**eat the oil in a soup pot over medium-high heat and cook the pancetta until it begins to brown. Stir in the onion and cook until softened. Stir in the garlic and red pepper flakes or paste and continue cooking until the garlic softens.

Lower the heat to medium and add the haddock. Stir gently for a few minutes; add the spinach, chicken broth, and evaporated milk. Bring the mixture to a gentle boil, and then reduce the heat to medium-low. The fish and spinach will cook in less than 5 minutes. As soon as the fish is opaque (white in color) add the peas. Cover and cook 1 minute. Stir in the thyme or basil off the heat, and add salt to taste. Serve very hot with crusty ciabatta bread drizzled with a good extra-virgin olive oil.

**NOTE:** *I have learned over the years just how much flavor fish heads add to a broth, so please do try it. I still prefer mine without, but everyone has a food phobia and this is mine.*

---

- **3 tablespoons extra-virgin olive oil**
- **¼ pound pancetta, diced**
- **1 medium red onion, peeled and diced**
- **1 garlic clove, minced**
- **1 teaspoon hot red pepper flakes or hot red pepper paste**
- **1½ pounds fresh haddock (head and skin removed), cut into 1-inch pieces**
- **1 pound spinach, washed, drained, stemmed, leaves shredded**
- **1 can (14½ ounces) light chicken broth**
- **1 can (12 ounces) low-fat evaporated milk**
- **1 cup peas**
- **⅓ cup minced fresh thyme or basil**
- **Salt**

# Sicilian-Style Mussel Soup

## Zuppa di Cozze alla Siciliana

4 pounds mussels, scrubbed, beards removed

½ cup white wine

2 garlic cloves, 1 minced, 1 left whole

½ cup extra-virgin olive oil

1 onion, chopped

1 tablespoon fennel seeds, crushed or fennel pollen

3 large plum tomatoes, peeled and chopped

2 cups bottled clam juice

1 package of saffron threads soaked in ¼ cup warm water

¼ cup minced flat-leaf parsley

Salt and black pepper

4 thick slices bread

*For Italians from* bella Sicilia *or* bella Napoli, *who made up the largest groups of immigrants coming to America, mussel soup (*zuppa di cozze) *was an endearing remembrance of home. It was an as-close-to-the-chest kind of dish that you could find. It was cheap to make, albeit the mussels were not the same as those in Italy. So what was available here was substituted instead. Mussels need to be looked over carefully; do not buy any cracked or open ones and use them the day of purchase.* **Serves 4**

Place the mussels in a large sauté pan or soup pot. Add the wine and the minced garlic. Cover the pan and slowly bring to a boil. Lower the heat to a simmer and cook just until the mussel shells open. Discard any mussels that do not open.

Transfer the mussels to a dish with a slotted spoon and strain the cooking liquid through a cheesecloth-lined sieve into a bowl and set aside.

When cool enough to handle, remove the mussel meat from the shells. Discard the shells. Set the mussels aside.

Return the pot to the stovetop and add the olive oil and onion and cook until the onion wilts. Stir in the fennel seeds or fennel pollen, tomatoes, and clam juice. Strain the saffron and add the liquid to the pot. Cook over low heat for 5 minutes. Add the shelled mussels and any juices that have collected in the bowl and cook 1 minute longer. Stir in the parsley and season with salt and pepper to taste. Cover and keep warm.

In a separate sauté pan, heat 2 tablespoons of olive oil over medium heat; add the bread slices and brown them on both sides. Transfer the slices to a cutting board and rub each one with the whole garlic clove.

Place a slice of bread in the bottom of each of 4 soup bowls and ladle the soup over the bread. Serve hot.

**Variation:** For a spicier version, add hot red pepper flakes.

**CHEF'S SECRET:** *Fennel pollen comes from fennel flowers and it takes a large amount to produce even a small amount of the pollen, making it almost as costly as saffron. But a little goes a long way—the flavor is intense. Fennel pollen is very popular in Italy.*

# Tiny Cheese Soup Dumplings

## Passatelli

*My mother made a coarse type of soup pasta called* passatelli *that was grated on a cheese grater and then cooked in boiling chicken broth. The pasta had a distinct lemon flavor because of the grated lemon zest that was mixed into the dough. This is a very old recipe with many variations and names.* **About 3 cups grated passatelli**

In a bowl, mix the flour, cheese, and bread crumbs together. In another bowl, mix the remaining ingredients, except the broth, together. Add to the flour mixture and mix well with your hands. Gather the dough into a ball; the dough will be quite rough. Wrap it in plastic and refrigerate for at least 6 to 7 hours, or overnight, until firm enough to grate.

Using a box grater, grate the dough through the large holes onto a clean kitchen towel. Spread the passatelli out on a towel as you make them.

In a large pot, bring the broth to a boil. Add 1½ cups of the passatelli and boil for about 3 minutes, or until the pasta floats to the surface. Serve immediately.

**NOTE:** *Uncooked passatelli freezes very well. Spread the grated uncooked pasta out on a floured, towel-lined baking sheet and freeze until hard. Transfer the passatelli to plastic bags. Do not defrost before cooking.*

½ cup plus 2 tablespoons unbleached all-purpose flour

¾ cup grated Parmigiano-Reggiano cheese

1 cup toasted fresh bread crumbs

Grated zest of 1 medium lemon

1½ teaspoons fresh lemon juice

2 large eggs, lightly beaten with a fork

Salt and black pepper

1 recipe Nonna Galasso's Chicken Soup (page 57) or other

# Shrimp Soup with Orzo and Farro

## Zuppa di Gamberetti con Orzo e Farro

*This healthy shrimp soup has many layers of flavor and, though it takes time to prepare, it can be considered a meal in itself. Farro, a strain of ancient wheat that is enjoying a comeback, packs this soup with both flavor and nutrition. Soak the farro the day before and cook the orzo or beans ahead to cut down on the cooking time. If you cannot find farro, substitute wheat berries.* **Makes 1¾ quarts**

½ cup farro or wheat berries

1 pound small shrimp in the shell

½ cup orzo, pearled barley, or small dried white beans

2½ pounds plum tomatoes, coarsely chopped

2 tablespoons extra-virgin olive oil

2 celery stalks, thinly sliced

1 small onion, minced

¼ cup minced flat-leaf parsley

4 cups hot chicken broth

2 teaspoons celery salt

½ teaspoon sea salt

Freshly ground black pepper

Place the farro in a medium bowl, cover with cold water, and soak overnight.

Place the shrimp in a small saucepan, and cover with cold water. Bring to a boil, and then simmer the shrimp for 3 minutes. Turn off the heat and allow the shrimp to cool in the water, then drain them, reserving the water. Peel the shrimp and set aside.

Pour the orzo into a 2-quart saucepan and cover with 3 cups of cold water. Bring to a boil, lower the heat to simmer, and cook about 15 to 20 minutes, just until al dente, firm but cooked. (If you are using dried beans, soak them overnight, then cook them about 30 minutes, or until tender but not mushy.)

Drain the farro and transfer it to the saucepan used to cook the orzo. Cover the farro with 3 cups of cold water and bring to a boil. Cook about 25 minutes, or just until the grains are cooked through but still remain firm. Drain and set aside.

Place the tomatoes in a food processor, food mill, or blender and puree until smooth. Pour the pulp into a fine-mesh strainer placed over a bowl. Press on the pulp with a spoon to release the juice. Discard the seeds and skins. There should be about 2 cups of tomato juice. If not, add water. Set aside.

Heat the olive oil in a 2-quart saucepan and stir in the celery, onion, and parsley. Cook until the vegetables soften. Pour in the chicken broth, reserved tomato juice, 1 cup of the reserved shrimp broth, celery salt, sea salt, and pepper and bring to a boil. Lower the heat and cook the mixture, covered, for 5 minutes. Stir in the orzo and farro. Stir in the shrimp. Cook over low heat for 3 or 4 minutes; do not let the soup boil or the shrimp will become tough.

Ladle the soup into bowls and pass olive oil to drizzle on top.

**NOTE:** *If you cannot find small shrimp, buy the 20- to 40-count and split them in half lengthwise.*

## Making Do In L'America

For my grandmothers Maria Assunta Saporito and Anna Galasso, coming to America was the bravest thing that they could have done. Everything that defined them—family, language, customs, dress, and memories—was left at the port of Napoli as they waved good-bye to their native land.

Nonna Saporito was tall with dark skin and short curly hair. She came from Caltanisetta, Sicily, as part of an arranged marriage. Nonna Galasso was short with fair skin and long hair worn as a bun atop her head and came from Naples. Her voyage was sponsored by relatives already here. Both these women were strong willed and butted heads often—most often over who was the better cook. It took them a long time to settle into their new surroundings with complaints about what was wrong with L'America. According to them, people did not eat right. Where were their beloved cardoons, fava beans, and crusty peasant breads? Why did L'Amerigan eat ghastly ravioli from a can? How come the sardines didn't taste like the ones in Italy? And worst of all, why is everyone in such a hurry?

Nonna Saporito had her own butcher shop in Fairport, New York, and she could wield a cleaver with great force. Just watching her singe the feathers off a chicken and cut it into pieces with lightning speed was mesmerizing. The flavor of her crusty chicken cooked to a deep brown glaze in red wine and falling off the bone was worth the two-hour drive to see her.

Nonna Galasso ran a boarding house in Depew, New York, and was the proud owner of the only bathtub in her neighborhood that she rented out for twenty-five cents per bath; you provided your own towel. Not bad for a woman with no English, no education, and eight children! She cooked and served all the meals for the boarders.

And while all that was before my time, I sure remember her braciole. It was lip-smacking legendary. She spent considerable time at the butcher's looking for an affordable cut of round steak to stuff with pecorino cheese, bread crumbs, parsley, garlic, and hard-boiled eggs. Rolled up and tied, she would brown it in lard, add other meats like spareribs and sausage, and cover everything with the canned tomatoes she put up each summer. I can still see her squeezing *each tomato between her chubby fingers as she added them to the pot. Cooked for hours, this would become her beloved ragu served with homemade spaghetti. In her later years, she would warn me as a young bride to never be swayed by sauce in a can. I never was and never tinkered with her recipe, making it over and over, even on national television, and our viewers loved it and adopted it as their own! Ironic. If you Google Anna Galasso, there her proud recipe will be. Anna Galasso, my Neapolitan grandmother, an obscure passenger in steerage on the ship Simon Bolivar, winds up a household name on the World Wide Web, and complete strangers are making her ragu sauce. Only in L'America.*

# Meatball Soup

## Zuppa di Polpettine

2 slices good-quality bread, crust removed

⅓ cup whole milk or ricotta cheese

½ cup grated Parmigiano-Reggiano or pecorino cheese

2 tablespoons minced flat-leaf parsley

1 tablespoon grated lemon zest

Salt and black pepper

¼ pound ground chuck

¼ pound ground pork

¼ pound ground veal

One 2-pound bag frozen mixed vegetables

One 14-ounce can cannellini beans, rinsed and drained

2 quarts canned low-sodium chicken or beef broth

One 28-ounce can diced plum tomatoes

1 cup water

1 teaspoon celery salt

1 whole bay leaf

*Filling meatball soup is one of my choices for weekend cooking. I have streamlined the process by using already cut-up mixed frozen vegetables and prepared broth. The meatballs can be made two days ahead and refrigerated.* **Serves 8 to 10**

Tear the bread into pebble-size pieces and place them in a bowl. Pour the milk over the bread or stir in the ricotta cheese. Let the mixture stand for 5 minutes. Stir in the grated cheese, parsley, lemon zest, and salt and pepper to taste and mix well. Add the meats and mix with your hands to combine the ingredients well.

Preheat the oven to 350°F.

Have a bowl of water handy to wet your hands as you form the meatballs. Scoop up about 2 teaspoons of the mixture and roll it into a small ball the size of a marble with your hands. Place the meatballs on a lightly oiled baking sheet. Continue making meatballs, placing them on a baking sheet and spacing them so they do not touch one another.

Bake them for about 8 minutes, or until they begin to brown. Transfer them with a slotted spoon to a soup pot or slow cooker.

Stir in the mixed vegetables, cannellini beans, and broth. Add the tomatoes. If you have no diced canned tomatoes on hand and only whole tomatoes, using clean kitchen scissors, cut them into bits right in the can; then add them to the soup.

Bring the mixture to a boil, add the water, celery salt, and bay leaf, then lower to a simmer and cook, covered, for 10 minutes.

Taste and correct the seasonings, if necessary. Remove and discard the bay leaf. Ladle the soup into bowls and top with extra grated cheese.

**Variation:** Add 1 cup cooked small pasta like ditalini or elbow macaroni to the soup.

**CHEF'S SECRET:** *To save time, keep a container of already grated cheese in the refrigerator.*

# Minestrone

## Minestrone

*"Do you have a good recipe for minestrone soup?"* This is what a large segment of our television family wants to know. Over the years I have scoured many sources regarding the meaning of the word minestrone and I always come up with the same definition—a big soup with lots of vegetables swimming in a savory broth. Minestrone is a soup of creativity, necessity, or what I call the original "kitchen sink" soup. It is found all over Italy made with a variety of ingredients. A good example is the region of Liguria where cooks stir in spoonfuls of pesto sauce made from the fragrant small-leafed basil which defines much of their cooking. One thing is for certain, vegetables, beans, and pasta will find their way into the minestrone soup pot. Don't be timid. Add those leftover vegetables, snippets of herbs, and bits of cheeses in your refrigerator to the soup. Minestrone is tolerant of whatever you are inspired to add to it, becoming a meal in itself. Serve it with good crusty bread and a green salad.  **Makes about 3 quarts**

2 tablespoons extra-virgin olive oil

1 medium onion, diced

¼ pound pancetta (or bacon), diced

10 whole black peppercorns

1 large sprig rosemary

Two 28-ounce cans whole peeled plum tomatoes, coarsely chopped

2 cups water

One 3-inch piece cheese rind

1 bay leaf

½ cup diced eggplant

1 cup sliced carrots

One 19-ounce can chickpeas, rinsed and drained

Salt

¾ cup ditalini, tubetti, or other small soup pasta, cooked, drained, and set aside

1 cup cooked green beans or peas

1 cup cooked, chopped broccoli

½ cup chopped basil leaves

**h**eat the olive oil in a soup pot, stir in the onions, pancetta, peppercorns, and rosemary and cook slowly until the onions are soft and the pancetta begins to brown. Stir in the tomatoes and water and continue to cook over low heat, uncovered, for 3 or 4 minutes. Stir in the cheese rind, bay leaf, eggplant, carrots, and chickpeas. Cover the pot and simmer the ingredients for 40 minutes.

Uncover the pot, stir in the pasta, green beans, and broccoli and cook 5 minutes longer. Stir in the basil and cook an additional 5 minutes. Season with salt to taste. Remove and discard the bay leaf and rosemary sprig. Serve piping hot.

**TIPS:** *Uncooked pasta can be added to the soup if a thicker soup is preferred since the pasta will absorb some of the liquid. Cooking it separately and adding it later allows for a thick but not chunky consistency.*

*After pouring out the canned tomatoes, pour the water called for in the recipe into the can and swirl it around to get the remaining tomato juices from the can.*

# Wedding Soup

## Minestra Maritata

*Who has not had wedding soup? It was served as a first course at my own wedding but it was never intended for such an occasion. It got its name from the fact that all the ingredients go together well just like a married couple. There are so many watered down versions of this soup. But here is what was served at mine.*
*Serves 8*

**S**tud the onion with the cloves and place in a large soup pot with the celery, carrots, bay leaf, parsley, thyme, chicken wings, and lemon slices. Cover the ingredients with water and bring to a boil. Reduce the heat to a simmer so that the water is barely moving. Cover the pot and cook for 1½ hours.

Meanwhile make the meatballs. In a small bowl, combine the bread crumbs with the milk and set aside.

In a medium bowl add the veal or chuck, egg, cheese, garlic, salt and pepper, and the soaked bread crumbs. Gently mix with your hands to combine the ingredients.

Preheat the oven to 350°F. Lightly oil a rimmed baking sheet.

Have a bowl of water ready to wet your hands as you form the meatballs. Scoop up about 2 teaspoons of the mixture and roll into meatballs the size of a marble.

Place the meatballs on the prepared sheet as you make them, spacing them so they do not touch one another.

Bake the meatballs in the preheated oven for 20 minutes, or until lightly browned.

Transfer the meatballs to a bowl and refrigerate them. The meatballs can be made three days ahead.

Remove the chicken wings from the pot and set them aside on a cutting board. Strain the broth through a sieve, pressing on the vegetables to extract as much liquid as possible. Discard the solids and return the broth to the

### BROTH

1 large onion, peeled

10 to 12 whole cloves

2 large celery stalks with leaves, cut into quarters

2 large carrots, scraped and cut into quarters

1 large bay leaf

1 small bunch flat-leaf parsley

3 sprigs thyme

3 pounds chicken wings

1 large lemon, thinly sliced into rounds, seeds removed

1 head escarole, well washed, coarsely chopped

Salt and black pepper

Grated pecorino cheese for sprinkling on top

### MEATBALLS

⅓ cup fresh bread crumbs, crust removed

*(cont'd)*

3 tablespoons whole
milk

½ pound ground veal
or chuck

1 small egg

¼ cup grated
pecorino cheese

1 garlic clove, minced

1¼ teaspoons salt

Freshly ground black
pepper

2 tablespoons extra-
virgin olive oil

pot. Bring to a boil and stir in the escarole. Cook 3 to 4 minutes, just until the escarole has wilted. Remove the meat from the chicken wings and add it to the broth. Add the meatballs to the broth. Reheat the soup. Taste and correct the seasoning, if needed. Serve hot with grated pecorino cheese sprinkled on top.

# Sausage and Barley Soup

## Zuppa di Salsiccia e Orzo

*Thick sausage and barley soup is perfect cold weather food and the vegetables can vary from kale to escarole to Swiss chard to spinach. The choice is yours.* **Serves 8**

**P**ut the barley in a large saucepan and cover it with 2½ cups of cold water. Bring to a boil, lower the heat, and cook until the barley is tender. Drain it in a colander and transfer to a bowl.

Heat the olive oil in a sauté pan over medium heat. When the oil is hot add the sausage and cook until it is nicely browned. Transfer the sausage to a cutting board and allow it to cool for 5 minutes. Slice it into ¼-inch-thick rounds and refrigerate it until needed.

Put the onion, celery, carrot, fennel, and bell pepper in a soup pot. Cover the ingredients with water by 2 inches. Bring to a boil then lower the heat to medium, cover, and allow the vegetables to cook until they soften.

Stir in the tomatoes with their juice and 2 cups of water. Bring the mixture to a boil, lower the heat to medium, and cook the soup for 5 minutes. Stir in the zucchini, parsley, and red pepper flakes and cook 2 minutes longer. (If using shredded kale, escarole, Swiss chard, or spinach, add it at this point.) Add the sausage and barley, cover, and cook about 5 minutes longer, just until everything is hot. Season with salt and pepper to taste and ladle into bowls.

**NOTE:** *Orzo is the Italian word for barley and also refers to a tiny soup pasta.*

**NOTE:** *If using leafy green vegetables, wash, drain, and shred them.*

⅔ cup pearled barley

1 tablespoon extra-virgin olive oil

1 pound sweet Italian sausage

1 medium onion, chopped

2 celery stalks, thinly sliced

2 large carrots, thinly sliced

1 small fennel bulb (white part only), chopped

1 sweet red bell pepper, cored, seeded, and chopped

One 28-ounce can diced plum tomatoes

1 medium zucchini, cut in half lengthwise, then cut into thin half-moons

¼ cup minced flat-leaf parsley

¼ teaspoon hot red pepper flakes

Salt and black pepper

# Pizza and Bread

PIZZA

Basic Pizza Dough

Classic Pizza

Genoa-Style Focaccia

Mom's Ricotta Cheese Calzones

Onion, Potato, and Pumpkin Seed

   Focaccia

Palermo-Style Pizza

Skillet Pizza

Spinach Pizza Roll

Prosciutto and Arugula Pizza

Pizza Sauce

BREAD

Homemade Bread

Mom's Cinnamon Rolls with

   Lemon Icing

Sicilian Bread

Walnut, Dried Fig, and Anise Bread

Whole Wheat Bread

# as good as bread

for Italians bread is more than something to eat, it is a sacred symbol. It makes a statement. If you have bread, you are not poor, you can survive. No Italian table is ever without bread and even stale bread is never wasted. It gets new life in the bottom of the soup bowl, finds its crumbled way into stuffings, forms a delicious coating on meats and poultry, and is often grated over pasta.

Bread is so revered in Italy that a popular saying is: *"é buono come il pane"* (he or she is as good as bread). It means that you can count on that person to always be there for you, dependable, helpful, and generous, just as bread will always be on the table.

Baking bread was a weekly ritual for my mother. It was nothing for her to turn out dozens of loaves of semolina bread, as well as rolls and pizza, all by hand. And there was nothing better than ripping open a piping hot slice of bread, smearing it with butter and salt, and sitting on the back porch just eating it with abandon. Mom gave a lot of what she baked away to neighbors, my nonna's friends, and of course our relatives, who all lived close by, some within walking distance. Even the monsignor at our church loved receiving a loaf of my mother's golden crumbed semolina bread or her chubby cinnamon rolls glazed with the creamiest and outrageously delicious lemon-flavored icing.

One day Mom announced to my father that she was thinking of opening a pizza stand at the end of the driveway so as people drove by, they could stop and buy a pizza. It seemed like a fine idea and I was proud that Mom was thinking like a corporate woman. After all, she should have her own pocket money. She would still be at home, juggle everything she needed to do, and still look out the kitchen window to see if anyone was in need of a pizza!

A sign was made: "LOUISE'S FRESH PIZZA." A stand was built and she was in business. Mom used flour by the fifty-pound bagfuls, which she bought in Canada because she considered their flour superior to the Robin Hood variety that she bought in her local A&P. Nothing was going to stop her from using the best ingredients. She insisted that fresh cake yeast gave the best rise and taste to bread and pizza. She used plum tomatoes, squeezed by hand and put up in jars the summer before, as the topping for the pizza and she sent my father all the way to Buffalo to the Broadway Market to get the best provolone, mozzarella, and salame.

At night after we had dinner, gotten our dose of cod liver oil, brushed our teeth, and done our homework, Mom would make pizza dough and let it rise overnight. In the morning a massive cloud of dough spilled out of the white tub where it had been rising. She would deal with that after we left for school.

Pizza with tomatoes and cheese, pepperoni pizza (an American invention), anchovy pizza, and mushroom pizza were her signature items. We waited for a car to stop . . . and waited. Finally, a customer! Mom, in her apron, sold her first pizza! She might as well have given it away because the costs of the ingredients and her time and labor were far more than what she charged. But that first sale gave her confidence, and the pizza business grew, slowly. Soon there were repeat customers who began to tell Mom how delicious her pizza was, which led to the downfall of the business because praises got them a free pizza! Hardly a way to make a profit but Mom was as good as bread—and that's as good as it gets.

# Basic Pizza Dough

*There is no question that the right flour makes the best pizza. Caputo flour, the very same flour used in Naples to make their famous pizzas, is a high-gluten flour, which has between 11 and 12 percent protein. This is a perfect ratio for making a dough that is not too heavy or too chewy. The characteristic of pizza Napoletana is a crust with a thin middle and a rim that balloons up in the oven. You can find Caputo flour online, or substitute 00 flour, which is Italian all-purpose flour and readily available from King Arthur Flour. Unbleached all-purpose flour will also give good results. This recipe uses Caputo flour so you may find yourself adjusting the amount of flour depending on what kind of flour you use. This dough is made very quickly in a food processor. You will note that only a teaspoon of yeast is used, which will result in a slow rise, giving a much better flavor to the dough.* **Makes 1¾ pounds of dough or enough to make two 13-inch pizzas**

1½ cups warm water (100°F)

½ teaspoon active dry yeast

3 to 3¾ cups Caputo flour

½ teaspoon sea salt

1 teaspoon extra-virgin olive oil

**P**our the water into the bowl of a food processor fitted with the dough blade. Sprinkle the yeast over the water and process for 30 seconds.

Add 2 cups of the flour and the salt to the bowl and process until blended. The mixture will look soupy. Add 1 more cup of the flour and process. The dough should begin to wind around the blade. Add only enough of the remaining flour to create a dough that feels just a bit tacky on your hands.

Pour the olive oil into a large bowl, add the dough, and coat it in the oil. Cover the bowl tightly with plastic wrap and allow the dough to rise for several hours, or until doubled in size. The dough can be made and refrigerated for several days after rising. Just punch it down and place it in a large ziplock plastic bag or plastic container and refrigerate. When ready to use, transfer the dough to a bowl and allow it to rise again, covered with plastic wrap, until doubled in size. Use the dough to make Classic Pizza Margherita (page 93).

## The Art of Getting By

*Before I went to Naples, everything that I knew about it came from what my Neapolitan nonna, Anna Galasso, told me. People were poor, living conditions were hard, food was scarce, there was crime, and it was hard to find work. These factors and others brought her to America around 1900, when she was in her early twenties.*

*When I finally went to Naples, I found a city of contrasts. My first encounter was the elegant hotels along the Via Partenope, one of the main streets along the seaside (lungomare) offering gorgeous views of the sea, and of large ships slowly passing by on their way to nearby Capri, Ischia, and other ports, as well as a panoramic sweep of the sleeping giant, Mount Vesuvius, looming in the not too far distance. Closer to shore, fishermen lowered and raised their nets as their vividly colored boats bobbed gently in the water.*

*Jutting out to sea across from Via Partenope was the foreboding-looking Castel Dell'Ovo (Castle of the Egg). This ancient fortress, the oldest castle in Naples, provides a dramatic backdrop where brides like to have their photos taken, and it is a favorite place for lovers to cozy up on the rocky ledges that flank the water's edge. It is also a spot for the polizia stradale (traffic police) to hover and at a moment's whim stop motorists for a check of their licenses while paying no attention at all to the hundreds of motorists whizzing by them without any concern for traffic lights or pedestrians.*

*Not far from Via Partenope is the expansive Piazza del Plebiscito with the impressive and opulent Palazzo Reale, a seventeenth-century royal palace built for the Spanish viceroys who ruled Naples. Opposite the palace is an architectural wonder, the nineteenth-century church of San Francesco di Paola, which bears a striking resemblance to the Pantheon in Rome. The space between these two monumental structures was originally intended for ceremonies and military parades, and is today a "communal living room" for Neapolitans of all ages to congregate with their families and friends. Here they gossip, sit on mopeds, eat gelato, read the paper, people-watch, and stroll arm-in-arm with no particular destination in mind. When I am in these settings it is an opportunity to see people for who they really are, and the Neapolitans exhibit a zest for life found nowhere* else in Italy that I have been. They live life on the edge, unabashed, and with gusto. They test fate at every turn, as is evidenced in the way they drive, argue, and turn negative situations to their advantage.

To experience the real and everyday Naples a visit to the old neighborhoods is a must, whether it is the Spanish quarter (Quartieri Spagnoli or Spaccanapoli, which means split Naples). If you are observant in these places you can get an idea of how Neapolitans live. These working neighborhoods are defined by narrow crowded streets shaded by buildings that appear to close in on themselves. Row after row of laundry, strung from building to building, block out the sunshine but make a statement about how to cope in confined spaces. Scores of people crowd the walkways on their way to shop or work; children play soccer in spaces no bigger than a closet, and some men pass the time of day amid all the chaos by claiming a small section of the sidewalk and enclosing themselves in a makeshift tent to play a game of cards.

There are shops of every description on these streets from butchers to bakers to tripe sellers, and open-air markets where fish from the tiniest of fresh sardines to huge tuna and swordfish are cut, sold, and wrapped in large paper cones. In the produce market every imaginable fruit or vegetable is available including carrots, celery, onions, and herbs already tied together like a bouquet ready to add to the soup pot, an indication that today's Neapolitan women do not have the time to spend in the kitchen like their nonnas did.

A walk down the famous Via San Gregorio Armeno reveals a colorful street made famous by the presepio trade, the handcrafted nativity figures made by local artists from terra-cotta and dressed elegantly in the costumes of old Naples. I stopped to look for figures in some of the jam-packed shops. I soon learned by observing that one of the elements of getting by was the ability to haggle. If you want to pay a fair price for a presepio, or anything, knowing how to strike a good deal and the art of persuasion are key.

Today's presepio reflects more than the manger scene of the Christ Child, shepherds, and Three Kings; there are figures of present-day politicians, Sophia Loren, the pizzaiola (pizza maker), the prosciutto-maker, the wet nurse, scenes of life in old Naples and the constant favorite, Pulcinella, the masked clown in baggy white pants, pointed hat, and ruffled shirt, who is the classic and complex character symbol of Naples, a symbol of fortune and fate, of laughter and tears, of good and evil, of conflict and resolve, of intrigue and innuendo, and who above all embodies l'arte di arrangiarisi, the art of living by your wits.

Coping and ingenuity go hand in hand in this crowded, boisterous city of contrasts. No matter what fate has in store for a Neapolitan, he or she will find a way to deal with it, whether it is the music grinder who positions himself strategically on the street playing for your entertainment while his hat becomes a receptacle for money, or the puppeteer who pulls all the right strings to amuse you and shame you into recognizing that his talents are not for free, or the trinket peddler who just wants to get by, and stands on a corner all day long repetitiously demonstrating how a battery-operated toy works. Even in restaurants you may be serenaded by a wandering musician who will expect you to show your satisfaction with a slip of a few euro.

In Naples, the game is life lived to the best of one's ability and for that we must all have a little bit of Pulcinella within us.

# Classic Pizza

## Pizza Margherita

*If your refrigerator contains fresh mozzarella cheese, fresh basil, and a simple sauce made from plum tomatoes, you have the makings of a classic Margherita pizza, named after Queen Margherita who visited Naples in the late nineteenth century. Why not start a tradition in your house and make Friday or Saturday pizza night? Your family will look forward to it and it will get them enthused about being in the kitchen and making something they love. With pizza for supper, you can plan ahead, and at the same time teach children about cooking skills. And you can teach them that pizza can be a good food if made properly, and the toppings are chosen wisely.* **Makes two 13-inch pizzas**

**P**reheat the oven to 450°F.

After the dough has risen, punch it down with your fists. Divide the dough in half and stretch each half out with wet hands on a floured work surface to a 13-inch round. Place each round on a lightly oiled pizza pan. Brush each round with 1 tablespoon of the olive oil. Divide and spread the tomato sauce evenly over the top of each pizza to within 1 inch of the border. Divide and sprinkle the cheese evenly over each pizza. Drizzle the tops of each pizza with a little olive oil and sprinkle with salt.

Bake each pizza until the edges begin to brown slightly and the underside is nicely browned. Remove the pizza from the oven, cut into wedges with a pizza cutter or kitchen scissors, and divide and scatter the fresh basil over the slices. Serve hot. Now that is true pizza!

I recipe Basic Pizza Dough (page 89)

2 tablespoons extra-virgin olive oil, plus extra for drizzling

1½ cups Pizza Sauce (page 105)

½ pound fresh mozzarella cheese, cut into small pieces

Salt

8 basil leaves, torn into small pieces

# Genoa-Style Focaccia
## Focaccia Genovese

1 teaspoon active dry
yeast

1½ cups warm water

3½ to 4 cups
unbleached
all-purpose flour

1 teaspoon salt

¼ teaspoon sugar

1 tablespoon extra-
virgin olive oil plus
extra for the pan

Coarse sea salt

*It's no secret that I love to work with yeast dough. I usually bake bread every week and Friday nights are reserved for homemade pizza. Focaccia Genovese, Liguria's answer to pizza, is something I like to make as well. If you have a food processor, stand mixer, or just a bowl, you can whip up this simple dough in no time. Serve the focaccia with a glass of wine, a few olives, and cheese and you will be satisfied. It is also great with the Fish Chowder on page 71.* **Makes one 14-inch round focaccia**

**d**issolve the yeast in ½ cup of the warm water in a mixing bowl, or the bowl of food processor or stand mixer. Allow to stand 5 minutes, then pour in the rest of the water. Mix in 3½ cups of the flour along with the salt, sugar, and olive oil. If the dough seems too wet and is really sticking to your hands, or does not wrap around the blade of the food processor or the dough hook in a stand mixer, add just enough of the remaining flour to obtain a smooth ball of dough.

Transfer the dough to a work surface and allow it to stand, covered with a kitchen towel, for 10 minutes.

Oil a 12- to 14-inch round pizza pan or nonstick, ovenproof skillet.

Transfer the dough to the pan or skillet and press it out with wet hands to the edges of the pan. Cover with a kitchen towel and let rise for 2 hours.

Preheat the oven to 425°F.

When ready to bake, using your thumb, make impressions all over the surface of the dough. Brush the dough liberally with olive oil and sprinkle with coarse sea salt.

Bake the focaccia for 30 to 35 minutes, or until golden brown. Serve hot, cut into wedges.

**Variations:** Rosemary leaves, pitted black olives, and grated cheese are also great toppings.

# Mom's Ricotta Cheese Calzones

## Calzone di Ricotta alla mamma

*Whenever I visited my mother, I would take her out to dinner at one of her favorite restaurants. Mom was never one about ambience; it was all about the food. So it was not surprising that she often liked to go to a nondescript, hole-in-the-wall diner where they made delicious ricotta cheese-filled calzones. They were as big as a platter and she often brought half of one home for lunch the next day. Mom could re-create anything, so instead of asking the diner folks how they made them, she created her own recipe with many filling variations, such as spinach and cheese or broccoli and cheese or sausage and cheese. Still, I loved the ricotta-filled ones the best because she did, too. The success of this recipe depends on the quality of the ricotta and mozzarella cheeses.*
**Makes 4 calzones**

In a bowl, combine the cheeses and salt and season generously with pepper and mix well. Cover and keep refrigerated while making the dough.

In a large mixing bowl or in the bowl of a stand mixer, combine the water, yeast, and sugar. Allow to stand for 5 minutes. Add the olive oil and 2½ cups of the flour and mix by hand or on medium speed with the dough blade until blended. Add additional flour ½ cup at a time until the dough begins to wind around the blade or is not sticking to your hands. Strive for a soft but not sticky dough.

Lightly flour a work surface and turn out the dough. With wet hands knead the dough until it is smooth and elastic. Divide the dough into four equal-size balls and place them on a clean kitchen towel. Cover and let rise until doubled in size.

Preheat the oven to 425°F. With a rolling pin, flatten each ball and roll into an 8-inch-diameter round. Spread ½ cup of the ricotta filling on one half of each round. Fold the other half of the round over the filling to create the calzone, or turnover, shape. Seal the edges with a fork that has been dipped in flour.

As you form the calzones, place them, 2 inches apart, on a parchment paper–lined baking sheet. Cover with a clean kitchen towel and let rise for 20 minutes.

Brush the tops of each calzone with the beaten egg; sprinkle with the coarse salt and make an X with a scissors in the top of each one.

Bake the calzones for 20 minutes, or until golden brown. Serve hot.

## FILLING

1 pound good-quality ricotta cheese, well drained

½ pound fresh mozzarella or provolone cheese, cut into bits

1½ teaspoons fine sea salt

Coarsely ground black pepper

## DOUGH

1 cup warm water (110°F)

1 package active dry yeast

1½ teaspoons sugar

3 to 3½ cups unbleached all-purpose flour

2 teaspoons salt

2 tablespoons extra-virgin olive oil

## TOPPING

1 large egg, lightly beaten with a fork

Coarse sea salt for sprinkling on top of calzones

# Onion, Potato, and Pumpkin Seed Focaccia

## Focaccia di Cipolla, Patate e Semi di Zucca

*I give credit to Nonna Galasso for the trick I have used on* Ciao Italia *to demonstrate how to make a good, light-tasting yeast dough. She always saved the water that potatoes were boiled in, or the water that peeled, uncooked potatoes were held in. In either case a lot of starch leaches out of the potatoes, and yeast just loves to feed on the sugars in potato starch. Nonna would always crumble her cakes of yeast into warm potato water. When I boil potatoes I make sure to drain off the water into containers that I can freeze. That way I always have potato water on hand. This dough is what is referred to as straight dough because it uses just water, active dried yeast, unbleached all-purpose flour, salt, and a little olive oil. Sometimes I add toasted pumpkin seeds to the dough; it adds nutty flavor, and texture. I top the dough with onions, paper-thin slices of potatoes, and fresh thyme to make a delicious focaccia, a flat, rectangular pizza that is a great starter for a rustic Italian dinner.* **Makes one 15 x 1½-inch focaccia**

**P**reheat oven to 325°F.

Spread the pumpkin seeds on a baking sheet and toast them for 8 minutes. You will hear a popping noise as they toast. Transfer the toasted seeds to a dish to cool.

Make the dough in a stand mixer, food processor, or by hand. Pour ½ cup of the water into a mixing bowl. Sprinkle the yeast over the water and stir it with a spoon. Allow the yeast to "proof" until bubbles appear on the surface. This will take about 5 minutes. Pour in the remaining water. Lightly spoon the flour into a 1-cup dry measure (stainless steel or plastic) and level off the top with a butter knife. Add to the proofed yeast. Stir in the salt and olive oil. Continue measuring and adding enough flour to create dough that moves away from the sides of the mixing bowl. The dough should be slightly tacky but not sticking to your hands.

Knead the dough a few times on a lightly floured work surface. Form the dough into a ball and place it in a large bowl. Cover the bowl tightly with plastic wrap and allow it to rise until double in size. Or make the dough a day ahead, and after it has

**DOUGH**

½ cup hulled, unsalted pumpkin seeds

1½ cups warm potato water (110°F)

1 package active dried yeast

3 to 3½ cups unbleached all-purpose flour

1½ teaspoons fine sea salt

1 teaspoon extra-virgin olive oil

**TOPPING**

6 tablespoons extra-virgin olive oil

1 large Yukon or red-skin potato

2 large red onions, peeled and thinly sliced

4 tablespoons of sugar

⅓ cup red wine vinegar

¼ cup fresh thyme leaves

½ teaspoon coarse ground black pepper

risen, punch it down, and place the dough in an olive oil–sprayed plastic bag. Refrigerate the dough overnight if you're not making the focaccia right away.

Remove the dough from the refrigerator, punch it down with your fists, and transfer it to a lightly floured work surface. Stretch out the dough with your hands into a roughly shaped round. Spread the pumpkin seeds on top of the dough. Fold the dough over the pumpkin seeds, and knead the dough until the seeds are evenly distributed throughout the dough.

Transfer the dough to a lightly greased 15 × 11½-inch rimmed baking sheet and stretch it out with your hands to fit the pan.

When ready to use, transfer the dough to a bowl; cover it with a towel and let it come to room temperature, and rise again until double in size.

Meanwhile make the topping.

Peel the potato, and cut it into paper-thin slices. (If you want to prep the potatoes ahead of time, place the slices in a bowl, and cover them with cold water to prevent them from discoloring. Then drain and dry the slices before sautéing them.)

Heat 3 tablespoons of the olive oil in a sauté pan over medium heat. Add the potatoes and sauté them, turning them frequently, just until they start to brown around the edges. Transfer the potatoes to a dish. Add the remaining 3 tablespoons of olive oil to the pan. Add the onions and cook, stirring them occasionally, until they soften. Stir the sugar into the onions and continue cooking them for 2 to 3 minutes. They should look creamy and glazed. Raise the heat to high and stir in the vinegar. Continue cooking and stirring until all the vinegar has evaporated. Transfer the mixture to a bowl and allow it to cool.

Spread all the potato slices over the top of the dough. Spread the onions evenly over the potatoes, and sprinkle the thyme and pepper over the onions. Cover with a clean dishtowel, and allow to rise for 20 minutes.

Preheat the oven to 400°F.

Bake the focaccia for 25 to 30 minutes or until the bottom crust is nicely browned. Cut the focaccia into squares and serve warm.

**Variation:** The dough and topping can be divided to make two smaller focacce.

Skillet ...

Pizza in P...

*This is not a trad...*
*no time to bake...*
*this method of n...*
**one 9- to 10-in...**

**h**eat a well-oil...
If you don't hav...
On a lightly...
than the diamet...
low it to cook u...
flip the dough o...
and scatter the c...
tinue to cook th...
Using the m...
with salt and dri...
over the wedge...

# Onion, Potato, and Pumpkin Seed Focaccia

## Focaccia di Cipolla, Patate e Semi di Zucca

*I give credit to Nonna Galasso for the trick I have used on Ciao Italia to demonstrate how to make a good, light-tasting yeast dough. She always saved the water that potatoes were boiled in, or the water that peeled, uncooked potatoes were held in. In either case a lot of starch leaches out of the potatoes, and yeast just loves to feed on the sugars in potato starch. Nonna would always crumble her cakes of yeast into warm potato water. When I boil potatoes I make sure to drain off the water into containers that I can freeze. That way I always have potato water on hand. This dough is what is referred to as straight dough because it uses just water, active dried yeast, unbleached all-purpose flour, salt, and a little olive oil. Sometimes I add toasted pumpkin seeds to the dough; it adds nutty flavor, and texture. I top the dough with onions, paper-thin slices of potatoes, and fresh thyme to make a delicious focaccia, a flat, rectangular pizza that is a great starter for a rustic Italian dinner.* **Makes one 15 x 1½-inch focaccia**

**P**reheat oven to 325°F.

Spread the pumpkin seeds on a baking sheet and toast them for 8 minutes. You will hear a popping noise as they toast. Transfer the toasted seeds to a dish to cool.

Make the dough in a stand mixer, food processor, or by hand. Pour ½ cup of the water into a mixing bowl. Sprinkle the yeast over the water and stir it with a spoon. Allow the yeast to "proof" until bubbles appear on the surface. This will take about 5 minutes. Pour in the remaining water. Lightly spoon the flour into a 1-cup dry measure (stainless steel or plastic) and level off the top with a butter knife. Add to the proofed yeast. Stir in the salt and olive oil. Continue measuring and adding enough flour to create dough that moves away from the sides of the mixing bowl. The dough should be slightly tacky but not sticking to your hands.

Knead the dough a few times on a lightly floured work surface. Form the dough into a ball and place it in a large bowl. Cover the bowl tightly with plastic wrap and allow it to rise until double in size. Or make the dough a day ahead, and after it has

**DOUGH**

½ cup hulled, unsalted pumpkin seeds

1½ cups warm potato water (110°F)

1 package active dried yeast

3 to 3½ cups unbleached all-purpose flour

1½ teaspoons fine sea salt

1 teaspoon extra-virgin olive oil

**TOPPING**

6 tablespoons extra-virgin olive oil

1 large Yukon or red-skin potato

2 large red onions, peeled and thinly sliced

4 tablespoons of sugar

⅓ cup red wine vinegar

¼ cup fresh thyme leaves

½ teaspoon coarse ground black pepper

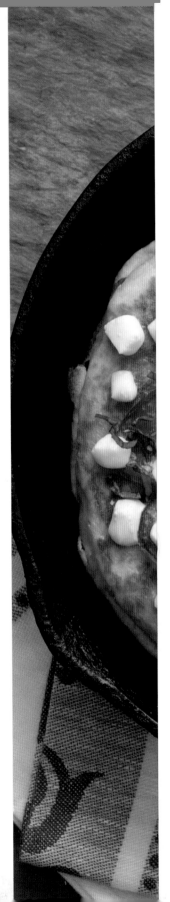

# Spinach Pizza Roll

## Rotolo di Spinaci

**DOUGH**

4 to 4½ cups unbleached all-purpose flour

2 teaspoons fine sea salt

1 package Fleischmann's pizza crust yeast

1¾ cups warm water (120°F)

1 tablespoon extra-virgin olive oil

**FILLING**

¼ cup extra-virgin olive oil

2 garlic cloves, minced

2 cups finely chopped cooked spinach

1½ cups diced salame

1 ball (6 ounces) fresh mozzarella cheese, diced

¼ pound provolone cheese, diced

Salt and black pepper

1 large egg, beaten with 1 teaspoon water for egg wash

Coarse salt

Sesame seeds

*I have been using Fleischmann's yeast my entire adult life and my mother used it as well. The good people at Fleischmann's know how busy a lot of people are these days so they developed a pizza crust yeast which is mixed directly with the dry ingredients and water, formed into dough, and rolled out for pizza with no rising time at all. This is a great boon for pizza lovers and now any night can be pizza night at home in less time than it takes to order takeout and have it delivered! Try your own toppings on the basic dough recipe given here or make this delicious spinach pizza roll.*   **Serves 8 to 10**

**C**ombine 4 cups of the flour, salt, and yeast in a large mixing bowl or food processor. Add the water and olive oil through the feed tube until a ball of dough forms. If more flour is needed, add it a little at a time until the dough comes away from the sides of the bowl.

Knead the dough a couple of times until you have a soft ball of dough that is slightly tacky but not sticking to your hands. Set aside.

Preheat the oven to 375°F. Lightly grease a baking sheet.

To make the filling, in a large frying pan, heat 3 tablespoons of the olive oil. Add the garlic and sauté until softened. Add the spinach and sauté for 2 to 3 minutes. Add the salame and cook for 2 to 3 minutes. Transfer the mixture to a bowl and let cool.

On a lightly floured work surface, roll the dough into a 12- to 14-inch-long rectangle. Lift the dough and place it on the prepared baking sheet; don't worry if the edges hang over the sides of the sheet at this point.

Brush the top of the dough with the remaining 1 tablespoon olive oil. Spread the cooled spinach mixture over the dough to within ½ inch of the edges. Scatter the cheeses over the dough and sprinkle with salt and pepper. Starting with a long side, roll the dough up tightly like a jelly roll. Pinch the seam to seal and position the roll on the baking sheet so the seam is on the bottom; tuck the two ends under the roll.

Brush the top of the roll with the egg wash. Sprinkle with salt and sesame seeds.

Bake the roll for 25 to 30 minutes, or until nicely browned. Let cool, then cut crosswise into thick slices.

# Skillet Pizza

## Pizza in Padella

*This is not a traditional way to make pizza, but so many people tell me t
no time to bake that one day while I was experimenting with dough, I
this method of making pizza in a stove-top skillet using store-bought do*
**one 9- to 10-inch pizza**

**h**eat a well-oiled, cast-iron, 10- or 12-inch skillet for 5 minutes over
If you don't have a cast-iron skillet, use a heavy nonstick frying pan.

On a lightly floured work surface, roll the dough out into a circle 1
than the diameter of the pan you are using. Place the dough in the ho
low it to cook until it begins to rise and the bottom is starting to bro
flip the dough over with a wide metal spatula. Lay the tomato slices ov
and scatter the cheese over the tomatoes. Lower the heat to medium-
tinue to cook the pizza until the cheese has melted.

Using the metal spatula, transfer the pizza to a cutting board. Sprir
with salt and drizzle with olive oil. Cut into wedges and sprinkle the sh
over the wedges.

# Palermo-Style Pizza

## Lo Sfincione alla Palermitano

*Sfincione, Sicilian pizza, is found in the province of Palermo and is a staple of the Christmas season. A peasant dish in origin, the word* sfincione *is often translated as meaning something being very soft* (muodda 'na sfinci), *and sfincione is very breadlike in texture and taste. Begin the dough with a starter dough called a* biga *or* madre, *which helps to enhance the the dough's rise and flavor. The topping is a very vibrant flavor combination of anchovies, cheese, and bread crumbs.* **Makes two thick 9-inch pizzas**

**i**n a medium bowl, dissolve the yeast in ½ cup of the water; stir in ¾ cup of the flour and mix well to form a ball. Allow to rest, covered with plastic wrap, for 30 minutes. This is the *biga* or *madre*.

Dump the remaining flour onto a work surface and make a hole in the center. Add the *biga* or *madre*. Work the flour and 2 teaspoons of salt into the *madre*. Add as much of the remaining 2 cups of water as needed to make a dough that is soft and elastic and not sticking to your hands. Add the 3 tablespoons of olive oil to the dough and work it in with your hands until it is completely absorbed. Cover with a bowl and allow the dough to rise until doubled in size.

Meanwhile, liberally oil two 9-inch cake pans and set aside. Simmer the onions in the water until they are soft. Drain and blot the onions dry. Sauté the onion in a tablespoon of olive oil until golden brown. Stir in the tomato sauce and simmer the ingredients for 10 minutes. Season to taste with salt and pepper.

After the dough has risen, punch it down with your fists and divide it in half. Spread each half in a prepared cake pan, spreading it out with your fingers so it covers the bottom in an even layer. Sprinkle the anchovies over each half, pushing them down into the dough as far as they will go. Spread the tomato and onion sauce evenly over the dough, then evenly scatter the cheese. Sprinkle coarse salt and a grinding of coarse black pepper over the sauce (to taste).

Mix the bread crumbs and oregano together and sprinkle them over the sauce. Cover the pans with a towel and allow the pizzas to rise for 2 hours.

Preheat the oven to 425°F. Bake the pizzas for 30 to 35 minutes, or until the crusts are golden brown. Drizzle the tops with olive oil. Cut into pieces and serve hot.

**DOUGH**

1 teaspoon active dry yeast

2½ cups warm water (110°F)

5½ cups unbleached all-purpose flour

Salt

3 tablespoons extra-virgin olive oil

**TOPPING**

1 large onion, peeled and thinly sliced

1 cup water

½ cup extra-virgin olive oil, plus more for drizzling

1½ cups tomato sauce

Coarse salt

Coarsely ground black pepper

8 anchovy fillets packed in oil, drained, and cut into small pieces

½ pound provolone or fresh mozzarella cheese, cut into bits

1 cup toasted bread crumbs

2 tablespoons dried oregano

# Spinach Pizza Roll

## Rotolo di Spinaci

*I have been using Fleischmann's yeast my entire adult life and my mother used it as well. The good people at Fleischmann's know how busy a lot of people are these days so they developed a pizza crust yeast which is mixed directly with the dry ingredients and water, formed into dough, and rolled out for pizza with no rising time at all. This is a great boon for pizza lovers and now any night can be pizza night at home in less time than it takes to order takeout and have it delivered! Try your own toppings on the basic dough recipe given here or make this delicious spinach pizza roll.* **Serves 8 to 10**

**DOUGH**

4 to 4½ cups unbleached all-purpose flour

2 teaspoons fine sea salt

1 package Fleischmann's pizza crust yeast

1¾ cups warm water (120°F)

1 tablespoon extra-virgin olive oil

**FILLING**

¼ cup extra-virgin olive oil

2 garlic cloves, minced

2 cups finely chopped cooked spinach

1½ cups diced salame

1 ball (6 ounces) fresh mozzarella cheese, diced

¼ pound provolone cheese, diced

Salt and black pepper

1 large egg, beaten with 1 teaspoon water for egg wash

Coarse salt

Sesame seeds

**C**ombine 4 cups of the flour, salt, and yeast in a large mixing bowl or food processor. Add the water and olive oil through the feed tube until a ball of dough forms. If more flour is needed, add it a little at a time until the dough comes away from the sides of the bowl.

Knead the dough a couple of times until you have a soft ball of dough that is slightly tacky but not sticking to your hands. Set aside.

Preheat the oven to 375°F. Lightly grease a baking sheet.

To make the filling, in a large frying pan, heat 3 tablespoons of the olive oil. Add the garlic and sauté until softened. Add the spinach and sauté for 2 to 3 minutes. Add the salame and cook for 2 to 3 minutes. Transfer the mixture to a bowl and let cool.

On a lightly floured work surface, roll the dough into a 12- to 14-inch-long rectangle. Lift the dough and place it on the prepared baking sheet; don't worry if the edges hang over the sides of the sheet at this point.

Brush the top of the dough with the remaining 1 tablespoon olive oil. Spread the cooled spinach mixture over the dough to within ½ inch of the edges. Scatter the cheeses over the dough and sprinkle with salt and pepper. Starting with a long side, roll the dough up tightly like a jelly roll. Pinch the seam to seal and position the roll on the baking sheet so the seam is on the bottom; tuck the two ends under the roll.

Brush the top of the roll with the egg wash. Sprinkle with salt and sesame seeds.

Bake the roll for 25 to 30 minutes, or until nicely browned. Let cool, then cut crosswise into thick slices.

# Palermo-Style Pizza

## Lo Sfincione alla Palermitano

Sfincione, *Sicilian pizza, is found in the province of Palermo and is a staple of the Christmas season. A peasant dish in origin, the word* sfincione *is often translated as meaning something being very soft (*muodda 'na sfinci*), and sfincione is very breadlike in texture and taste. Begin the dough with a starter dough called a* biga *or* madre, *which helps to enhance the the dough's rise and flavor. The topping is a very vibrant flavor combination of anchovies, cheese, and bread crumbs.* **Makes two thick 9-inch pizzas**

In a medium bowl, dissolve the yeast in ½ cup of the water; stir in ¾ cup of the flour and mix well to form a ball. Allow to rest, covered with plastic wrap, for 30 minutes. This is the *biga* or *madre.*

Dump the remaining flour onto a work surface and make a hole in the center. Add the *biga* or *madre.* Work the flour and 2 teaspoons of salt into the *madre.* Add as much of the remaining 2 cups of water as needed to make a dough that is soft and elastic and not sticking to your hands. Add the 3 tablespoons of olive oil to the dough and work it in with your hands until it is completely absorbed. Cover with a bowl and allow the dough to rise until doubled in size.

Meanwhile, liberally oil two 9-inch cake pans and set aside. Simmer the onions in the water until they are soft. Drain and blot the onions dry. Sauté the onion in a tablespoon of olive oil until golden brown. Stir in the tomato sauce and simmer the ingredients for 10 minutes. Season to taste with salt and pepper.

After the dough has risen, punch it down with your fists and divide it in half. Spread each half in a prepared cake pan, spreading it out with your fingers so it covers the bottom in an even layer. Sprinkle the anchovies over each half, pushing them down into the dough as far as they will go. Spread the tomato and onion sauce evenly over the dough, then evenly scatter the cheese. Sprinkle coarse salt and a grinding of coarse black pepper over the sauce (to taste).

Mix the bread crumbs and oregano together and sprinkle them over the sauce. Cover the pans with a towel and allow the pizzas to rise for 2 hours.

Preheat the oven to 425°F. Bake the pizzas for 30 to 35 minutes, or until the crusts are golden brown. Drizzle the tops with olive oil. Cut into pieces and serve hot.

**DOUGH**

1 teaspoon active dry yeast

2½ cups warm water (110°F)

5½ cups unbleached all-purpose flour

Salt

3 tablespoons extra-virgin olive oil

**TOPPING**

1 large onion, peeled and thinly sliced

1 cup water

½ cup extra-virgin olive oil, plus more for drizzling

1½ cups tomato sauce

Coarse salt

Coarsely ground black pepper

8 anchovy fillets packed in oil, drained, and cut into small pieces

½ pound provolone or fresh mozzarella cheese, cut into bits

1 cup toasted bread crumbs

2 tablespoons dried oregano

## Pizza in Padella

*This is not a traditional way to make pizza, but so many people tell me that they have no time to bake that one day while I was experimenting with dough, I came up with this method of making pizza in a stove-top skillet using store-bought dough.* **Makes one 9- to 10-inch pizza**

**1 pound store-bought dough, at room temperature**

**1 medium ripe tomato, thinly sliced**

**¼ pound fresh mozzarella cheese, cut into bits**

**Coarse sea salt**

**Extra-virgin olive oil for drizzling**

**½ cup shredded basil leaves**

**h**eat a well-oiled, cast-iron, 10- or 12-inch skillet for 5 minutes over medium heat. If you don't have a cast-iron skillet, use a heavy nonstick frying pan.

On a lightly floured work surface, roll the dough out into a circle 1 inch smaller than the diameter of the pan you are using. Place the dough in the hot pan and allow it to cook until it begins to rise and the bottom is starting to brown. Carefully flip the dough over with a wide metal spatula. Lay the tomato slices over the dough and scatter the cheese over the tomatoes. Lower the heat to medium-low and continue to cook the pizza until the cheese has melted.

Using the metal spatula, transfer the pizza to a cutting board. Sprinkle the pizza with salt and drizzle with olive oil. Cut into wedges and sprinkle the shredded basil over the wedges.

# Spinach Pizza Roll

## Rotolo di Spinaci

### DOUGH

4 to 4½ cups unbleached all-purpose flour

2 teaspoons fine sea salt

1 package Fleischmann's pizza crust yeast

1¾ cups warm water (120°F)

1 tablespoon extra-virgin olive oil

### FILLING

¼ cup extra-virgin olive oil

2 garlic cloves, minced

2 cups finely chopped cooked spinach

1½ cups diced salame

1 ball (6 ounces) fresh mozzarella cheese, diced

¼ pound provolone cheese, diced

Salt and black pepper

1 large egg, beaten with 1 teaspoon water for egg wash

Coarse salt

Sesame seeds

*I have been using Fleischmann's yeast my entire adult life and my mother used it as well. The good people at Fleischmann's know how busy a lot of people are these days so they developed a pizza crust yeast which is mixed directly with the dry ingredients and water, formed into dough, and rolled out for pizza with no rising time at all. This is a great boon for pizza lovers and now any night can be pizza night at home in less time than it takes to order takeout and have it delivered! Try your own toppings on the basic dough recipe given here or make this delicious spinach pizza roll.* **Serves 8 to 10**

Combine 4 cups of the flour, salt, and yeast in a large mixing bowl or food processor. Add the water and olive oil through the feed tube until a ball of dough forms. If more flour is needed, add it a little at a time until the dough comes away from the sides of the bowl.

Knead the dough a couple of times until you have a soft ball of dough that is slightly tacky but not sticking to your hands. Set aside.

Preheat the oven to 375°F. Lightly grease a baking sheet.

To make the filling, in a large frying pan, heat 3 tablespoons of the olive oil. Add the garlic and sauté until softened. Add the spinach and sauté for 2 to 3 minutes. Add the salame and cook for 2 to 3 minutes. Transfer the mixture to a bowl and let cool.

On a lightly floured work surface, roll the dough into a 12- to 14-inch-long rectangle. Lift the dough and place it on the prepared baking sheet; don't worry if the edges hang over the sides of the sheet at this point.

Brush the top of the dough with the remaining 1 tablespoon olive oil. Spread the cooled spinach mixture over the dough to within ½ inch of the edges. Scatter the cheeses over the dough and sprinkle with salt and pepper. Starting with a long side, roll the dough up tightly like a jelly roll. Pinch the seam to seal and position the roll on the baking sheet so the seam is on the bottom; tuck the two ends under the roll.

Brush the top of the roll with the egg wash. Sprinkle with salt and sesame seeds.

Bake the roll for 25 to 30 minutes, or until nicely browned. Let cool, then cut crosswise into thick slices.

2 po
    b
    d
1 tal
    vi
    m
    th
16 sl
    P.
2 cu
    so
Salt
½ cu
    nu
1 me
    ar
    st
    ar
2 tea
    ba

# Mom's Cinnamon Rolls with Lemon Icing

*My mother could make anything from donuts to puff pastry. One of her Sunday morning specialties was cinnamon rolls. This was her concession to baking American-style sweet rolls. I craved them then and I still do now.* ***Makes 18 rolls***

**t**o make the dough in a stand mixer, combine 4½ cups of the flour, the granulated sugar, salt, and yeast. Combine the water, milk, eggs, and butter. Add to the dry ingredients and process until a ball of dough forms around the blade. If the dough is sticky, add more flour, a tablespoon at a time, until a soft, but not sticky, ball of dough forms.

Transfer the dough to a lightly floured work surface and knead with your hands until it is smooth and no longer sticky, adding more flour if necessary. Transfer the dough to a lightly buttered bowl and cover tightly with plastic wrap. Allow the dough to rise in a warm, but not hot, place (72°F is ideal) until doubled in size.

Meanwhile mix the cinnamon and granulated sugar together in a small bowl. Set the filling aside.

When the dough has risen, punch it down and roll it out on a lightly floured work surface into a large 18 × 12-inch rectangle.

Brush the dough with the melted butter and evenly sprinkle the cinnamon-sugar mixture over the top. Sprinkle the raisins over the sugar. Start at the longest side nearest you and roll the dough up on itself tightly, forming a long log. Pinch the seam and the ends closed.

Preheat the oven to 375°F. With a knife cut eighteen 1-inch slices and place them on lightly greased baking sheets about 1 inch apart.

Cover the rolls with a towel and allow them to rise again until doubled in size.

Bake the rolls until lightly browned, about 25 to 30 minutes. Transfer the rolls to a wire rack to cool slightly. Use a fork dipped in the glaze and drip it over the tops of the rolls. These are best eaten warm.

## DOUGH

- 4½ to 5 cups unbleached all-purpose flour
- ½ cup granulated sugar
- 1½ teaspoons salt
- 1 package active dry yeast
- ¼ cup warm water (110° to 115°F)
- ½ cup warm milk (110° to 115°F)
- 3 large eggs, at room temperature
- 8 tablespoons (1 stick) unsalted butter, melted and cooled

## FILLING

- 2¼ teaspoons ground cinnamon
- 1⅔ cups granulated sugar
- 4 tablespoons (½ stick) unsalted butter, melted and cooled
- 1¾ cups raisins, soaked in warm water and drained

## LEMON GLAZE

Double glaze from page 397

# Sicilian Bread

## Pane Siciliano

### CRESCIUTA

¼ teaspoon active dry yeast

½ cup warm water (110° to 115°F)

½ cup unbleached all-purpose flour

### DOUGH

1 teaspoon active dry yeast

2 cups warm water (110° to 115°F)

4 to 5 cups fine durum semolina flour

1 teaspoon wheat gluten

2 teaspoons fine sea salt

Cornmeal for sprinkling, or parchment paper

⅓ cup sesame seeds

*Sicilian bread is special; it has a golden crumb due to the fine durum semolina flour used to make it and a nice nutty taste from the sesame seeds on the crust. Begin the bread's life by making a biga (a mother dough) or what the Sicilians call a cresciuta. The mother dough gives added strength to the dough, helps it rise, and provides wonderful flavor.* **Makes 1 large loaf or 2 smaller ones**

To make the *cresciuta*, in a small bowl, dissolve the ¼ teaspoon yeast in the water and let stand 10 minutes until foamy. Stir in the flour, cover the bowl with plastic wrap, and let the mixture sit in a warm place for at least 4 hours, or overnight.

In a large bowl, dissolve the 1 teaspoon yeast in 2 cups of the warm water. Let stand, covered, for 5 minutes, or until foamy.

Stir the *cresciuta* into the yeast and water mixture and blend well. Add 2 cups of the semolina flour, the wheat gluten, and the salt and mix until a pancake-like batter forms. Add additional flour, a little at a time, until a smooth ball of dough is obtained that is soft but not sticking to your hands.

Turn the dough out onto a floured work surface and knead it for about 10 minutes. Place it in a large bowl and cover with plastic wrap. Let it rise until doubled, about 1½ hours.

Punch down the dough, divide it in half, and roll each half into a 30-inch-long rope. Curl the dough back and forth on itself leaving a 6- to 7-inch tail.

Lay the tail over the top of the loaf. Do not tuck it under. This form is called *mafalda*. The dough may also be formed into the eyes of Saint Lucy (an S shape).

Place the dough on a peel sprinkled with cornmeal or lined with parchment paper. Cover with a towel and let rise in a warm place until doubled in size.

Place a baking stone on the bottom rack and preheat oven at 375°F for at least 30 minutes.

Brush the top of the dough with water and sprinkle with sesame seeds. Lightly press the seeds in.

If using cornmeal, sprinkle it on the baking stone. Slide the loaf from the peel onto the stone. Bake the bread for 30 minutes, or until nicely browned and sounds hollow when tapped on the bottom. Let the bread cool on a rack before slicing.

# Walnut, Dried Fig, and Anise Bread

## Pane di Noce, Fico Secco e Anice

*I learned to bake bread from my mother. I find manipulating dough and coaxing it to do what you want is a very meditative process. For me it is almost second nature to work with dough. But I am also keenly aware that a lot of people are afraid to work with yeast dough. So years ago I wrote a book entitled* What You Knead *that took the novice bread baker step-by-step into the world of bread baking and demonstrated what you could do to change the character of a simple loaf like this recipe for fig and anise bread. This bread is easy to make and produces two exceptional-tasting loaves. The whole process can be done in a stand mixer. Start the dough early in the day, or the night before. The wheat gluten used in this recipe is available online or in the baking section of grocery stores. It is a good bread-baking aid that helps to develop a better rising dough. Be sure to use pure anise extract and not just a weak, watered down imitation.* ***Makes 2 loaves***

- 1 cup coarsely chopped walnuts
- ½ cup warm water (110° to 115°F)
- 1 tablespoon active dry yeast
- 7½ cups (approximately) unbleached all-purpose flour
- 5 ounces dried Calimyrna figs (about 13 whole), stemmed
- 1½ cups plus 1 tablespoon warm milk
- 6 tablespoons (¾ stick) unsalted butter, softened
- ⅔ cup granulated sugar
- 1¾ teaspoons pure anise extract
- 2 large eggs, slightly beaten
- 1 tablespoon wheat gluten
- 2½ teaspoons salt
- ½ cup confectioners' sugar

Place the nuts on a baking sheet and toast them in a preheated 350°F oven until they smell fragrant and are lightly browned. Transfer to a small bowl and set aside.

Pour the water into a small bowl and stir in the yeast. Stir in ½ cup of the flour to make a loose dough. Cover the bowl tightly with plastic wrap and let it rest at room temperature for 2 to 3 hours, or overnight; the dough will look spongy with lots of holes.

Place the figs in another bowl, cover them with water, and let stand at room temperature for 1 hour to soften them. Drain the water, dry the figs, and dice them. Set aside.

When you are ready to make the dough, transfer the yeast mixture to the bowl of a stand mixer fitted with the paddle attachment. Add 1½ cups milk, the butter, granulated sugar, 1½ teaspoons of the anise extract, eggs, wheat gluten, and salt to the bowl and combine the mixture on medium speed.

Begin adding the remaining flour 1 cup at a time and mix on high speed to combine the ingredients. Add only enough flour to achieve a dough that begins to come away from the side of the bowl and is not sticky on your hands.

Transfer the dough from the mixer bowl to a lightly floured work surface. Push the dough down with your hands to flatten it. Place the walnuts and figs on top of the dough, then fold the dough over to cover them. Knead with your hands to evenly distribute the walnuts and figs in the dough. Shape the dough into a large round and place it in a large lightly buttered bowl. Cover the bowl tightly with plastic wrap and allow the dough to rise for 2 hours or until doubled in size.

Preheat the oven to 375°F. Line two baking sheets with parchment paper.

Punch the dough down with your hands and transfer it to a work surface. With a knife, divide the dough into two equal pieces. Working with one piece at a time, roll each piece under the palm of your hands into a 46-inch-long rope. Starting at one end of the rope, coil the dough up tightly and place it on one of the parchment paper–lined baking sheets. Repeat with the second piece of dough.

Cover the baking sheets with a clean kitchen towel and allow the bread to rise for 20 minutes.

Bake the bread for 40 to 45 minutes, or until the crust is evenly browned on the top and bottom. Insert an instant-read thermometer in the center of the dough to determine if the bread is cooked. If the thermometer registers between 200° and 210°F, transfer the bread to a wire rack and cool until warm. If not, bake a few minutes longer.

Meanwhile in a small bowl, combine the confectioners' sugar, the 1 tablespoon milk, and the remaining ¼ teaspoon anise extract. Stir the ingredients together to make a glaze.

Using a spoon, drizzle the top of the breads with the glaze. Serve the bread warm or at room temperature.


**NOTE:** *To freeze the bread, allow it to cool completely, then wrap the unglazed bread well in aluminum foil.*

# Whole Wheat Bread

## Pane Integrale

*I developed this wheat bread by changing the ratio of unbleached flour to whole wheat flour, and added malt barley because the sugars in it causes rapid multiplication of yeast cells. Malt barley is used by many bread bakers in Italy to help give color and rise to their breads. You can purchase it in health food stores or by mail order from King Arthur Flour. Add an equal amount of sugar if malt barley is not available.* **Makes 1 large loaf**

1 tablespoon active dry yeast

1¾ cups warm water (110° to 115°F)

2 teaspoons malt barley or sugar

1 cup whole wheat flour

3 cups unbleached all-purpose flour

½ teaspoon salt

1 tablespoon extra-virgin olive oil

1 large egg, slightly beaten

1 tablespoon wheat bran

In a large bowl, dissolve the yeast in ¼ cup of the warm water. Allow the yeast to proof until it is foamy, about 10 minutes. Add the remaining 1½ cups water and the malt barley (or sugar) and mix well. Set the bowl aside.

In a separate bowl, mix the whole wheat flour, 2 cups of the all-purpose flour, and the salt. Add to the yeast mixture and mix with a wooden spoon. At this point, the mixture will be very soft. Add the remaining flour and mix with your hands until a ball of dough is formed. Add additional all-purpose flour as needed to make a soft dough.

Place the dough on a floured work surface and knead it for 5 to 10 minutes, folding the dough over on itself several times, until it is shiny and elastic. Let the dough rest, covered with a kitchen towel, on a floured surface for 5 minutes.

Grease a bowl with the olive oil. Put the dough in the bowl and turn the dough a few times to coat with the oil. Cover the bowl tightly with plastic wrap and then a clean kitchen towel, and let the dough rise in a warm place until doubled, about 1 hour.

Punch the dough down and knead it a few times on a floured work surface. Shape the dough into a round, oval, or braid and place on a baking sheet. Cover the bread with a clean kitchen towel, and let rise about 20 minutes.

Preheat the oven to 375°F. Grease a baking sheet.

Just before baking, brush the top of the loaf with the beaten egg and sprinkle on the wheat bran. Make a couple of ½-inch slashes in the top of the dough with a sharp knife or a bread lame.

Bake the bread for 30 to 35 minutes, or until the top and bottom are nicely browned. Remove the bread to a rack to cool completely.

# Pasta

Homemade Tagliatelle

Homemade Pasta

Spinach Pasta

Baked Macaroni and Cheese

Farfalle with Pistachio Nuts

Fettuccine with Mixed Mushroom Sauce

Macaroni Frittata

Paccheri with Mushroom Sauce

Mini Macaroni and Cheese

Penne with Vodka Sauce

Pasta Salad

Rigatoni with Onion Sauce

Whole Wheat Penne with Cauliflower

Pasta with Lemon

Lasagne Verdi Bologna Style

Little Ears with Pork Ragu

Tagliatelle with Bolognese Meat Sauce

Baked Ziti Casserole with Meatballs

Guy's Whole Wheat Spaghetti
with Tuna and Lemon

Pasta with Seafood Sauce

Vermicelli with Clams

Whole Wheat Spaghetti in White Clam
Sauce

Paccheri with Shrimp

Potato Gnocchi with Fontina Sauce

Ricotta Cheese and Zucchini Gnocchi

Sardinian Gnocchi with Pork Ragu

White Frittata

# from maccarun to macaroni to pasta

**a** Mount Vesuvius mountain of flour sits on my mother's thick butcher-block table. A couple of dozen fresh eggs from the "chicken man" are nearby. A broom handle, long and thin rolling pin, and a ravioli cutter come out of the pantry. Now my mother and Nonna Galasso, donned in fresh, flowered aprons, can get down to the business at hand, making fresh macaroni. This was a weekly ritual because macaroni was the centerpiece for Sunday dinner and it would have been outside the realm of reason in my ancestral home to ever have started any Sunday, or special occasion dinner, without some sort of macaroni. It was expected. Macaroni was defined as spaghetti, rigatoni, shells, lasagne, ravioli, gnocchi, and bow ties. Of those, only the shells and bow ties came from a box. Everything else was *fatto a mano* (made by hand).

In Naples, where the art of making and drying macaroni was perfected, Neapolitans were lovingly called *mangiamaccheroni* (macaroni eaters) by their more northern Italian neighbors who were affectionately known as *mangiafagioli* (bean eaters) and *mangiapolenta* (cornmeal eaters).

We never called macaroni by its more fashionable name of pasta because it was always *maccarun* (mock-a roon) to Nonna and macaroni to the rest of us. We understood its role in our lives, its character, and its goodness because it was made *a mano* (by hand). That was tradition.

I watched as Nonna gingerly cracked each egg with its deep orange-colored yolk into the middle of the flour mountain (known as the *fontana*) where my mother had made a wide hole. Then they dove right in with their hands, mixing the eggs and flour so fast that even a food processor would be envious! In no time a silky, yellow smooth ball of dough was born. I never understood why, but as soon as it was made, Nonna covered it with her huge yellow spongeware bowl and said that the dough had to "sleep." She would sit nearby and wait for the dough to "wake up" and tell me how it used to be made in Naples, in huge vats where the dough was kneaded with your feet!

Years later when I made my own macaroni, I came to understand that it was much easier to roll out a rested dough, after the gluten had relaxed, then to try and roll out a dough immediately when it would just resist your efforts. While the dough "slept," Nonna placed wooden rods that looked like thin broom handles across two kitchen chairs. My mother laid newspapers on the floor under the chairs to catch any falling pieces of macaroni as it dried. Now the dough was cut into pieces and rolled out as thin as a piece of paper. I can still hear the slapping noise of the dough as Nonna rolled and unrolled it on her pin, causing it to get larger and thinner with each slapping pass. My mother cut the sheets of dough with the ravioli cutter, making long, thin strands. These strands were draped over the rods. A big paper sign was placed near them that warned us not to touch or bump the chairs for fear that the delicate strands would go crashing to the floor. I loved how they dried, their ends curling slightly upward. When the macaroni was brittle dry, my mother placed it in flat cardboard boxes for storing. Dried, it could keep for months. And it made great gifts when someone came to visit. Just think, a box of handmade macaroni to take home!

Every Sunday without fail, huge platters of macaroni made their steamy way down the long dining room table. Macaroni thin as shoelaces and tossed in Mom's best tomato sauce was a culinary triumph. It defined what Sunday was all about in an Italian American home.

As time went on, Nonna and Mom gave in to new ways of doing things in the kitchen and purchased a hand crank pasta machine. They took to it immediately like a child with a new toy. Now they could make macaroni whenever they wanted to, not just for Sunday. They could put the dough into the rollers of the machine to flatten it, so the rolling pin wasn't needed as much and they could cut the dough, too, in the rollers for vermicelli and fettuccine.

When I got married, they gave me a hand crank machine because they wanted to be sure that I would carry on the tradition. (I later added a small motor to the handle so I did not have to hand-turn it.) I still use the "fontana" method of making pasta by hand on a wooden board and barreling down with my fist into a slightly smaller mountain of flour than what Mom and Nonna used. And when I am in a hurry, I make pasta using my food processor (which I know they would frown on), but one thing has never changed: I still call it macaroni even though the rest of the world may know it as pasta.

# Homemade Tagliatelle

*Tagliatelle are narrow ¼-inch ribbons of pasta. The name comes from the word "tagliare," meaning "to cut." They are a staple of the cooking of Bologna, where fresh pasta rules. As with many Italian foods, tagliatelle has a legend behind it. It is said that these golden yellow strands of dough were made in honor of the blond tresses of Lucrezia Borgia upon the occasion of her marriage in Ferrara to the Duke of Este.* *Makes about 2 pounds tagliatelle*

8 large eggs

6 cups unbleached all-purpose flour

Whirl the eggs in the bowl of a food processor, and slowly add the flour, cup by cup, until you have a dough that winds around the blade and cleans the sides of the bowl. Gather the dough up into a ball and place it on a lightly floured work surface. Cover the dough with a bowl and allow it to rest for 30 minutes.

Alternatively, make the dough by hand. Mound the flour on a work surface; make a hole in the center of the flour and crack the eggs into it. Break the eggs up with a fork, taking care not to break through the wall of flour. Gradually bring in the flour from the inside of the flour wall and mix with the eggs until a ball of dough forms. You may not need all the flour; push the excess aside. Knead the dough until it is smooth and allow it to rest as above.

Divide the dough into 4 equal pieces and flatten each one with a rolling pin into roughly 4 × 5-inch pieces. Thin the dough in a hand crank pasta machine using the settings on the knob. Pass the dough through the rollers and thin them until you can see your hand behind it. Allow the sheets to dry on a flat, floured surface until they are just damp to the touch, and then pass them through the cutter for fettuccine. At this point you can either cook them immediately by dropping the strands into boiling salted water or dry them for future use.

To dry them, separate the strands and hang them on a drying rack or on dowel rods propped between two chairs. They are totally dry when the ends curl. Slide the strands off the dowel rods onto a sheet of aluminum foil, seal, and save for future use. They will keep for up to one year.

# Homemade Pasta

## Pasta Fatta in Casa

*Homemade pasta is something wonderful, endearing, comforting, satisfying, and a nod to the way things used to be. Who has time to make it anymore? True, the nonnas (grandmothers) and zie (aunts) of yesterday had the care and feeding of their families as their central focus. And there was a time not so very long ago when an Italian bride to be had to master the making of pasta before getting married. Now instead of reaching for a rolling pin, we can reach for a box of pasta all ready to cook. But I think it is worth knowing how to make fresh pasta, the basis of so many great classic dishes like Lasagne Verdi alla Bolognese (page 146), ravioli, linguine, and spaghetti. The reward for your hard work is in the first forkful. And as a concession to the "no-time-to-cook" mantra, make it in minutes in a food processor.   Makes about 1 ¼ pounds*

4 large eggs

⅛ teaspoon salt

3 cups unbleached
  all-purpose flour

**W**hirl the eggs with the salt in a food processor until blended. Begin adding the flour a cup at a time and process until a ball of dough forms and leaves the sides of the bowl; you may not need all the flour. The dough should be soft but not sticking to your hands. Place the dough on a lightly floured work surface and cover it with a bowl. Let it rest for 30 minutes to relax the gluten and allow the flour to absorb the liquid.

After the dough has rested, cut it into 4 equal pieces. Work with one piece at a time, keeping the others covered so they do not dry out.

Using a rolling pin flatten the dough into a 5-inch-wide by 4-inch-long piece.

Using the settings on a hand crank pasta machine, thin the dough until you can see your hand behind it.

To make lasagne sheets cut the dough into 4 × 8-inch rectangles and place them on clean cotton kitchen towels in a single layer.

Use the cutter feature on your machine to make linguine, fettuccine, or ravioli.

When you are ready to cook the pasta, bring 4 quarts of water to a rolling boil in a large pot and add 1 tablespoon of salt. Add the pasta and cook no longer than 3 to 4 minutes; fresh pasta cooks in no time. Drain the pasta and sauce it as you wish.

If you are making lasagne sheets, have a shallow baking dish of ice cold water handy to cool the sheets after they are boiled. Add 6 to 8 sheets at a time and cook for 2 minutes, no longer. Scoop the sheets out of the water with a handheld strainer and place them immediately in the ice water. When they are cool enough to handle, place them in single layers on cotton towels and damp dry them. The lasagne sheets are now ready for assembly.

If making lasagne sheets for *Lasagna Verdi alla Bolognese,* make the sheets with spinach dough (page 127).

## Sunday Dinner with the Relatives

They came right after the late morning Sunday mass, Nonna Galasso's children all parading in to pay their respects to Ma. There were eight of them, my mother being one of four sisters and her four brothers. Since Nonna lived with us, our house was the meeting place and that meant no visit could take place just for a visit's sake—there must be dinner.

And that was the weekly duty of my mother, who never failed in this task. But she did not understand the word basta, which means enough, because for her, there was never enough food.

From my upstairs bedroom, I could hear her early on Sunday morning getting her cooking pots ready. I would mosey downstairs, still drowsy, and I could tell before she even said a word that getting ready for the noonday meal was going to consume a lot of my time, too.

There would be the roast, of course. To this day, I can still taste those crunchies that formed at the bottom of the roasting pan as the pot roast cooked to a deep brown color. The flavor was memorable, and I have never even come close to duplicating that taste in my own kitchen.

Nonna sat quietly at the kitchen table, sipping coffee and trimming the green beans that would go with the roast as well as the potatoes that would cook alongside the roast until they were browned to perfection. I was assigned to cleaning the salad greens. There were always tomatoes, cucumbers, fennel, and lettuce in the salad and Mom loved to add canned black olives, which I told her in later years was one of the only faux pas she made as a cook!

The tomato sauce for the macaroni, made with tomatoes that Mom had put up the summer before, simmered away. The whole house smelled like a fine-dining restaurant, which come to think of it now, was what it was! While we waited for the "guests" to arrive, I set the large conference-size dining room table according to Mom's instructions, with the best china and silverware, as if the most important people were coming. To me, a mere teenager, they were just the relatives.

When all was ready, I joined my dad, reading the Sunday paper, comfortably ensconced in his favorite chair. I scrambled through the sections until I came to the *funnies and caught up on the doings of Dick Tracy. No sooner had I read the strip than the door opened and in came uncles Emil, Tony, Gus, and Louie, followed by aunts Martha, Nancy, and Jenny and their wives, husbands, and children! Nonna Galasso held court, greeting each one with kisses and Italian words of wisdom. Then we ate and shared our life stories of the week.*

*And although at that time I looked upon Sunday dinners as nothing but added work, they were a time of closeness and family bonding. Sunday dinners have all but disappeared from today's lifestyle and we need to bring this rich time of togetherness back because when all is said and done, nothing will ever replace the power of sharing a meal together with family—the power to heal, to love, to laugh, and, of course, to eat well.*

# Spinach Pasta
## Pasta Verde

*Spinach-flavored pasta is an integral part of making a true lasagne verdi alla Bolognese. I prefer to make the dough in a food processor as described on page 123 instead of by hand because the spinach blends in more easily with the eggs, producing a dazzling brilliant green color.* **Makes about 1 pound pasta**

10 ounces fresh spinach, well washed and stemmed

2 large eggs

3 to 3½ cups unbleached all-purpose flour

**P**lace the spinach leaves in a pot without any additional water, cover, and wilt them down; this will take just a few minutes. As soon as the spinach has wilted, drain it in a colander and, when cool enough to handle, squeeze it *very* dry. It is important to get out all the excess water otherwise you will have to use too much flour.

Place ⅓ cup of the squeezed spinach in the bowl of a food processor fitted with a steel blade. Reserve any remaining spinach for another use.

Add the eggs and pulse to combine well.

Add the flour 1 cup at a time and process until a ball of dough forms around the blade that is not tacky or sticky and cleans the sides of the bowl. You may or may not need additional flour. Transfer the dough to a floured work surface.

Knead the dough with your hands for 2 or 3 minutes, then place a bowl over it and allow it to rest to relax the gluten.

Follow the directions on page 123 for rolling and assembling the pasta for the Lasagne Verdi Bolognese Style (page 146).

*NOTE: This dough can also be cut into spaghetti, linguine, or fettuccine.*

# The Case for Pasta

*You will probably notice that this book gives a lot of attention to pasta and that is because I love it and make no secret about it! No matter what the food police dictate about pasta, like calling it a forbidden food or a carb with consequences, it will always stand the test of time as good and wholesome food when prepared correctly and in keeping with tradition.*

*If you have followed my books over the years, you already know the good and the bad about pasta. You know that fresh and dried pasta cook differently. Fresh pasta is made from eggs and flour, although there are some regional variations; some use a larger ratio of egg yolks to whole eggs as in the Piedmont, and some use white wine in place of eggs in the dough as in Liguria.*

*Dried pasta, made from semolina flour and water, was born in Naples, and it became the pasta epicenter for the rest of the world. And even though there are many superior dried types of pasta imported from all over Italy, I will always prefer freshly made pasta to dry. It is lighter, cooks faster, and has nuances that manufactured boxed pasta could never have. And the bad? That depends on who is preparing it and how it is consumed. Always a first course, it is never the meal unless it is part of a casserole like a timballo. It is never drowned in sauce but rather lightly coated so there is a nice balance of flavor between pasta and sauce. And, four ounces is an average serving!*

*Keep those rules in mind and you can enjoy pasta every day just like the Italians, and walk away from the table guiltfree.*

# Baked Macaroni and Cheese
## Maccheroni al Formaggio

*Macaroni and cheese is without question one of those Italian American dishes that says comfort food. Some myths link Thomas Jefferson with introducing it at a White House dinner. He may have imitated the English version of macaroni and cheese, which was baked in the oven with cream. The dish was known in Europe and mainly enjoyed by the upper classes. After the American Civil War, a number of pasta-making factories opened, which allowed macaroni products to become more affordable to all. Needless to say there are countless versions of the dish, embellished with everything from vegetables to cured meats and leftovers such as chicken and turkey. Suffice it to say that macaroni and cheese is here to stay and will always be evolving into something grander than its original form. This version is a favorite of my children.*   *Makes 8 to 10 servings*

**O**n the stovetop, over low heat, melt the butter in a deep (10 × 13-inch), heatproof casserole or a Dutch oven. Stir in the flour and whisk to make a smooth paste; do not let it brown. Raise the heat to medium, and slowly whisk in the milk and dry mustard. Continue whisking until the sauce begins to thicken and coats the back of a spoon. Do not make the sauce too thick. Season with salt and pepper to taste. Add 2 cups of the cheese and stir until the mixture is smooth. Turn off the heat. Stir in the macaroni, ham, and broccoli and mix well. Taste and correct the seasonings if necessary.

Sprinkle the remaining cup of cheese evenly over the top of the casserole. Cover and bake for 30 to 35 minutes. Uncover and bake 10 minutes longer, or just until the cheese forms a nice brown crust. Serve directly from the casserole or Dutch oven.

2 tablespoons unsalted butter

2 tablespoons all-purpose flour

Three 12-ounce cans low-fat evaporated milk

1 teaspoon dry mustard

Salt and black pepper

3 cups grated Swiss, Italian fontina, or cheddar cheese

1 pound cooked bow ties, elbows, or rigatoni, slightly undercooked

2½ cups cooked ham, cubed

2 cups cooked broccoli florets, cut into small pieces

# Farfalle with Pistachio Nuts

## Farfalle ai Pistacchi

*Nonna Saporito frequently made this macaroni dish with pistachio nuts that are so popular in the town of Bronte, Sicily, where each year in September a festival takes place* (sagra del pistacchio) *celebrating the pistachio nut. The Arabs introduced them into Sicily, and Bronte is the center for their cultivation. Known as the "green gold" of Etna because of their intense green color, pistachio nuts are used as an ingredient in everything from pastries to fillings for vegetables to flavoring local salame, and in pasta dishes like this one.* **Serves 8 as a first course**

4 tablespoons extra-virgin olive oil, plus more if needed

1 medium yellow onion, minced

½ cup shelled natural pistachio nuts, coarsely chopped

1 teaspoon hot red pepper flakes or hot red pepper paste

Fine sea salt

1 pound farfalle or penne

Freshly ground black pepper

⅔ cup grated pecorino cheese

In a large sauté pan, heat the olive oil over medium-high heat. Add the onion and cook until soft but not brown. Stir in nuts and cook 1 minute. Turn off the heat and stir in the red pepper flakes or pepper paste. Add a little more olive oil if the mixture seems dry. Cover and keep warm.

Bring 4 quarts of water to a rapid boil in a large pot and add 1 tablespoon of salt. Add the pasta and cook until al dente. Drain, reserving ¼ cup of the cooking water, and transfer the pasta to the sauté pan. Reheat slowly, stirring in the reserved water and combining the ingredients well. Season with salt and pepper to taste. Stir in the cheese. Transfer the pasta to a shallow platter and serve immediately.

## To the Tooth

Ah, al dente! Roughly translated it means "to the tooth" and is the universal directive slogan for cooking pasta that is neither too hard nor too mushy but just right. Easier said than done. Let me give you a good example. Rigatoni is a popular tubular short cut of pasta that should hold its shape after it is cooked. How many times have you seen it arrive on your plate flat as a pancake? That is an example of overcooked pasta.

There is a point of no return as to when pasta is really cooked. After the water comes to a boil, throw the pasta in, then fish a piece out of the cooking water occasionally before the recommended cooking time labeled on the box is up and break the pasta in half, be it rigatoni, spaghetti, or any other unfilled pasta, and look to see if there is any white uncooked flour where you have broken it. If so, the pasta needs more time. If no flour can be detected, it is cooked. Drain, do not rinse, and toss with your favorite sauce. In Italy pasta is always served much firmer than here.

# Fettuccine with Mixed Mushroom Sauce

## Fettuccine ai Funghi Misti

*Italians go out of their way to cook with mushrooms, often meticulously foraging for their beloved wild porcini. We should be so lucky! In my opinion, mushrooms do not get the respect they deserve here in the United States. So I like to get away from predictable recipes like stuffed mushrooms, and do something magical with them, such as this earthy-tasting mixed mushroom sauce. Use your imagination, combining what varieties are available but don't use portobellos, which would turn the sauce dark. Save those for the grill. A combination of oyster, shiitake, and button mushrooms, all available in supermarkets, provides a nice balance of flavors in this sauce and a generous splash of white wine makes these flavors even better.*   **Serves 6 to 8**

Clean all the mushrooms with a mushroom brush or damp paper towels. Cut all the mushrooms into thin slices. Set aside.

Heat the olive oil and butter in a large 12- to 14-inch sauté pan. When the butter has melted, add the garlic and cook until softened. Stir in all the mushrooms and cook them over medium heat without turning until they begin to exude their water. Turn the mushrooms and continue cooking until they begin to brown around the edges. Raise the heat to high and add the wine; continue cooking for 3 minutes. Lower the heat to medium; add salt and pepper to taste. Stir in the cream, parsley, and thyme. Cook just until the sauce is slightly thickened. Cover and keep warm.

Bring 4 quarts of water to a rapid boil in a large pot and add 1 tablespoon of salt. Add the farfalle or fettuccine and cook until al dente. Drain, reserving ¼ cup of the cooking water.

Transfer the drained pasta and reserved water to the sauté pan with the mushroom sauce and reheat everything quickly over medium heat. Transfer the mixture to a serving platter. Serve hot and pass the grated cheese for sprinkling on top.

½ pound button mushrooms, stemmed

½ pound oyster mushrooms, separated into individual pieces

¼ pound shiitake mushrooms, stemmed

4 tablespoons extra-virgin olive oil

4 tablespoons (½ stick) unsalted butter

1 large garlic clove, minced

⅓ cup dry white wine

Salt and black pepper

⅓ cup heavy cream

¼ cup minced flat-leaf parsley

2 tablespoons fresh thyme leaves

1 pound farfalle or fettuccine

Grated Parmigiano-Reggiano cheese for sprinkling

# Macaroni Frittata

## Frittata di Maccheroni

4 tablespoons extra-virgin olive oil, plus more for pan

1 small onion, chopped

1 garlic clove, peeled and halved

2 tablespoons tomato paste

One 28-ounce can plum tomatoes, chopped

Salt and black pepper

1 pound vermicelli

4 large eggs

½ cup grated Parmigiano-Reggiano or pecorino cheese

¼ cup minced basil

¼ cup minced flat-leaf parsley

*This is the classic macaroni frittata that I remember from home. My mother always used vermicelli, which are thinner strands of spaghetti, but any good cut of macaroni will do.*
*Serves 6*

heat 2 tablespoons of the oil in a 2-quart saucepan. Add the onion and cook until softened but not browned. Add the garlic and press on the cloves as they cook until the edges begin to brown. Remove the garlic. Stir in the tomato paste and cook for several minutes, stirring often. Add the tomatoes and salt and pepper to taste. Bring to a boil, then lower the heat and simmer for 5 to 6 minutes.

Bring 4 quarts of water to a rapid boil in a large pot and add 1 tablespoon of salt.

Cook the vermicelli until al dente. Drain and mix in a large bowl with 2 cups of the sauce. Set aside.

Beat the eggs with a fork in a separate large bowl; stir in the cheese, basil, parsley, and salt and pepper to taste.

Combine the vermicelli and egg mixture well.

Heat the remaining olive oil in a nonstick, 12-inch sauté pan. Transfer the vermicelli mixture to the pan, pressing on the ingredients to achieve an even thickness. Cook the frittata until it moves easily from side to side in the pan. Place a dish larger than the diameter of the pan over the top of the frittata and flip it out. The bottom is now on top. Carefully slide the frittata back into the pan and cook the other side.

Transfer the frittata to a plate. Cut into wedges and serve with extra sauce on the side.

# Paccheri with Mushroom Sauce

## Paccheri con La Salsa di Funghi

*Paccheri fascinate me. They look like giant rigatoni. They are normally served with some type of seafood, usually shrimp or lobster. But try them with fresh oyster mushrooms for an exquisite taste treat.* **Serves 4**

**M**elt the butter in a medium saucepan and add the pine nuts and 1 cup of the mushrooms; cook over medium heat until very soft. Puree the mixture and keep warm.

Heat the oil in a 12- to 14-inch sauté pan. Stir in the garlic and cook until the garlic softens. Add the remaining mushrooms and cook 3 to 4 minutes. Add the wine and salt and continue to cook for a few minutes. Stir in the mushroom puree. Keep sauce warm while the paccheri are cooking.

Bring 2 quarts of water to a rapid boil in a large pot and add tablespoon of salt.

Add the paccheri and cook until al dente. Drain, reserving ½ cup of the cooking water. Add the paccheri and reserved water to the sauce. Reheat and mix the paccheri and sauce well. Serve with a generous grinding of black pepper and a sprinkling of Parmigiano-Reggiano cheese.

4 tablespoons (½ stick) unsalted butter

¼ cup pine nuts

⅔ pound fresh oyster mushrooms, wiped clean with a damp paper towel, stemmed, and sliced

⅓ cup extra-virgin olive oil

2 garlic cloves, minced

½ cup dry white wine

Salt and black pepper

1 pound paccheri

½ cup grated Parmigiano-Reggiano cheese

# Mini Macaroni and Cheese

## Piccole Casseruole di Pasta al Formaggio

*Mom made macaroni and cheese a lot but with a twist. She would bake individual servings in her muffin pans. She called them "casserolettes." Use a standard-size, non-stick, 12-cup muffin pan. Mini macs can be individually wrapped and frozen for future use and are great for portion control. Take them out as you need them. (Mom was so clever.) And there are so many ways to present them; how about at your next ladies' bridge lunch, a bridal luncheon, or as a starter to a casual dinner party. The kids will love them, too.*   **Makes 12 mini macs**

2 tablespoons extra-virgin olive oil

1 small onion, peeled and diced

2 tablespoons all-purpose flour

2½ cups fat-free evaporated milk

1 teaspoon dry mustard

2 teaspoons salt

Freshly ground black pepper

2 cups grated reduced-fat Swiss cheese

½ pound elbow or other small macaroni like pennette

Preheat the oven to 350°F. Lightly grease a 12-cup muffin pan with melted butter.

In a medium saucepan, heat the olive oil over medium heat and stir in the onion. Cook until the onion is very soft but not brown. Sprinkle the flour over the onion and stir to combine. Slowly pour in the milk and stir over medium heat to combine the ingredients. Add the mustard and salt and pepper to taste and continue to stir until the sauce thickens enough to coat the back of a spoon. Do not make the sauce too thick. Stir in 1½ cups of the cheese and stir until melted. Set the sauce aside off the heat, covered.

Bring 6 cups of water to a boil in a 2-quart pot and add 1 teaspoon of salt. Add the elbow macaroni and cook just until the macaroni begins to soften. Do not overcook the macaroni because it will cook more when it is baked.

Drain the macaroni in a colander and transfer it to a large bowl. Pour the sauce over the macaroni and combine well. Using a ¼-cup measure, scoop and fill the pan with the macaroni mixture. Be sure to evenly fill each muffin well right to the rim.

Place the pan on a larger baking sheet to catch any spills.

Sprinkle the remaining ½ cup of cheese evenly over each mini mac.

Bake the mini macs for 30 minutes, or just until set. Turn on the broiler and broil just until the tops are crusty brown.

Let the mini macs cool slightly in the pan before removing them individually with the aid of a butter knife. Serve hot, or wrap and freeze for future use.

# Penne with Vodka Sauce

## Penne alla Vodka

4 tablespoons (½ stick) unsalted butter

1 garlic clove, minced

1 teaspoon hot red pepper paste (or more to taste)

2 cups pureed fresh or canned plum tomatoes

½ cup vodka

1 cup heavy cream

1 cup grated Parmigiano-Reggiano cheese

Fine sea salt

1 pound penne rigate (penne with lines)

*Is penne alla vodka a traditional dish found on menus across Italy? The answer depends on who you ask. Certainly it is a dish that frequently appears on Italian American restaurant menus. I personally have never seen this dish on any menu in Italy. I have asked countless Italian friends from the north to the south if they know of this dish and they just give me a quizzical look. Penne alla vodka is nothing more than a tomato sauce laced with cream, vodka, and hot pepper paste, and is used to dress a slant cut of pasta called penne (which means "pen"). According to some foodies, the original recipe called for pepper-flavored vodka but now hot pepper paste has taken its place.*

*In the research that I have done it appears that this dish was introduced into Italy sometime in the early 1970s. It was brought by vodka distillers who wanted restaurants and their chefs to promote the consumption of vodka to the Italians. Besides enjoying it in chilled vodka glasses, they even suggested that Italian chefs dream up ways to cook with it! So this may have been when penne alla vodka appeared in Italy. The craze did not last long because Italians are very fussy and traditional when it comes to tinkering with their national dish. They frequently add wine to tomato sauce but vodka? Not in my grandmother's day. How about the cream? Again, tomato sauce hails from the south of Italy, particularly the region of Campania, and being of Neapolitan ancestry, I can tell you that cream is not something you would ever find in tomato sauce.*

*The debate will rage on. Meanwhile, if you want to try making this dish, here is one that I concocted.* **Serves 8**

Melt the butter in a 12- to 14-inch sauté pan. Add the garlic and cook over medium heat until soft. Stir in the red pepper paste and cook about 1 minute.

Add the tomatoes and vodka and cook for about 5 minutes, stirring occasionally.

Reduce the heat to low and slowly pour in the cream and cook for an additional 5 minutes. Add half the cheese, cover, and keep the sauce warm while the pasta is cooking.

Bring 4 to 6 quarts of water to a rapid boil and add 1 tablespoon of salt. Add the pasta and cook until al dente. Drain the penne, reserving ¼ cup of the cooking water.

Transfer the penne and reserved cooking water to the sauce and stir the ingredients well over medium heat until hot. Sprinkle on the remaining cheese and stir to blend.

Transfer the penne to a serving platter. Serve immediately.

# Pasta Salad

## Insalata di Pasta

2 tablespoons minced red onion

1 garlic clove, minced

½ cup extra-virgin olive oil

1 teaspoon salt

Juice of 2 large lemons

1 pound bow ties, ziti, or spirals

1 large avocado, cut in half, seed removed, flesh scooped out with a large spoon, and thinly sliced

1 cup chopped walnuts

1 cup halved cherry tomatoes

6 to 8 basil leaves, torn into bits

1 small ball fresh mozzarella cheese, cut into bits

Freshly ground black pepper

1 small head radicchio, washed, leaves separated

*I normally would not include a recipe for a cold pasta salad in a collection of Italian recipes as it is not something Italians traditionally eat, but I do like it as a summer salad on hot days.* **Serves 6 to 8**

In a jar with a lid combine the onion, garlic, olive oil, salt, and 2 tablespoons of the lemon juice. Cap the jar and shake well. Set aside. The dressing can be made a couple of days ahead and refrigerated. Bring to room temperature before using.

Bring 4 quarts of water to a rapid boil and add 1 tablespoon of salt. Add the bow ties and cook until al dente; firm but not mushy. Drain the bow ties and transfer them to a large bowl. Pour the dressing over them and toss well. Season with salt and pepper to taste and set aside.

In a small bowl toss the avocado with the remaining lemon juice and set aside.

Add the walnuts and tomatoes to the bow ties and toss. Add the avocado and lemon juice and toss gently. Add the basil, mozzarella, and a grinding of black pepper.

Toss everything gently and serve on a bed of radicchio leaves.

*NOTE: On average, Italians consume over sixty pounds of pasta per person per year. Americans consume about twenty pounds per person. In order to fill worldwide demand, pasta is mass-produced around the world but the time-tested artisan production in Italy still adheres to traditional methods, which in turn creates superior pasta.*

# Rigatoni with Onion Sauce

## Rigatoni con La Salsa di Cipolla

*This clever and inexpensive sauce for rigatoni starts with common yellow onions. I love its earthy flavor and was introduced to it in Perugia while I was enrolled in cooking school. What made it so memorable was the use of homemade lard; I have substituted lean salt pork and like the results. You will, too.*   *Serves 4 to 6*

**b**ring 4 quarts of water to a rapid boil in a large pot and add 1 tablespoon of salt. Add the rigatoni. Stir once or twice and cook until the rigatoni are al dente; firm but cooked through and holding their shape. Drain the rigatoni and transfer them to a large bowl. Add the butter, toss well, cover, and set aside.

Cook the salt pork and onions together in a 12- to 14-inch sauté pan over medium heat until the salt pork has browned and rendered its fat. Sprinkle the flour over the salt pork and onions and stir to blend.

Add the rigatoni and half the beef broth and combine well. Stir in the cheese and the remaining broth and combine well. Add a grinding of black pepper, and when everything is hot, transfer the rigatoni and onion sauce to a serving platter or bowl and serve immediately.

Salt

1 pound rigatoni

2 tablespoons unsalted butter, melted

¼ pound lean salt pork, finely diced

2 medium yellow onions, peeled and thinly sliced

1 tablespoon unbleached all-purpose flour

1 to 1½ cups hot homemade or canned low-sodium beef broth

¼ cup plus 2 tablespoons freshly grated Parmigiano-Reggiano cheese

2 teaspoons coarsely ground black pepper

# Whole Wheat Penne with Cauliflower

## Penne Integrale con Cavolfiore

4 tablespoons extra-virgin olive oil

½ teaspoon fennel pollen (see Note) or 2 tablespoons minced fennel leaves

1 teaspoon fine sea salt

Freshly ground black pepper

1 medium head cauliflower, core removed, head cut into 1-inch florets

¼ pound pancetta, diced

1 medium red onion, minced

2 large garlic cloves, minced

3 tablespoons salt-packed capers, well rinsed, minced

1 cup dried tomatoes packed in olive oil, drained and diced (about 8 large tomatoes)

1 cup dry white wine

*Why doesn't cauliflower get the attention it deserves? I can only surmise that it is because it has been prepared badly in the past and by that I mean just boiled in water until it was mushy soft and served with some insipid fake cheese sauce. There is a much better way to enjoy this vegetable known as cavolfiore. Roast it! Three things will happen: there will be no residual sulfur odor in your kitchen; the natural sugars in the cauliflower will add a mild sweetness, and it will become a family favorite like this easy-to-make whole wheat penne and roasted cauliflower casserole, ready in 30 minutes. The secret ingredient in this dish is fennel pollen, which imparts just a hint of sweetness.*   **Serves 6 to 8**

Preheat the oven to 350°F.

Pour 2 tablespoons of the oil into a medium bowl. Add the fennel pollen, salt, and black pepper. Stir in the cauliflower florets and mix well with the seasonings.

Transfer the mixture to a rimmed baking sheet and roast for 12 minutes, or until the florets are fork-tender and lightly browned. Set aside. While the florets are roasting, make the sauce.

Pour the remaining olive oil into a medium, 12- to 14-inch sauté pan. Stir in the pancetta and cook over medium heat until the pancetta begins to render its fat. Stir in the onion and cook until wilted. Stir in the garlic and continue to cook until the garlic has softened. Stir in the capers and tomatoes and continue cooking for 2 to 3 minutes, stirring a couple of times. Raise the heat to high and stir in the wine, scraping the bottom of the pan to get all those flavorful cracklings. After 2 or 3 minutes, reduce the heat to simmer and stir in the cauliflower. Keep the mixture warm while you cook the penne.

Bring 4 quarts of water to a rapid boil in a large pot and add 1 tablespoon of salt. Add the penne and cook until al dente. Drain and immediately transfer the penne to the pan with the cauliflower sauce. Raise the heat to medium and stir to combine the ingredients well. Stir in the parsley. Serve very hot with grated cheese for sprinkling if desired. I would suggest an aged pecorino Romano.

1 pound whole wheat penne

¼ cup minced flat-leaf parsley

Grated cheese for serving

NOTE: *Fennel pollen is a spice made from the tiny yellow flowers of the fennel plant. It is sometimes referred to as "the spice of the angels." Find it in the specialty food store or online.*

*Cauliflower is available* year-round. Peak seasons are spring and fall. Purchase thick, compact heads of creamy white florets. The head should be heavy for its size and the leaves surrounding it should be bright green and with no signs of wilting. Store cauliflower in the refrigerator stem side down. This will avoid excess moisture that hastens deterioration. Store for 5 to 7 days.

## Pasta Is New Again

*Just about everyone was enjoying twirling noodles until the pasta police arrived and ruined not only Wednesdays, but every day with their emphatic declaration that white was not right! Growing up in a large southern Italian family, pasta was always a central dish. But eating habits change with time and so it is with pasta. Ever since carbohydrates were declared enemies of the plate, many of us have had to reluctantly resign ourselves to a single reality—our beloved pasta had been banished from the garden of eating. Pasta as we knew it had to go—a health ruination, a weight gain menace, a carb with consequences. What to do? Enter the world of whole-grain pasta! We are saved. Hooray! We can twirl linguine once again!*

*Choosing to incorporate whole-grain pasta in your diet will definitely affect your health. You'll get more minerals and vitamins, that's for sure. You won't have to worry so much about packing on the pounds because whole grains are absorbed slowly into your system, leaving you with that full feeling while eating less. You'll have more energy, too!*

*Pasta is a food of the ancient world, but the world of whole-grain pasta is in its infancy. Open a box and discover the satisfaction and surprise that comes from adding whole-grain pasta to your diet.*

# Pasta with Lemon

## Tagliolini al Limone

*This is one of my favorite ways to serve pasta when hot summer days dictate something light and refreshing. I took my inspiration for this lemony-tasting pasta from a trip to Amalfi where I was surrounded by the most fantastic lemons I have ever seen. They were as big as grapefruit and their taste sweet and refreshing.* **Serves 6 to 8**

**b**ring 4 quarts of water to a rapid boil in a large pot and add 1 tablespoon of salt. Add the tagliolini and cook until al dente. Drain in a colander. Return the tagliolini to the same pot and over low heat stir in the butter, lemon juice and zest, heavy cream, cheese, parsley, and salt and pepper to taste. Mix well to combine. Transfer the tagliolini to a shallow platter and serve with additional cheese passed on the side.

Salt

1 pound tagliolini (fettuccine), store-bought or homemade

4 tablespoons (½ stick) unsalted butter, at room temperature

Zest and juice of 2 large lemons (use 4 if they are medium)

½ cup heavy cream

½ cup freshly grated Parmigiano-Reggiano cheese

2 tablespoons minced flat-leaf parsley

Coarsely ground black pepper

# Lasagne Verdi Bologna Style

## Lasagne Verdi alla Bolognese

1 recipe Basic White
(béchamel) Sauce
(page 177)

1 recipe Spinach
Pasta (page 127)

1 recipe Ragu
Bologna Style
(page 188)

1 cup grated
Parmigiano-
Reggiano cheese

*Lasagne Verdi alla Bolognese is one of those timeless classic dishes that every cook should know how to prepare. Unfortunately it comes in many guises, most of them poor shadows of the original made by well-meaning chefs. So when I wanted to make it as it should be, I went to Bologna and met with Giovanni Tamburini, the owner of Tamburini, that venerable food emporium that stocks the prized ingredients and prepared foods of the region known as Emilia-Romagna, which many consider the gastronomic center of Italy.*

*Making this lasagne is a labor of love but well worth the time for a true and delicious payoff. Both the béchamel and the ragu sauces can be made several days ahead and refrigerated. Reheat them slowly when you are ready to assemble the lasagna. If the béchamel sauce is too thick, thin it down with a little milk.  Serves 8 to 10*

Preheat the oven to 350°F. Butter a 14 × 11 × 3-inch deep lasagne pan or baking dish.

Spread a thin coating of the béchamel sauce in the bottom of the pan or dish.

Place a layer of the pasta sheets over the sauce. Spread another thin coating of the béchamel sauce over the pasta and then a thin coating of the ragu sauce over the béchamel. Sprinkle the top with about 2 tablespoons of the cheese.

Continue making layers as above, reserving about ½ cup of the béchamel sauce and ⅓ cup of the cheese for the top layer. Be sure to spread the sauce evenly over the top layer to completely cover the pasta.

Cover the pan or dish tightly with aluminum foil and bake about 30 minutes. Uncover and continue baking until the lasagne is hot and the top has a nice crust.

Loosely cover the lasagne with aluminum foil and allow it to rest for 10 minutes before cutting it; the cuts will not come out as even blocks but be rather loose. Serve immediately.

# The Road Not Taken

*I am baffled as to why the city of Bologna does not get the same kind of attention from tourists in Italy as, say, Rome, Florence, and Venice. Bologna should get the same attention for it is a grand city of learning, boasting the oldest, continuing university in the world. For that reason it has the endearing name of* La Dotta, *the learned. But it is also called* La Grassa, *meaning "the fat" in the sense that the cuisine is very rich.*

*My first trip to Bologna began right at Tamburini, on Via Caprarie. This beautiful food emporium right in the heart of the city is a visual library of all of the regional foods of Emilia-Romagna. There I met owner Giovanni Tamburini, a towering figure who is passionate about promoting awareness of the exquisite foods that this region has to offer. Giovanni gave me a food tour and tasting that has had lasting memories.*

*All the big cured-meat and artisan-cheese players from mortadella to prosciutto di Parma to Parmigiano-Reggiano, culatello, coppa, and sausage were brilliantly displayed. And when it comes to fresh pasta, Bologna cannot be surpassed. Classic filled pasta like tortelli, tortellini, ravioli, and lasagne verdi are just some of the choices.*

*When I asked about the tempting pans of green lasagne ready for customers to buy and bring home, Giovanni got teary-eyed as he explained its ethereal qualities and dismissed with one wave of his hand what the rest of the world passes off as the la vera lasagne verdi alla Bolognese (true lasagne, Bologna style). He insists that I taste, and when I do, I know what La Grassa truly means: a rich, velvety mouthfeel and light-as-a-feather strips of pasta hiding just a whiff of cream sauce and ragu sauce between its many layers. It goes down easily and has none of that I-ate-too-much feeling one sometimes gets with the more densely packed versions of American lasagne.*

*Lasagne verdi alla Bolognese is made with fresh spinach pasta. There is no fork in the road (so to speak) in deviating from that rule. So if you want to try it, see the recipe on page 147 and be aware that making this is a labor of love. To minimize the work, make both sauces several days ahead of time and refrigerate. The spinach dough can be made quickly in a food processor, and a hand crank pasta* machine will roll out the dough in but a few minutes' time. When all is ready and baked, your first forkful will convince you that there is no going back to premade store-bought lasagne or to making the American versions packed with everything from ricotta cheese to mushrooms and peppers and smothered in tomato sauce.

If I had not taken the road to Bologna, I would have missed one of its most beloved and classic dishes. And I would not have been able to share it with you.

# Little Ears with Pork Ragu

## Orecchiette al Ragù

3 tablespoons extra-virgin olive oil

1 onion, peeled and minced

2 garlic cloves, minced

¼ teaspoon hot red pepper flakes

1 teaspoon fennel seeds, crushed

1 pound ground pork

2 teaspoons fine sea salt

Freshly ground black pepper

1 cup dry white wine

1¼ cups hot chicken or vegetable broth

1 pound orecchiette

½ cup grated pecorino cheese, plus more for serving

¼ cup minced flat-leaf parsley

*Orecchiette (little ears) is pasta that with a stretch of the imagination looks like ears. The little impressions in the orecchiette are perfect for trapping all kinds of sauces like this delicious ground pork ragu.*   **Serves 6**

Heat the olive oil in a 12- to 14-inch sauté pan. When the oil is hot, stir in the onion and cook until it begins to soften. Stir in the garlic, red pepper flakes, and crushed fennel seeds and cook 1 minute. Stir in the pork and cook until browned. Season with salt and pepper to taste.

Raise the heat to high, pour in the wine, and cook, stirring occasionally, until most of the wine has evaporated. Pour in the chicken broth, lower the heat to a simmer, and cook until the liquid is reduced by half.

While the sauce simmers, bring 4 quarts of water to a rapid boil in a large pot and add 1 tablespoon of salt. Add the orecchiette and cook until al dente. Drain the pasta in a colander and transfer it to the sauté pan. Stir in the cheese and parsley and reheat everything until the sauce is hot and has thickened slightly. Serve immediately and pass additional grated cheese on the side.

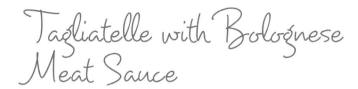

# Tagliatelle with Bolognese Meat Sauce

## Tagliatelle al Ragù alla Bolognese

*Ragù alla Bolognese is the traditional sauce used to dress tagliatelle pasta, another hallmark of the region's cuisine. Tagliatelle are long flat ribbon noodles about ¼ inch wide, and folklore tells us that they were first made by a Bolognese chef in service to the court in honor of the golden tresses of Lucretia Borgia who married the Duke of Este in the fifteenth century and became Duchess of Ferrara.*   **Serves 6**

If making the tagliatelle by hand, follow the directions for homemade pasta on page 123 and after thinning the sheets of dough, cut them into strands using the fettuccine setting on the pasta machine. As you cut them, hang them over a drying rack or place them loosely scattered on lightly floured cotton towels.

Bring 4 quarts of water to a rapid boil in a large pot and add 1 tablespoon of salt. Add the tagliatelle and cook until al dente.

Drain the tagliatelle in a colander, leaving a little water clinging to the strands. Immediately return the tagliatelle to the pot and, over low heat, stir in the ragu sauce and combine well until the strands are well coated. Transfer to a serving platter and serve immediately.

Pass grated Parmigiano-Reggiano cheese on the side.

1 pound fresh or
   store-bought
   tagliatelle

Salt

2 cups Ragu Bologna
   Style (page 188)

Grated Parmigiano-
   Reggiano cheese
   for sprinkling

# Baked Ziti Casserole with Meatballs

## Ziti al Forno Con Polpettine

*One of the most popular and recognized short cuts of tubular pasta is ziti, which means "groom" in Italian. In the south of Italy, especially in Puglia, Campania, and Sicily, baked ziti casseroles have long been associated with weddings. This one is my favorite and was made for me by my friend Lina DiGesù when I was in Puglia to film some segments of my television program.* **Serves 8**

To make the ragu: Heat the olive oil in a 2-quart saucepan. Stir in the onion and cook until it is limp. Stir in the sausage and cook until it is browned. Combine the tomatoes with the wine and stir into the sausage. Season with salt and pepper to taste. Cook, uncovered, at a simmer for 30 minutes. Stir in the basil. Set aside.

In a bowl, mix all the ingredients for the meatballs together except the olive oil, mozzarella cheese, and ziti.

Make tiny meatballs the size of marbles. Pour a thin layer of olive oil in a sauté pan and fry the meatballs in batches. Or bake the meatballs on a lightly oiled baking sheet at 350°F for 12 minutes.

Transfer the meatballs to a large bowl and mix them with 1 cup of the sauce. Set aside.

Bring 4 quarts of water to a rapid boil in a large pot and add 1 tablespoon of salt.

Add the ziti and cook just until softened but still a bit firm. They will finish cooking in the oven. Drain them and transfer them to a bowl. Toss them with 1 cup of the sauce and set aside.

Preheat the oven to 375°F.

Spread a thin layer of the ragu sauce in a large, heavy ovenproof dish or lasagne pan. Spread one-third of the ziti over the sauce. Make a second layer of the meatballs mixed with half of the cheese.

Spread 1 cup of the sauce over the cheese. Make a second layer like the first. Spread the remaining ziti over the second layer and top with the rest of the sauce.

Bake, covered with aluminum foil, for 30 minutes. Uncover and bake 10 to 15 minutes longer. The top should be very crispy.

### PORK SAUSAGE RAGU SAUCE

1 tablespoon extra-virgin olive oil

1 medium onion, minced

1/2 pound ground pork sausage

6 cups canned plum tomatoes

1/2 cup red wine

Salt and black pepper

6 or 7 basil leaves

### MEATBALLS

1/4 pound ground beef

1/4 pound ground pork

1/4 cup grated pecorino cheese

1/4 cup soft bread crumbs

2 tablespoons minced flat-leaf parsley

1 teaspoon minced garlic

2 large eggs

Olive oil for frying

1 pound ziti

1 pound fresh mozzarella cheese, cut into bits

# Guy's Whole Wheat Spaghetti with Tuna and Lemon

## Spaghetti Integrale al Tonno e Limone

4 tablespoons extra-virgin olive oil

1 small onion, peeled and chopped

2 garlic cloves, minced

¼ teaspoon hot red pepper flakes

½ cup dry white wine

2 tablespoons capers packed in brine, drained and coarsely chopped

Two 6-ounce cans tuna fillets, packed in olive oil (see Note)

¼ cup minced flat-leaf parsley

Juice of 1 large lemon

Salt and black pepper

1 pound whole wheat spaghetti or linguine

*My husband Guy is not only a great gardener, supplying me with all the fresh produce that I need when Ciao Italia is in production, he is also very knowledgeable about Italian wines, baking bread, and whipping up some delicious pasta dishes in no time. Case in point is what he did with tuna fillets in olive oil and whole-wheat pasta. It is critical to use good tuna fillets in olive oil. You'll see why when you try this recipe. Serves 6 to 8 as a first course or 4 as a main course*

heat the olive oil in a 12- to 14-inch sauté pan, over medium heat. Add the onion, stir, and cook until the onion is soft, but not brown. Stir in the garlic and cook until softened. Stir in the red pepper flakes and cook 1 minute.

Raise the heat to high, pour in the wine, and cook until most of it has evaporated. Lower the heat to medium, stir in the capers, and cook 1 minute longer. Turn off the heat.

In a bowl, flake the tuna fillets in large chunks. Add them to the pan along with the parsley, lemon juice, and black pepper. Stir the ingredients and add salt to taste. Keep the sauce covered and warm while you cook the spaghetti.

Bring 4 quarts of water to a rapid boil in a large pot and add 1 tablespoon of salt. Add the spaghetti, cover the pot, and bring the water back to a boil. Uncover the pot and cook until the spaghetti is al dente, still firm but cooked all the way through.

Drain the spaghetti in a colander and immediately transfer it to the pan with the tuna sauce. Reheat, gently mixing the ingredients to combine and until very hot. Serve with an additional grinding of black pepper.

*NOTE: It is traditional that no cheese is ever used on fish dishes; Italians believe the flavors would be in direct competition.*

*NOTE: Marinella or Wild Planet are good brands of tuna.*

# Pasta with Seafood Sauce

## Scialatielli

**SAUCE**

¼ cup extra-virgin olive oil

1 minced garlic clove

1 handful minced flat-leaf parsley

4 pounds clams or mussels, scrubbed

1 cup dry white wine

2 cups halved cherry tomatoes

Salt and black pepper

**DOUGH**

1 extra-large egg

2 tablespoons extra-virgin olive oil

⅓ to ½ cup whole milk

½ teaspoon salt

2½ cups 00 flour

1 tablespoon grated pecorino cheese

2 tablespoons minced basil or parsley leaves

*Scialatielli is a very popular pasta in Naples that is not often made at home anymore. It resembles short, stubby spaghetti. Besides eggs and flour, the dough contains milk, grated cheese, and parsley or basil and is most often served with a seafood sauce. Serves 4*

Heat the olive oil in a 12- to 14-inch sauté pan. Add the garlic, parsley, and clams and toss for a couple of minutes, Add the wine, cover the pan, and cook until the clams open; discard any that do not. Reserve a few clams in their shells for garnish. Set aside.

Remove the clams from their shells, working over a bowl to catch the juices. Set the clams aside in another bowl. Strain the liquid and set aside.

Return the clams to the sauté pan and add the cherry tomatoes. Add the reserved clam juices. Season with salt and pepper. Set the sauce aside while you cook the pasta. Reheat the sauce when pasta is ready.

Make the pasta. Place egg, olive oil, ⅓ cup milk, and salt in bowl of food processor and whirl until smooth. Add flour and pulse until mixture is grainy looking. Add the parsley or basil and pulse just until the dough begins to leave sides of bowl. If the dough is too dry, add a little of the remaining milk until you can pinch a piece of dough between your fingers and it does not crumble.

Transfer the dough to floured surface and knead it into a smooth ball. Place a bowl upside down over the dough and allow it to rest for 30 minutes to relax the gluten and make it easier to roll.

Divide the dough into quarters and keep three covered while working the first piece. Flatten the first piece of dough to a 4-inch-wide piece. Place it through the rollers of a hand crank pasta machine set to the fattest setting (#1). Set the rollers to the next fattest setting down (#2) and run the dough through again.

Using a small knife, cut the dough into ⅛-inch-wide strips and place the strips on a clean towel. Repeat with the remaining dough.

Bring 4 quarts of water to a rapid boil in a large pot and add 1 tablespoon of salt. Add the scialatielli and cook for 2 to 3 minutes. Drain, reserving ¼ cup of the cooking water. Add the scialatielli and reserved water to the sauce pan, toss well and reheat. Serve hot garnished with the reserved clams in the shell.

NOTE: Fare la scarpetta *is a phrase used when a dish of pasta is so good that any sauce that is left behind in the dish is mopped up with pieces of bread.*

# Vermicelli with Clams

## Vermicelli alle Vongole

*Spaghetti with clams, better known in Naples as vermicelli with clams, is subject to much interpretation when it comes to adding or not adding fresh peeled tomatoes or prepared tomato sauce. As the Neapolitans say it is a matter of "a piacere," or "how you like it." I prefer fresh tomatoes, which give the dish a lighter taste and do not mask the flavor of the clams as a tomato sauce would. Vermicelli, a thin spaghetti, is the perfect foil for the sweet-tasting clams.   Serves 6 to 8*

3 pounds fresh clams, well scrubbed and rinsed

½ cup dry white wine

½ pound vermicelli, linguine, or spaghetti

Fine sea salt

⅓ cup extra-virgin olive oil

2 garlic cloves, minced

1 teaspoon hot red pepper flakes

2 cups skinned, seeded, and chopped plum tomatoes

Freshly ground black pepper

2 tablespoons minced flat-leaf parsley

discard any clams that are open or have broken shells. Place the clams and wine in a 12- to 14-inch sauté pan and set over medium-high heat. Cook, covered, until the clams open. Discard any clams that do not open.

Drain the clams and their juices through a fine-mesh sieve lined with a damp cheesecloth, set over a bowl. Reserve 6 to 8 clams in the shell for garnish and set aside. Remove the rest of the clams from their shells and place in a bowl. Set aside.

Bring 2 quarts of water to a rapid boil in a large pot and add tablespoon of salt. Add the vermicelli and cook until al dente. Drain in a colander.

Return the sauté pan to the stovetop, add the olive oil, and place over medium heat. Stir in the garlic and red pepper flakes and cook until the garlic softens. Add the tomatoes and the reserved clam juice and cook over medium-low heat 2 to 3 minutes. Stir in the clams and season with salt and pepper to taste.

Add the vermicelli to the sauté pan and reheat slowly, mixing the ingredients well. Stir in the parsley.

Transfer the vermicelli to a platter and garnish with the reserved clams in the shell. Serve hot.

CHEF'S SECRET: *To keep prepared pasta hot for serving, heat an ovenproof shallow platter or bowl in a preheated 200°F oven while the pasta is cooking. After draining and saucing the pasta, transfer it to the heated platter or bowl and it will stay hot for as long as it takes to enjoy the pasta.*

# Whole Wheat Spaghetti in White Clam Sauce

## Spaghetti di Farina Integrale alle Vongole in Bianco

3 pounds Littleneck or other fresh clams in the shell, well scrubbed and rinsed

3 garlic cloves, minced

1 medium onion, minced

½ cup minced flat-leaf parsley

⅔ cup dry white wine

2 tablespoons extra-virgin olive oil

1 tablespoon hot red pepper flakes or hot red pepper paste (or more to taste)

2 tablespoons salt-packed capers, well rinsed and minced

Juice of 2 lemons

Salt and black pepper

1 pound whole wheat spaghetti or linguine

2 lemons, sliced into wedges

*I get a lot of e-mails from viewers who have been to Italy and want to duplicate the foods they enjoyed there at home. Easier said than done. I try not to blow the lid off of their enthusiasm but let them down slowly and tell them that they can approximate the flavors but never duplicate them. Case in point: spaghetti alle vongole (spaghetti with clams), a classic Neapolitan dish. A good start is with the spaghetti, which we can get imported from Italy, and canned San Marzano plum tomatoes. But clams, stop right there. Vongole veraci, the typical clams found in Naples, are not available here. Tiny and sweet, the Neapolitans adore them. To approximate this dish at home, use Little-neck, Rhode Island, mahogany clams, or whatever is available. And even though regular spaghetti is the most popular choice for this dish, I have substituted whole wheat spaghetti; the slightly nutty flavor really marries well with the spicy clam sauce. Be sure to purchase clams that feel heavy in your hand, have no cracks, and are not open. Serves 6 to 8*

discard any clams that are open or have broken shells. Place the clams in a 12- to 14-inch sauté pan. Add half the garlic, the onion, and half of the parsley and pour in the wine. Cover the pan and bring to a boil. Lower the heat to medium and cook until the clams have opened, about 4 minutes. Discard any clams that do not open. Reserve 6 to 8 whole clams in the shell for garnish and set aside.

Drain the clams and their cooking liquid through a fine-mesh sieve lined with damp cheesecloth, over a bowl. When cool enough to handle, remove the clams from their shells, working over a bowl to catch any juices, and place them in another bowl. Add any juices to the bowl with the clam cooking liquid.

Wipe out the sauté pan, add the olive oil, and place over medium-high heat. Stir in the remaining garlic, parsley, red pepper flakes or paste, and capers. Cook over medium heat until the mixture softens.

Slowly pour in the reserved liquid and the lemon juice. Bring the mixture to a boil, then reduce the heat to a simmer and cook for 2 minutes. Season with salt and black pepper to taste. Turn off the heat. Chop the clams and add them to the pan. Cover and keep warm while you cook the spaghetti.

Bring 4 quarts of water to a rapid boil in a large pot and add 1 tablespoon of salt.

Cook the spaghetti until al dente, reserving 2 tablespoons of the cooking water. Drain the spaghetti and add along with the reserved water to the sauté pan with the clams. Reheat slowly, stirring constantly, until the mixture is hot. Transfer the mixture to a platter and garnish with the reserved clams in the shell and the lemon wedges.

NOTE: *You can make the sauce ahead of time and refrigerate for up to 3 days; it will taste even better.*

# Paccheri with Shrimp

## Paccheri con Gamberi

3 tablespoons extra-virgin olive oil

2 garlic cloves, minced

1 cup cherry tomatoes, halved

1 teaspoon hot red pepper paste

½ cup dry white wine

2 pounds rock shrimp (about 6 to 8 per pound) in the shell

½ pound paccheri

Salt and black pepper

*I first encountered* paccheri *while filming a segment on short cuts of dry pasta in Molise. The story goes that this particular pasta served as a hiding place for, of all things, garlic cloves that were smuggled into Austria. Why smuggled? Because Italian garlic was far superior to the weak type produced by Austrian farmers and highly sought after by the aristocracy. In order to protect the production of Austrian garlic, the border between Italy and Austria was closed! But those who craved garlic smuggled it in, safely stuffed inside the paccheri! Paccheri are best served with seafood but they are equally as good tossed with a ragu sauce. Can't find paccheri? Use the largest rigatoni you can find.*
*Serves 4*

heat the olive oil in a 12- to 14-inch sauté pan. Add the garlic, and when it has softened stir in the cherry tomatoes and hot pepper paste. Cook 1 or 2 minutes, then add the wine and bring to a boil. Lower the heat and add the shrimp. Cover with a lid and cook about 8 minutes.

While the shrimp cook, bring 2 quarts of salted water to a boil in a large pot (see Note). Cook the paccheri until al dente. Drain the paccheri, reserving ½ cup of the cooking water, and add them to the sauté pan with the shrimp along with the reserved cooking water. Cook a few minutes, stirring to combine. Season to taste with salt and pepper.

*NOTE: Paccheri tend to split in rapidly boiling water, so once the water comes to a boil, turn it down so the paccheri are cooking at a gentle boil.*

# Potato Gnocchi with Fontina Sauce

## Gnocchi alla Bava

*All gnocchi are not created equal. The most popular and familiar is potato gnocchi but there is also pumpkin, ricotta, semolina, spinach, squash, and even prune gnocchi depending on where you find yourself in Italy. Gnocchi alla Bava is what you will find in northern Italy in the Valle d'Aosta. The word* bava *means stringy and refers to the sauce, which is made with fontina. As with all gnocchi made with potatoes, the less flour added, the lighter the consistency will be.* **Serves 6 as a first course**

**t**o make the gnocchi, bake or microwave the potatoes and cool. When cool, peel them, cut them into chunks, and pass through a ricer or food mill into a large bowl. Do not use a food processor or hand masher; this will make the potatoes too gummy.

Add just enough of the flour to make a soft dough that does not stick to your hands (see Note). Divide the dough into quarters and work with one piece at a time.

Roll each piece under the palms of your hands into a long rope the thickness of your middle finger. Cut each rope into 1-inch pieces and roll each piece off the tines of a fork to create ridges.

Place the gnocchi on baking sheets lined with a clean kitchen towel as you make them, keeping them in a single layer.

To make the sauce, place the milk and fontina cheese in a saucepan and heat it slowly over low heat until the cheese has melted. Season the sauce with salt and the nutmeg. Keep covered and warm while the gnocchi boil.

Lightly butter a baking dish and set aside. In a large pot, bring 4 quarts of water to a rapid boil and add 1 tablespoon of salt. Add the gnocchi in batches of 24 and boil them gently until they rise to the surface. Use a skimmer or hand strainer to scoop them out of the water, shaking off any excess, and place them in the prepared dish. Spoon some of the sauce over the gnocchi and mix gently to lightly coat them. Serve immediately and spoon the remaining sauce over the top of each serving.

*CHEF'S SECRET: Once you have made the gnocchi dough, test a few gnocchi for consistency by cooking one or two in a small pot of boiling water. If they hold together, enough flour has been added; if they fall apart, add more flour to the dough a little at a time.*

## GNOCCHI

1 pound Yukon Gold potatoes, about 4

1¼ cups unbleached all-purpose flour

## SAUCE

1 cup whole milk

⅔ pound Italian fontina cheese, diced

Salt

¼ teaspoon freshly grated nutmeg

# Ricotta Cheese and Zucchini Gnocchi

## Gnocchi di Ricotta e Zucchine

*If ever there was a homemade pasta that put the fear of God into cooks, it has got to be gnocchi, those light-as-a-feather dumplings that sometimes turn out all wrong, tasting heavy and chewy. Most people are familiar with potato gnocchi tossed in to-mato sauce, and over the years I have showcased these and many other types on* Ciao Italia, *including squash, semolina, spinach, and my daughter Beth's favorite, ricotta cheese and zucchini gnocchi. The technique for making them has everything to do with a light hand and a nimble thumb. Using ricotta cheese in place of potatoes makes a cloud-light dumpling with a very tender texture. Adding the zucchini gives great taste, and is a novel way to get veggies into your diet. Most important, knowing how much flour to add when making the dough is the key to perfect gnocchi. There are many sauces for gnocchi besides tomato, including butter and cheese, sage and butter, pesto sauce, and parsley sauce.   Makes 12 dozen gnocchi*

1 medium zucchini, ends trimmed, halved

1½ cups unbleached all-purpose flour

1 teaspoon plus 1 tablespoon salt

3 tablespoons grated pecorino cheese, plus more for sprinkling

One 16-ounce container whole milk ricotta cheese, well drained

1 large egg slightly beaten

Extra-virgin olive oil

2 cups prepared tomato sauce (enough to sauce 4 dozen gnocchi)

grate the zucchini on the smallest holes of a box grater. Wrap the zucchini in a double thickness of paper towels and squeeze the excess water out. The zucchini needs to be very dry otherwise too much flour will be used and your gnocchi will have you tearing out your hair. Aim for 1 cup of well-squeezed zucchini. Set aside.

Heap the flour on a work surface, add the salt and pecorino cheese and blend well with your hands. Make a hole in center of the flour mixture and plop the ricotta cheese in it. Flatten the ricotta a bit with a spoon to make a slight depression in the center of the cheese and add the egg and grated zucchini. It will look like a mess.

Roll up your sleeves and use your hands to blend everything into a ball of dough. It will be a bit sticky, but only add more flour if the dough is so soft that it will not form a slightly tacky ball. Otherwise leave it alone and allow it to rest, covered with a bowl, for 5 minutes while you wash the excess dough bits off your hands.

You will find that as the dough rests, it will be easier to handle. Use a dough scraper to help you move and turn the dough to knead it. It does not have to be smooth, but just holding together. To test see note on page 163.

Divide the dough ball in half, then divide each half into quarters. Roll each quarter out on a lightly floured work surface into an 18-inch-long rope the thickness of your middle finger.

Using a small knife cut each rope into 1-inch pieces.

Here's the fun part: Use a fork or butter paddle to roll each gnocchi with your thumb off the tines of the fork or butter paddle to create ridges on one side. As you do this, a little depression will form on the other side. Alternatively, you can just use the cut pieces without forming the ridges (yawn).

As you form them, place the gnocchi on baking sheets lined with clean kitchen towels, keeping them in a single layer.

To cook and sauce: Decide how many gnocchi you wish to serve. Gnocchi are traditionally served as a first course, so 4 dozen gnocchi will serve 8. To cook 4 dozen gnocchi, bring 2 quarts of water to a boil and add 1 tablespoon of salt. Heat the sauce in a saucepan and keep warm. By hand, drop the desired amount of gnocchi a few at a time into the pot of boiling water and cook them just until they bob to the surface.

Use a pasta scoop with a handle, or a handheld strainer, to fish them out of the water; be sure to shake off all the excess water and transfer them to a skillet with the waiting tomato sauce.

Heat the gnocchi in the sauce and toss them gently to coat well.

Serve them as a first course and pass the cheese for sprinkling on top.

*NOTE: Want to make gnocchi ahead? Cooked gnocchi freeze beautifully. Flash-freeze your cooked gnocchi frozen on baking sheets in a single layer. When frozen, transfer to plastic ziplock bags. They will keep for 3 months. When ready to cook, take out as many as you wish and allow them to defrost then reheat them in the sauce of your choice.*

# Sardinian Gnocchi with Pork Ragu

## Malloreddus al Sugo

*Sardinian gnocchi are called* malloreddus *and are very easy to make. I learned how from my friends Giulia and Mario Cocco, who live in Cagliari, an important Sardinian port city.* Malloreddus *are served with a simple pork sausage ragu sauce flavored with saffron.*  **Serves 6**

In a bowl, dissolve the salt in the warm water. Combine the semolina and unbleached flours and mound the flours on a work surface. Make a well in the center and add the water along with the olive oil. Using your hands, gradually bring the flour mixture from the inside wall of the well into the center. Continue adding flour until a ball of dough forms; push any excess flour aside. Knead the dough with your hands until it is smooth. Cover the dough with a bowl and allow it to rest for 30 minutes.

Meanwhile make the sauce. Heat the olive oil in a heavy-bottomed, 2-quart saucepan over medium-high heat. Add the onions, bay leaf, and salt. Reduce the heat to medium-low and cook, stirring occasionally, for about 5 minutes. Stir in the sausage and cook for 10 minutes. Add ¼ cup water, the wine, and the saffron. Reduce the heat to a simmer and cook about 10 minutes. Add the tomatoes, cutting them up in the can with a scissors or breaking them up with your hands. Simmer the sauce, covered, for 1 hour. Season to taste with salt and pepper. Keep warm.

To make the gnocchi, divide the dough into 4 equal pieces and roll each piece into a long rope about the thickness of your middle finger. Cut each rope into ¼-inch pieces. Press each piece against the tines of a fork or a ridged butter paddle to make the classic ridges in the gnocchi.

As you make them spread them out on baking sheets lined with clean kitchen towels, keeping them in a single layer.

To cook the gnocchi, in a large pot, bring 4 quarts of water to a boil and add 1 tablespoon of salt. Add the malloreddus and cook for about 5 minutes. Using a pasta scoop or a handheld strainer, scoop them out of the water and drain well. Transfer the gnocchi to the saucepan with the ragu over medium heat and toss them until well coated with the sauce.

Serve immediately and pass the cheese for sprinkling on top.

## DOUGH

- 1 teaspoon fine sea salt
- ¾ cup warm water
- 1¼ cups fine semolina flour
- ¾ cup unbleached all-purpose flour
- 2 teaspoons extra-virgin olive oil

## RAGU

- 1 tablespoon extra-virgin olive oil
- 1 medium onion, finely chopped
- 1 whole bay leaf
- 1 teaspoon salt
- 1 pound Italian sweet sausage, casing removed
- ½ cup dry white wine
- ¼ teaspoon saffron
- One 28-ounce can whole tomatoes with their juice
- Salt and black pepper
- ½ cup grated pecorino Sardo cheese for sprinkling

# White Frittata

## Frittata Bianca

Salt and black pepper

½ pound vermicelli, spaghetti, or linguine

6 tablespoons (¾ stick) unsalted butter

1 cup grated Parmigiano-Reggiano cheese

4 large eggs

½ cup minced basil

¼ cup minced flat-leaf parsley

*Neapolitans love their frittatas, known to the rest of the world as omelets. Made with eggs and whatever else comes to mind like leftover vegetables, meat, and even pasta, it can be a picnic food, lunch, or easy supper. This so-called white frittata comes from the fact that there is little color to the dish, but the taste makes up for it!* **Serves 6 to 8**

bring 4 quarts of water to a rapid boil in a large pot and add 1 tablespoon of salt.

Add the vermicelli and cook until al dente. Drain and transfer to a large bowl. Stir in 4 tablespoons of the butter, the cheese, and salt and pepper to taste. Set aside.

In a separate bowl, beat together the eggs, basil, and parsley with a fork until foamy. Season with salt and pepper to taste. Pour the eggs over the pasta and stir to combine well. Set aside.

In a 12-inch, nonstick sauté pan, melt the remaining 2 tablespoons of butter over medium heat. Add the vermicelli mixture, smoothing it out with a wooden spoon to an even thickness. Cook until the mixture holds together as one piece when the pan is shaken. Place a plate larger than the diameter of the pan over the top of the frittata and flip it out onto the plate. Return the frittata to the pan to finish cooking the underside.

Serve either hot or cold, cut into wedges.

# Sauces

Tomato Sauce

Spicy Tomato Sauce

Sun-Dried Tomato Sauce

Basic White Sauce

Uncooked Cherry Tomato Sauce

Pesto

Garlic and Oil Sauce with Walnuts and
    Pecorino Cheese

Oven Baked Beef Shin Tomato Ragu

Nut Sauce

Ricotta Cheese Sauce

Sicilian Lemon and Olive Oil Sauce

Ragu Bologna Style

Nonna Galasso's Stuffed Rolled Beef

Orange Sauce

Tuscan-Style Meat Sauce

Dried Tomatoes in Olive Oil

# sauce ability

**r**ich, cloying sauces have never been a part of regional Italian cooking. As a matter of fact, there are no rules, no classic formula, and no agreement on what constitutes a sauce. Every Italian cook will have a particular way of making them and claim that theirs is the best. From town to town, and neighbor to neighbor, sauce components will vary, maybe by just one ingredient.

But I think that most Italians (and certainly Italian Americans) would agree that tomato sauce is the identifying benchmark of Italian sauces because it is the most familiar one. But there were other sauces used like oil and garlic, parsley and walnut, and ragu. Cream- and milk-based sauces were very rarely used unless for a labor-intensive casserole or a Lasagne Verdi Bologna Style (page 146).

The collection of sauces in this chapter are ones that I use most frequently. Feel free to adapt them as you see fit because ultimately it is the ability of the cook who determines just what a sauce will be.

# Tomato Sauce

## La Salsa di Pomodoro

¼ cup extra-virgin olive oil

3 garlic cloves, finely chopped

4 cups (about 8 medium) coarsely chopped fresh plum tomatoes or one 28-ounce can plum tomatoes

1½ tablespoons chopped fresh oregano or 1 tablespoon dried

2 teaspoons fine sea salt

¼ cup chopped basil leaves

*I could make tomato sauce in my sleep. That's because my dad taught me all about planting plum tomatoes—every summer we harvested bushels and bushels of the red beauties—and Mom and I turned them into a delicious and light-tasting sauce that we put up in jars for winter use. Contrary to what some people think, it takes very little time to make it. Fresh plum tomatoes are best, but if you do not have access to fresh tomatoes, then canned are fine. Just make sure the label specifies they are San Marzano plum tomatoes.* **Makes about 3½ cups**

In a saucepan, heat the olive oil over medium-heat. Add the garlic and sauté until soft. Add the tomatoes, oregano, and salt. Simmer over low heat for about 15 minutes, until slightly thickened. Remove from the heat and stir in the basil.

For a smoother sauce, puree the tomatoes in a food processor or food mill before adding to the saucepan.

# Spicy Tomato Sauce

## La Salsa Puttanesca

*When Dad's tomatoes (page 174) were ripe for the picking, one of his requests was for my mom to make him puttanesca sauce. My dad said that the name derived from the word* puttana *which means whore. We snickered at that but Mom said it had more to do with the spiciness of the sauce. Not only was it a great way to use fresh garden tomatoes but Dad also loved the kick provided from the hot red pepper.* **Makes about 2¼ cups**

In a large skillet, heat the olive oil over medium heat. Add the hot pepper and garlic and cook, pressing on the pepper and garlic with a wooden spoon until the pepper begins to soften and the garlic begins to color. Remove the pepper and discard. Add the anchovies and swirl them in the oil until they begin to dissolve. Add the tomatoes, capers, and olives, and cook, covered, for 5 minutes longer. Add the salt. Keep the sauce warm while you cook the pasta. This recipe makes enough sauce to dress a pound of pasta such as spaghetti or rigatoni.

¼ cup extra-virgin olive oil

1 small, fresh, hot red pepper, slit lengthwise

1 large garlic clove, minced

One 2-ounce can anchovies packed in olive oil, drained and chopped

8 large ripe plum tomatoes, peeled, seeded, and chopped

¼ cup capers packed in brine, rinsed and coarsely chopped

½ cup chopped, pitted, oil-cured black olives

1 teaspoon fine sea salt

## For the Love of a Tomato

We would need more than a whole book to talk about the role that tomatoes (*pomodori*) play in the Italian diet. We all know that they define much of southern Italian cooking and that they put Naples on the map with pizza and spaghetti, and that in New Jersey, tomato sauce is lovingly referred to as "gravy." But what I want to tell you about is my dad's tomatoes. His mom and dad were from Sicily, the land of plum tomatoes, so you can imagine how much they were a part of his diet. So much so that one day when I was home from college, he announced that he was going to plant a variety of plum and beefsteak tomatoes for everyone in the family in our backyard. That meant all my aunts, uncles, and grandparents would receive bushels. A huge task, but Dad, undaunted, got to work with his one hundred-plus plants.

My mother excitedly went along with it because her idea of cooking was to always think globally. I cringed because I knew what was coming, the tedious task of peeling, cutting, and cooking tomatoes for tomato sauce. And not only that, it was always my job to prepare the endless canning jars that would be used. Okay, I could understand the value of having fresh, homemade tomato sauce to take us through the winter months, but when Mom announced that we were going to make our own ketchup, too, well, that's when I saw red!

What I learned from Mom and Dad was that there was nothing, nothing like fresh tomatoes and that is why I have carried on the tradition of growing them in my own garden, albeit not one hundred plants but close—sixty!

When the last tomato comes out of my garden, I eat it gingerly because my rule is that no tomato shall pass my lips again until the next tomato season! Fall and winter store-bought tomatoes are bad imitations of the real thing and for me, a true waste of money. So I put up as many tomatoes as the garden will yield. Cherry tomatoes get tossed into plastic bags and frozen for soup, stew, and sauce. Plum tomatoes get dried and jarred in olive oil to eat as is or to toss on crostini or pizza or as an ingredient in many dishes, and also pureed into a pesto-style sauce (page 181) for short cuts of pasta. Only beefsteak-type tomatoes are not good candidates for sauce because they are watery and seedy. These tomatoes are best used for salads and sandwiches.

If you are a tomato lover but don't have room to plant your own, buy yours at farmers' markets. You would be surprised at how many varieties of heirloom tomatoes are available. I particularly love Brandywine as an eating tomato, and am fortunate enough to be able to grow it. It is a big, pink-skinned tomato that is very velvety in texture. Brandywines are a late-season tomato.

Never refrigerate fresh tomatoes as the cold destroys their flavor. Just keep them on your kitchen counter where you can admire them and be reminded that the season is all too short.

Some of my favorite Italian tomato varieties include:

CUORE DI BUE. A huge salad or sauce tomato tinged with green, which has a wrinkled skin; it is flavorful and acidic.

CAMONE. A very popular greenish tomato originally from Sardinia and Sicily. It is very good in salads and sandwiches.

COSTOLUTO GENOVESE. This pulpy tomato is best for making sauce.

SAN MARZANO. This is the king of plum tomatoes and the one most readily found canned. It is grown in Campania near Naples. It has smooth skin and peels easily.

PENDOLINO. These are cherry tomatoes from southern Italy where they hang in bunches from balconies and dry naturally for use during the winter season. They are used to make conserva, tomato paste.

# Sun-Dried Tomato Sauce

## La Salsa di Pomodori Secchi

1 cup oil-packed,
   sun-dried tomatoes

1 garlic clove, minced

¼ cup dry red wine

¼ teaspoon salt

*In the summer I dry loads of plum tomatoes and preserve them in olive oil. They are perfect for topping bruschetta or for adding great flavor to chicken dishes, but my favorite way to use them is as a sauce for short cuts of pasta like rigatoni or farfalle. This sauce can be made in less than ten minutes. Sun-dried tomatoes you make yourself are so much better in flavor than store-bought. See page 195 on how to dry them.*
**Makes 1 cup**

drain 2 tablespoons of the olive oil from the jar of tomatoes and place it in a small saucepan. Place the tomatoes in a food processor.

Cook the garlic in the oil until it is soft but not brown. Transfer it with the oil to the food processor. Pulse the tomatoes and garlic until a thick paste forms.

Scoop out the tomatoes and garlic paste and return it to the saucepan. Stir in the wine and salt and cook over medium heat for 2 or 3 minutes to blend the ingredients. Use the sauce immediately, or transfer it to jar and refrigerate it for up to 2 weeks.

# Basic White Sauce

## Salsa di Besciamella

Besciamella, *white sauce, is most often associated with northern Italian cooking and is used in oven-baked pasta dishes like Lasagne Verdi Bologna Style (page 146) or with vegetables or fish. It can be made ahead and refrigerated for 3 or 4 days but will thicken as it sits. When you reheat it, thin the sauce with a little milk. The basic recipe does not have the addition of herbs or spices. Those ingredients should be added after the sauce is cooked and should be tailored to the dish being prepared.*   **Makes 4 cups**

8 tablespoons (1 stick) unsalted butter

½ cup unbleached all-purpose flour

4 cups hot milk

Fine sea salt

Ground white pepper

**I**n a 1½ quart saucepan, melt the butter over medium-low heat; do not let the butter brown. Whisk the flour into the butter and cook it without browning until a uniform paste is formed and no streaks of flour remain. Slowly whisk in the milk. Cook about 10 minutes, stirring slowly, until the sauce coats the back of a wooden spoon. Season with salt and pepper to taste. Add herbs if desired.

**TIP:** *Adding hot milk will prevent bringing down the temperature of the ingredients.*

# Uncooked Cherry Tomato Sauce

## La Salsa di Pomodorini Crudi

2 cups whole cherry tomatoes, stemmed, washed, dried, and halved

1 teaspoon sugar

½ teaspoon salt

¼ cup minced flat-leaf parsley

1 garlic clove, minced

4 tablespoons extra-virgin olive oil

1 tablespoon white wine vinegar

*Take advantage of this no-cook, marinated tomato sauce when sweet cherry tomatoes are in season. Use this sauce at room temperature on hot pasta. The recipe makes enough sauce to dress a pound of a short cut pasta such as farfalle, rigatoni, or fusilli.*
***Makes 2 cups***

In a medium bowl, combine the tomatoes with the sugar, salt, parsley, garlic, olive oil, and vinegar. Toss well. Cover and marinate several hours at room temperature.

# Pesto

## Pesto Genovese

*The word pesto comes from* pestare, *to pound, because this classic fresh basil sauce from Genoa is traditionally made by pounding the leaves into a pulp using a mortar and pestle. Since most people do not have a mortar and pestle, using a food processor is a good alternative. Pesto's sweet, slightly peppery flavor marries well with many foods. Try to use small leaf basil for the recipe as it has much better flavor than larger leaves. Use pesto to dress pasta or stir it into minestrone soup or baste it on grilled fish, chicken, or pork.* **Makes 2 cups**

¼ cup pine nuts or walnuts

3 garlic cloves, peeled

1 teaspoon coarse sea salt

1½ packed stemmed basil leaves

3 tablespoons grated Parmigiano-Reggiano or pecorino Romano cheese

½ cup extra-virgin olive oil

Place the pine nuts, garlic, and coarse salt in the bowl of a food processor and pulse 2 or 3 times. Add the basil leaves and pulse 2 times. With the motor running, pour the olive oil, a little at a time, through the feed tube and continue processing until a smooth sauce consistency is obtained. You may not need all the oil. Stir in the cheese.

**NOTE:** *You can also make this pesto the traditional way using a mortar and pestle. Grind the basil and garlic together to a coarse puree. Add the nuts and grind to a smooth puree. Blend in the cheese. Blend in the oil a little at a time. Season to taste with salt.*

# Garlic and Oil Sauce with Walnuts and Pecorino Cheese

## La Salsa Aglio e Olio con Noci e Pecorino

1 cup fruity, extra-virgin olive oil

2 garlic cloves, finely minced

1 teaspoon salt

Freshly ground black pepper

⅓ cup minced flat-leaf parsley leaves

½ cup minced walnuts

¼ cup grated pecorino cheese

*If there is a sauce more classic than tomato it has to be* aglio e olio, *garlic and oil, and who does not have those two healthy ingredients on hand? This sauce exudes comfort; it is what I crave when I want something light, something that is not an assault on my stomach, and something that just plain puts me in a good mood. This sauce is sheer perfection and really is a great example of using the best ingredients for tasty results. Use a good, fruity, extra-virgin olive oil, fresh garlic, and fresh parsley. It is that simple. But if you want to take it one step further, add minced walnuts and pecorino cheese. The recipe makes enough to dress a pound of spaghetti or linguine, and can easily be doubled to serve more.* **Makes 1¾ cups**

In a 12-inch sauté pan, heat the olive oil slowly over medium-low heat. When it begins to shimmer at the edges, stir in the garlic and cook, pressing on it with a wooden spoon, until the garlic begins to turn golden brown; take care not to let it burn or you will have to discard it and start over. Turn off the heat and stir in the salt, pepper, parsley, walnuts, and cheese. Keep the sauce warm while you cook the pasta.

**CHEF'S SECRET:** *Use a Microplane grater to mince garlic. Just grate unpeeled cloves where you need it; the thin outer paper layer of the cloves is left behind.*

# Oven Baked Beef Shin Tomato Ragù

## Ragù al Forno

*Beef shin is a tough cut of meat also called the shank and is cut from the front lower leg of a steer. It needs to cook slowly in order to tenderize it and bring out its delicious flavor. Some people braise it in a small amount of liquid for a long time and Nonna Saporito used it to make a flavorful beef soup. I oven cook it with onions, pancetta, and tomatoes to make a ragu for short cuts of pasta like ziti. It is equally delicious mixed into rice, lentils, and as a sauce for polenta. I start the preparation on the stovetop and finish it in the oven.* **Makes 3½ to 4 cups ragu sauce**

**2 tablespoons extra-virgin olive oil**

**¼ pound pancetta, diced**

**1 medium onion, peeled and diced**

**3 garlic cloves, peeled and minced**

**3 tablespoons tomato paste (such as Mutti brand)**

**1 teaspoon fine sea salt**

**Freshly ground black pepper**

**1¼ pounds beef shin (center cut)**

**One 28-ounce can pureed plum tomatoes**

**¼ cup red wine vinegar**

**1 tablespoon sugar**

**4 tablespoons minced basil**

**I**n a Dutch oven or other heavy-duty ovenproof casserole, heat the olive oil over medium heat. Add the pancetta and onions and cook until the pancetta renders its fat and begins to brown. Stir in the garlic and continue to cook for one or two minutes, or until the garlic softens. Stir in the tomato paste, coating the pancetta mixture well, and season with salt and pepper to taste.

Transfer the mixture to a small bowl and set aside.

Preheat the oven to 325°F.

In the same pan, over medium-high heat, brown the meat well on both sides and season with salt and pepper. Turn off the heat.

In a medium-size bowl combine the tomatoes, vinegar, and sugar. Pour the mixture over the meat. Cover the pot with a tight-fitting lid and bake for 2⅓ hours or until the meat is fork tender.

With a slotted spoon remove the shank to a cutting board and, when cool enough to handle, shred the meat into small pieces and add back to the pot with the sauce. Discard the bone.

Stir the basil into the sauce. Check the seasoning and add more salt and pepper if desired.

Two cups of the sauce is enough to coat a pound of ziti, rigatoni, or fusilli.

The sauce can also be frozen for future use.

# Nut Sauce

## La Salsa di Noci

2/3 cup bread crumbs

2 tablespoons whole milk

1/2 cup walnut meats

1/2 cup pine nuts

1/2 cup grated pecorino cheese

5 tablespoons extra-virgin olive oil

Salt and black pepper

1 pound cappellini or other thin pasta

1/2 cup grated Parmigiano-Reggiano cheese

*This nut sauce is a good one to use on thin pasta such as cappellini or spaghettini because it adheres very well. I like using a combination of walnuts and pine nuts.*
***Makes 2¾ cups***

**I**n a small bowl moisten the bread in the milk.

Grind the nuts together in a food processor until they are coarse. Add the moistened bread crumbs and pecorino cheese and pulse again but do not make the mixture too smooth. Drizzle in the olive oil through the feed tube until a sauce is obtained. Do not overprocess or the sauce will have no texture. Transfer the sauce to a bowl, season with salt and pepper to taste, and set aside.

In a large pot, cook the pasta in 4 to 6 quarts of salted water until al dente. Drain the pasta reserving 2 tablespoons of the cooking water. Return the pasta to the pot, stir the reserved water and the sauce into the pasta, and mix well over low heat. Refrigerate the remaining sauce covered in a jar for up to 2 weeks. Serve hot sprinkled with the grated Parmigiano-Reggiano cheese.

# Ricotta Cheese Sauce

## La Salsa di Ricotta

*Have you ever thought of using ricotta cheese as a sauce for pasta? It is one of my favorites and the key is to use fresh, thick, whole milk ricotta; the skim milk variety is too thin and watery. Lots of grated lemon zest gives this sauce a very clean taste. This recipe makes enough sauce to dress one pound of pasta.* **Serves 4 to 6**

**I**n a large bowl, whisk the ricotta cheese, salt, and pepper together until well blended. Set aside.

In a large pot, cook the pasta of your choice in 4 quarts of rapidly boiling salted water until al dente. Drain the pasta in a colander, reserving ⅓ cup of the cooking water.

Return the pasta to the pot and, over low heat, add the ricotta cheese mixture, the reserved water, zest, and grated cheese. Mix everything well and serve when hot.

1½ cups whole milk ricotta cheese, well drained

1 teaspoon fine sea salt

½ teaspoon freshly ground black pepper

2 tablespoons freshly grated lemon zest (from 2 large lemons)

½ cup grated Parmigiano-Reggiano cheese

# Sicilian Lemon and Olive Oil Sauce

## La Salsa Salmoriglio

Salmoriglio *is a Sicilian sauce that a lot of people have never heard of. The name is derived from* salamoia, *which means "brine". Made with lemon juice, water, and olive oil, this quick sauce is perfect for basting grilled fish or to use at the table as a condiment for grilled meats. Old recipes say that the ingredients should be whisked together in a double boiler to insure a creamy emulsion but I find that a good whisk and some fast arm action is just as good.* **Makes about ¾ cup**

**C**ombine all the ingredients except the salt and pepper in a medium bowl and whisk until the ingredients are well blended. Season with salt and pepper to taste. Refrigerate and use to baste grilled fish, meat, or even poultry. Or pass it at the table as a condiment for grilled meats.

**Juice of 2 large lemons**

**½ cup extra-virgin olive oil**

**¼ cup hot water**

**1 garlic clove, minced**

**2 tablespoons minced flat-leaf parsley**

**1 teaspoon dried oregano**

**Fine sea salt**

**Freshly ground black pepper**

# Ragù Bologna Style

## Ragù alla Bolognese

¼ pound pancetta

1 medium onion, quartered

1 medium carrot, peeled and quartered

1 celery stalk, quartered

2 tablespoons extra-virgin olive oil

½ pound ground chuck

½ pound ground veal

½ pound ground pork

½ to 1 teaspoon fine sea salt

¼ teaspoon freshly ground black pepper

4 tablespoons tomato paste

½ cup dry red wine

½ cup whole milk or cream

*Bolognese* ragù *is the signature meat sauce of the region of Emilia-Romagna. It is simmered for at least an hour to develop a complex layer of flavors and proper consistency. Cooking the ragu in a heavy-bottomed pot will hold the heat steady and give a velvety texture to the ragu. Bolognese ragu is a classic sauce for lasagne verdi and tagliatelle. The sauce also freezes beautifully.* **Makes 4 cups**

**m**ince the pancetta, onion, carrot, and celery, mix together, and set aside.

Heat the olive oil in a heavy-bottomed pot or Dutch oven. Add the pancetta and minced vegetable mixture and cook over low heat, uncovered, for 30 minutes, stirring occasionally. Stir in the ground meats, salt, and pepper, and brown the meats completely. Stir the tomato paste into the wine and add it to the meat mixture. Simmer the ingredients, uncovered, for 45 minutes, adding the milk or cream a little at a time to keep the mixture from sticking while it cooks. The milk also lends richness and creaminess to the sauce. The sauce should have a thick consistency.

## Tomato Paste with Attitude

*I learned the art of making estrattu (that's dialect for tomato paste) in Sicily. It is a very dense and concentrated tomato paste that no Sicilian cook of any merit would be without. It takes about 10 pounds of the tomato pulp to dehydrate sufficiently into a concentrate to fill just one jar. Think of it as tomato paste with attitude. The handmade paste is a backbreaking, hot summer job, and the flavor is very intense.*

*First you must start with fresh plum tomatoes with skins and seeds removed. The tomatoes are cooked into sauce with the addition of onions, local herbs like oregano and basil, and salt and spices. There is no standard recipe since the method varies from place to place and every cook will tell you that his or her method is the tried-and-true one. The sauce is spread on long boards or placed in shallow metal pans, topped with screens to keep the bugs away, and placed in the searing Sicilian sun where it is frequently moved back and forth by hand with small implements resembling paddles to help it dry and remove the excess liquid. This process takes days. The whole idea is to wind up with a very pastelike consistency that is called estrattu, strattu, or strattu ri pumaroru, i.e., tomato paste.*

*Obviously it would be impossible to re-create estrattu here because of the radical difference in climate. But there is a way to make something similar by using a dehydrator.*

*To prepare it, use ripe plum tomatoes that have been washed, dried, and cored. Cut them in half lengthwise and place them, cut side down, in the dehydrator and dry them according to the manufacturer's instructions. Remove them when they are the consistency of dried apricots. This could take a day or two depending on the dehydrator and the size of your tomatoes. No dehydrator? Place the cut tomatoes on racks placed over baking sheets and place them in a 250°F oven. But note, this could take even longer.*

*Place the dried tomatoes in a food processor and puree them into a paste. Through the feed tube add just enough extra-virgin olive oil to smooth out the tomatoes but don't add too much. The mixture should remain thick with the consistency of peanut butter. Transfer the paste to a bowl and add salt and black pepper to taste. Fill new sterilized jars with the paste, cap, and refrigerate or freeze. Add the tomato paste in small amounts to really beef up the flavors.*

# Nonna Galasso's Stuffed Rolled Beef

## Braciolone alla Nonna Galasso

*Nonna Galasso's braciolone, or rolled stuffed beef, was a great favorite in our house. Top round steak was stuffed, rolled, and tied. After browning it well, she cooked it for hours over low heat with some of her usual ingredients for making tomato sauce. That way the sauce could be mixed with pasta for the first course while the braciolone was served as a secondo (second course), with some of the same sauce spooned over the meat.*

*Variations on the stuffing could include pine nuts, raisins, and olives. The sauce was used for rigatoni, spaghetti, lasagne, and potato gnocchi.* **Serves 6 to 8**

**t**o make the braciolone, lay the meat out flat and pound it with a meat mallet to flatten it slightly to a uniform thickness, about ¼-inch thick. Be careful not to tear the meat.

Wipe the meat dry with paper towels. Rub it all over with salt and pepper.

Mince the garlic, parsley, and walnuts together and spread it all over the surface of the meat.

Lay the egg slices down the center of the meat, slightly overlapping. Starting at a long side, roll up the meat like a jelly roll. Tie the roll with string at 1 inch intervals. Set aside.

To make the sauce, heat the olive oil in a large deep saucepan. Add the onions and cook until they soften. Add the meat to the pan and brown it on all sides.

Lower the heat to medium-low and add all the remaining ingredients; season with salt to taste. Stir to blend well. Simmer the meat, covered, for 1½ hours, or until tender.

Remove the meat from the sauce and let it rest for 5 to 10 minutes. Remove the strings and cut the braciolone into 1-inch-thick slices. Arrange the slices on a serving platter, spoon some sauce over the top, and serve.

**BRACIALONE**

2 pounds top round steak, about ¼ inch thick

2 teaspoons fine salt

1 tablespoon ground black pepper

4 garlic cloves

1 bunch flat-leaf parsley

½ cup walnuts

½ cup grated pecorino Romano cheese

3 hard-boiled eggs, cut into slices

**SAUCE**

⅓ cup extra-virgin olive oil

1 onion thinly sliced

4 cups crushed tomatoes (fresh or canned)

⅓ cup water

1 cup dry red wine

1 whole bay leaf

1 small bunch basil, tied with twine

Salt and black pepper

# Orange Sauce

## La Salsa di Arancia

2 tablespoons
  unsalted butter

3 large egg yolks

¼ cup red wine
  vinegar

1 tablespoon orange
  zest

Juice of 1 orange

Salt and black pepper

*This velvety orange sauce is perfect drizzled over grilled asparagus or fennel. It is best made with blood oranges but when they are not in season, navel oranges will do.*
***Makes about ⅔ cup***

**m**elt the butter in the top of a double boiler set over medium-low heat. Whisk in the egg yolks and cook until the yolks are well blended with the butter. Watch the heat and keep it low so the yolks do not scramble.

Slowly whisk in the vinegar, orange zest, and juice. Season with salt and pepper to taste and whisk until the sauce is smooth. Serve warm over grilled asparagus or fennel.

# Tuscan-Style Meat Sauce

## Ragù alla Toscana

*There are as many regional variations of ragu sauces among Italian cooks as there are stars in the sky! Just one variation of an ingredient is what makes it your own, and that pretty much sums up what is meant by "Italian cooking." Unlike Ragu Bologna Style on page 188, this ragu, typical of Tuscany, does not use milk or cream and is flavored with rosemary. Use it for short cuts of pasta like penne or rigatoni. The recipe makes a lot of sauce, but it freezes beautifully.* **Makes about 3 quarts**

4 tablespoons extra-virgin olive oil

2 celery stalks, diced

1 large carrot, peeled and diced

1 medium red sweet onion, peeled and diced

1 garlic clove, peeled and minced

2 tablespoons minced rosemary

1 pound ground beef

1 pound pork sausage, casings removed

Two 28-ounce cans whole peeled plum tomatoes

Salt and black pepper

1 cup dry red wine

heat the olive oil in a 2-quart, heavy-bottomed pot or Dutch oven. Add the celery, carrot, and onion and cook slowly over medium-high heat until the mixture softens. Do not let it burn. Stir in the garlic and rosemary and cook until the garlic has softened. Stir in the beef and pork and cook over high heat until the meat is browned.

Lower the heat to medium and, using your hands, squeeze the tomatoes and add them to the pot along with any juices. Season with salt and pepper to taste. Stir the mixture to combine the ingredients and add the wine. Bring the mixture to a boil, then lower the heat to a simmer, and cook, covered, for 1½ hours. Uncover and cook for 30 minutes more. The sauce should be very thick.

# Dried Tomatoes in Olive Oil

## Pomodori Secchi Sott'Olio

*Plum tomatoes are perfect for drying for winter use. To make them you will need a dehydrator, fresh plum tomatoes free of any blemishes or bruises, and sterilized new jars. Once you make your own, there is no going back to store-bought varieties that are often too salty and costly. Double or triple the recipe below to make more.* **Makes four 6-ounce jars**

**W**ash and dry the tomatoes. Core them and cut them in half lengthwise.

Place the tomatoes, cut side down, on the racks of a dehydrator and dry according to the manufacturer's instructions until they are shriveled but still bendable like a dried apricot.

Heat the vinegar in a large nonreactive pot and bring to a boil. Add the tomatoes and cook 1 minute. Using a slotted spoon, remove them and place them in a colander.

Layer the tomatoes into the jars and add the basil, capers, peppercorns, and salt, dividing them equally among the jars.

Slowly add the olive oil to each jar and fill to the top.

With a wooden spoon, press down on the tomatoes to submerge them under the oil. *This is a critical step.* No tomatoes should be above the olive oil. The oil prevents air from getting into the jars. Add more olive oil if necessary.

Cap the jars and allow them to sit on your counter for a day. Then open the jars to see if more oil is needed.

Cap the jars and store them in the refrigerator. Bring to room temperature when needed. Return what you do not use to the refrigerator. The tomatoes keep for several months.

14 meaty plum tomatoes

3 cups red wine vinegar

8 basil leaves, washed and dried

3 tablespoons capers packed in brine, drained

2 tablespoons whole black peppercorns

2 teaspoons fine sea salt

3 cups extra-virgin olive oil

4 sterilized 6-ounce jars

# Rice

Pumpkin Risotto

Risotto with Tomato and Wine

Asparagus Risotto Squares

Classic Risotto Milan Style

Risotto with Dried Porcini Mushrooms

Little Rice Cakes

Risotto with Portobello Mushooms and
Mascarpone Cheese

Risotto with Pork Sausage and Beet
Greens

Strawberry Risotto

Neapolitan Rice, Pork, and Vegetable
Mold

Rice Omelet

Barley and Mushroom "Risotto"

# italian rice
. . . . . . . . . . . . .

**r**ice is one of the oldest and most primary food sources for over half the world's population and according to recent scientific studies, Stone Age paddy fields tended by the world's earliest-known rice farmers have been uncovered in a swamp in China. Once cultivation began, it quickly spread westward. By medieval times, southern Europe saw the introduction of rice as a hearty grain.

In Italy rice *(riso)* was thought of as a mysterious plant and only used as a medicinal remedy. Then in the late fifteenth century, farmers in the Po Valley of Italy decided to plant some seeds and that was Italy's beginning as the largest rice producer in Europe. Northern Italy, especially the regions of the Piedmont, Lombardy, and the Veneto are the prime rice-growing regions because they have the right climate and the abundance of water needed for plants to grow.

Italy grows a short-grain, starchy rice that is perfect for making classic risotto, which requires a rice that can absorb a lot of liquid and produce a creamy consistency that the Venetians say needs to be *all onda* (on the wave). In other words, the rice must flow off the spoon in waves and not be lumpy.

There are several varieties of rice grown in Italy: *comune* (common), *semifino* (semifine), *fino* (fine), and *superfine* (super fine). Arborio rice is the most well-known of the superfino types and the one most readily available for making risotto. But there are other types also good for risotto such as Carnaroli and Vialone Nano.

If you want to make a good risotto, here are a few rules to keep in mind. First, start with a heavy-bottomed pot, which will deliver maximum heat during cooking. Second, make sure the rice is well coated in the oil or butter before adding the liquid; this will help to keep the grains separate, allowing the risotto to flow freely off the spoon when finished. Third, don't be in a hurry when stirring in the liquid; each addition should be fully absorbed by the rice before adding more liquid. Fourth, know when to stop stirring. Stop when the rice is still firm but cooked through. Taste it. It should not be hard or mushy, just creamy.

Risotto is an ever-changing dish with an endless variety of ingredients that can be added to it. For instance, in Milan it is saffron and Parmigiano-Reggiano cheese, in Venice it is seafood, or peas for the classic *risi e bisi* (rice and peas). But that is just the beginning of what you can do with Italian rice.

# Pumpkin Risotto

## Risotto alla Zucca

*Part of the fun of making risotto is coming up with all kinds of ingredients to combine with it, such as pumpkin. This creamy pumpkin risotto comes from my friend Terry Rozzi, whose home is Cremona in northern Italy. Adding pumpkin provides not only a delicate color but also a slightly sweet taste. Use pie pumpkin to approximate the taste of the zucca gialla (yellow pumpkin) of Cremona.*  **Serves 4**

**C**ut off and discard the pumpkin stem and, using a vegetable peeler, remove the skin. Cut the pumpkin in half and remove and discard the seeds and stringy center. Dice enough fresh pumpkin into ¼-inch pieces to make 1 cup. Reserve the rest of the pumpkin for another use.

In a heavy-bottomed, 2-quart saucepan, melt the butter over medium heat. Add the pumpkin and leek and cook, stirring often, until the vegetables soften. Stir in the rice and coat it with the butter mixture. Cook, stirring constantly, until the rice begins to make a crackling sound, about 4 to 5 minutes. Do not let the rice brown.

Add the wine and cook, stirring constantly, until the rice has absorbed all the liquid. Add ½ cup of the broth and continue to cook and stir until the rice has absorbed the broth. Continue adding the broth ½ cup at a time, allowing the rice to absorb each addition before adding more. Cook until the rice is still firm but cooked through. As the rice cooks it will increase in volume and should become creamy and fluid.

Taste the rice for doneness. Stir in the cheeses and blend well. Taste and season with salt as needed.

Serve immediately.

---

1 small pie pumpkin (about ½ pounds)

6 tablespoons (¾ stick) unsalted butter

1 large leek, white part only, halved lengthwise, well rinsed, and finely chopped

1½ cups Arborio rice

½ cup dry white wine

3½ cups hot home-made chicken broth

¼ cup mascarpone cheese

½ cup freshly grated Parmigiano-Reggiano cheese

Fine sea salt

# Risotto with Tomato and Wine

## Risotto Rosso

3½ to 4 cups home-made fresh cherry tomato juice, heated, or store-bought tomato juice

¼ pound pancetta, diced

2 tablespoons extra-virgin olive oil

1 small onion, minced

2 cups Arborio rice

1 cup dry red wine

½ cup grated Asiago cheese

¼ cup minced basil leaves

*I love the perky taste of summer in this tomato- and wine-flavored risotto. I make it when fresh cherry tomatoes are in season.*  **Serves 6**

**t**o make cherry tomato juice, with an immersion blender or food processor, puree 3 pints of washed and stemmed cherry tomatoes. Transfer the pulp to a fine-mesh sieve placed over a large bowl and strain out the juice. Discard the seeds and skins.

In a heavy-bottomed, 2-quart saucepan, brown the pancetta until crisp. With a slotted spoon transfer the pancetta to a dish and set aside.

Add the oil to the saucepan, add the onions, and cook over medium heat until very soft but not browned. Stir in the rice and coat well in the onion-oil mixture. Stir in the wine, ½ cup at a time, and cook, stirring constantly, until the wine has been absorbed.

Add ½ cup of the tomato juice to the pan and cook, stirring, until the juice has been absorbed. Continue adding more tomato juice, ½ cup at time, allowing the rice to absorb each addition before adding more.

As the rice cooks it will increase in volume and become creamy. Taste the rice for doneness. It should still be firm but be cooked through. If it is not, add more juice and continue to cook.

Stir in the cheese and basil. Return the pancetta to the saucepan and stir it in well.

Serve immediately.

# Asparagus Risotto Squares
## Quadri di Asparagi

*Here is a clever way to use Arborio rice in a do-ahead preparation. Unlike classic risotto, which must be served immediately, this recipe allows the rice mixture to firm up overnight and is then cut into squares and browned just before serving.* **Serves 6**

Preheat the oven to 350°F. Butter a baking sheet.

Toss the asparagus pieces with the olive oil; place them on a rimmed baking sheet and roast them until the tip of a knife is easily inserted, about 3 to 5 minutes. Season the asparagus with salt and pepper and keep warm.

Melt 2 tablespoons of the butter in a 2-quart saucepan over medium heat. Stir in the onion and prosciutto and cook until the onion is soft but not browned.

Stir in the rice and cook, stirring, for 1 to 2 minutes, evenly coating the rice with the butter-onion mixture. When the rice begins to make a crackling sound, reduce the heat to medium low and add the wine. Cook, stirring constantly, until all the wine has been absorbed.

Add the broth, ½ cup at a time, stirring constantly until the liquid has been absorbed. Continue adding broth ½ cup at a time, cooking and stirring until the broth has been absorbed before adding more. Taste the rice for doneness; it should be firm but cooked through. If it is not, add more broth and continue to cook.

Stir in 4 tablespoons of the remaining butter and the cheese. Carefully fold in half of the asparagus pieces. Refrigerate the remaining asparagus until ready to serve the squares.

Pour the mixture onto the prepared baking sheet and smooth it out to a thickness of ½ inch. Form the risotto into a 6 × 6-inch square. Lightly score the top of the rice into six 3-inch squares. Refrigerate, covered, for at least 1 hour or overnight.

Cut the chilled rice mixture into squares.

Melt the remaining 2 tablespoons of unsalted butter in a large sauté pan and fry the squares until golden brown. Add additional butter if the pan seems dry. Transfer to a warm platter and keep covered.

In the same pan, reheat the reserved asparagus and top each square with a few pieces. Serve hot.

1 pound asparagus, tough ends trimmed and spears cut into 1-inch-long diagonal pieces

1½ tablespoons extra-virgin olive oil

Salt and black pepper

8 tablespoons (1 stick) unsalted butter

1 medium onion, diced

½ cup diced prosciutto

1 cup Arborio rice

½ cup dry white wine

4 to 5 cups hot vegetable or chicken broth

⅔ cup grated Parmigiano-Reggiano cheese

# Classic Risotto Milan Style

## Risotto alla Milanese

1 tablespoon saffron
 threads

2 tablespoons warm
 water

6 tablespoons
 (¾ stick) unsalted
 butter

½ cup finely minced
 onion

2 cups Arborio rice

½ cup dry white wine

4½ to 5 cups hot
 homemade
 chicken broth

¾ cup grated
 Parmigiano-
 Reggiano cheese

*There is an art to making a well-prepared risotto that may just be the most richly layered and flavorful dish you will ever eat. Risotto develops unique character and layers of flavor depending on the ingredients added to it, which can include anything from vegetables to seafood to sausage.* Risotto alla Milanese *is the most famous Italian rice dish and its origins are probably Spanish since Spain ruled over Milan for two centuries. However, folklore tells us that the use of saffron (the stigma of the Crocus sativus flower) was the brainstorm of an artist who was known as Zafferano because he always added a pinch of saffron when mixing his colors. One day he decided to add it to the rice being prepared for a nobleman's daughter's wedding. The yellow-hued rice made such an impression that* risotto alla Milanese *was born. Risotto is traditionally served as a first course but when fish, vegetables, or meat is added, it can be served as a main course.* **Serves 6**

Place the saffron in a small bowl and pour the warm water over it. Set aside.

In a heavy-bottomed, 2-quart saucepan melt 3 tablespoons of the butter over medium heat; do not let it brown. Stir in the onion and cook until the onion is very soft but not browned; it should remain colorless and almost dissolve into the butter.

Stir in the rice and cook for 1 to 2 minutes, evenly coating the rice in the butter-onion mixture. When the rice begins to make a crackling sound, reduce the heat to medium-low and add the wine.

Cook, stirring constantly, until all the wine has been absorbed. Add ½ cup of the broth and continue to cook and stir until the rice has absorbed the broth. Continue adding the broth, ½ cup at a time, allowing the rice to absorb each addition before adding more.

As the rice cooks it should increase in volume, and become creamy and fluid. Taste the rice for doneness. It should be firm but cooked through. If it is not, add more broth and continue to cook.

Strain the saffron threads and add the liquid to the rice; this will provide a lovely yellow color. Off the heat, stir in the remaining 3 tablespoons of butter and the cheese.

Serve immediately.

# Risotto with Dried Porcini Mushrooms

## Risotto ai Funghi Porcini Secchi

*When serving risotto became all the rage, restaurants went to the mat with it, tweaking the ingredients and its preparation to offer patrons something new. And even though this classic rice dish originated in Milan, it is made all over "the boot" today imbued with local ingredients. No other food culture treats rice quite like Italy. To begin a successful risotto, the right rice is toasted, not boiled. Toasting keeps the kernel separate during the cooking process. Made with the proper ingredients, homemade risotto will have a fairly authentic taste. A favorite winter version is made with dried porcini mushrooms, Parmigiano-Reggiano cheese, and wine.* **Serves 4**

½ cup dried porcini mushrooms (about one 1-ounce package)

6 tablespoons (¾ stick) unsalted butter

2 large shallots, peeled and minced

1½ cups Arborio rice

4 cups hot chicken or beef broth

½ cup dry white wine

¼ cup minced flat-leaf parsley

1 cup grated Parmigiano-Reggiano cheese

Fine sea salt

Freshly ground black pepper

**P**ut the mushrooms in a bowl and pour a cup of boiling water over them. Set aside for 10 minutes.

Melt 4 tablespoons of the butter in a heavy-bottomed, 2-quart saucepan. Add the shallots and cook them over medium heat until they begin to take on a light brown color. Transfer them with a slotted spoon to a bowl.

Add the rice to the saucepan and stir it over medium heat until it becomes translucent and begins to make a crackling sound. Do not let the rice brown.

Return the shallots to the saucepan. Add the wine and cook, stirring constantly until the wine has been absorbed. Add the broth, a ladleful at a time, and continue to cook and stir until the rice has absorbed the broth.

Drain the mushrooms and reserve the soaking liquid. Strain the liquid to remove any bits of sediment. Chop the mushrooms and then add them to the rice along with the reserved liquid, stirring occasionally to keep the rice from sticking.

Continue adding broth, a ladleful at a time, until the rice has tripled in volume and is creamy and fluid. Taste rice for doneness. It should be firm but cooked through.

Turn off the heat and stir in the parsley, the remaining 2 tablespoons butter, and half the cheese. Season with salt and pepper to taste. The risotto should be free flowing off your spoon, not a congealed ball of rice. Practice makes perfect.

Serve hot and pass the remaining cheese on the side.

# Little Rice Cakes

## Tortine di Riso

4 to 5 tablespoons extra-virgin olive oil

1 cup Arborio rice

¼ cup minced onion

3 cups hot vegetable broth

1 large egg, slightly beaten

1 cup grated pecorino cheese

2 tablespoons minced flat-leaf parsley

Juice of 1 lemon

Salt and black pepper

*Ever wonder what else you could make with Arborio rice besides risotto? How about savory little rice cakes? These are a great side to any main dish and a nice change of pace from potatoes or just plain rice. The best part is that unlike making risotto where constant stirring is important to keep the mixture smooth, in this recipe, the pot needs no watching. Add different flavorings to the rice to suit your taste, like herbs, cheeses, and bits of ham or salame.* **Makes 8 rice cakes**

heat 2 tablespoons of the olive oil in a 2-quart saucepan. Add the rice and cook, stirring occasionally, until all the grains are coated and you hear a crackling sound. Stir in the onion and cook until the onion is soft but not browned. Add the broth and bring to a boil. Lower the heat and simmer until the liquid has been absorbed, about 20 minutes, and the rice is still firm but cooked through.

Transfer the rice to a bowl and stir in the remaining ingredients. Mix well and season with salt and pepper to taste. Allow the mixture to cool. Using wet hands, form 8 patties about 3 inches in diameter.

Heat the remaining olive oil in a large nonstick pan and brown the risotto cakes well on each side, about 4 minutes per side. Serve hot.

# Risotto with Portobello Mushrooms and Mascarpone Cheese

## Risotto con Cappellone e Mascarpone

3 tablespoons extra-virgin olive oil

1 large portobello mushroom (about 6 ounces), stemmed, cleaned, and diced

Fine sea salt

4 tablespoons (½ stick) unsalted butter

3 medium shallots, diced

2 cups Arborio rice

4 cups hot chicken broth

½ cup dry white wine

¼ cup mascarpone cheese

½ cup freshly grated Parmigiano-Reggiano cheese

*Wild funghi are unearthed from wooded areas all over Italy. They come in various shapes, sizes, and textures, but their whereabouts are usually a well-kept secret. Porcini are probably the most well-known of the hundreds of species of Italian mushrooms. But the deep brown, smooth-textured portobello mushroom, which is neither Italian in origin nor wild, is a work of art and is wonderful, grilled and sprinkled with just a whiff of balsamic vinegar. I use portobellos for ravioli filling, for sauces for pasta, and in this wonderful risotto. To clean mushrooms, use a mushroom brush or a damp clean sponge or paper towel to wipe them off. Do not rinse them under running water, which will make them difficult to saute.* **Serves 6 to 8**

heat the olive oil in a medium sauté pan over medium heat. Add the mushrooms and cook them until they are lightly browned, about 5 minutes. Season with salt to taste and set aside.

In a large heavy saucepan or a Dutch oven, melt the butter. Add the shallots and cook over low heat until they are very soft but not browned. Add the rice and stir to coat it evenly with the butter. Cook, stirring continuously, for about 5 minutes. Add about ¼ cup of the chicken broth and stir until the rice has absorbed the liquid. Add a little of the wine and stir constantly until absorbed. Continue adding the broth and wine alternately, cooking and stirring until the rice is still firm, but cooked through.

Add the mushrooms, mascarpone cheese, and Parmigiano-Reggiano cheese and stir to combine. Season with salt to taste and serve immediately.

**NOTE:** *One pound of fresh mushrooms is equal to 6 cups sliced or 3 ounces dried.*

# Risotto with Pork Sausage and Beet Greens

## Risotto con Salsicce e Bietole

*In my kitchen, a risotto made with beet greens and pork sausage is a requested favorite. I serve this as a main dish and team it with a salad and fresh fruit for a healthy and balanced meal.* **Serves 6**

**d**rop the beet greens into a pot of boiling water and cook them just until wilted. Drain, cool, squeeze dry, and coarsely chop them. Set aside.

Heat 1½ tablespoons of the oil in a medium sauté pan and add the garlic and the greens. Cook for 2 minutes over medium heat. Transfer the mixture to a bowl and set aside.

In a heavy-bottomed, 2-quart saucepan, heat the remaining 1½ tablespoons olive oil. When it is hot, stir in the onion, red pepper flakes, and sausage. Cook until the onion softens and the meat begins to brown slightly. Stir in the rice and mix to coat the rice well. Pour in the wine and stir until it evaporates.

Begin adding the tomato juice in ½-cup increments and allow the rice mixture to absorb each addition before adding more.

Add the broth in ½-cup increments, continuing to cook and stir until the rice mixture is creamy and the rice is still firm but cooked through. You may not need all the broth. Stir in the beet greens and grated cheese. Season with salt and pepper to taste and serve immediately.

½ pound beet greens, spinach, or Swiss chard, stemmed and washed

3 tablespoons extra-virgin olive oil

1 garlic clove, minced

1 small onion, peeled and diced

½ teaspoon hot red pepper flakes or hot red pepper paste

½ pound sweet Italian sausage, casings removed

1½ cups Arborio rice

½ cup dry white wine

2 cups hot tomato juice

2½ to 3 cups hot chicken broth

½ cup grated Parmigiano-Reggiano cheese

Salt and black pepper

# Strawberry Risotto

## Risotto con Fragole

*Fruit-flavored risotto is made in some parts of Italy in* alta cucina *(gourmet cooking) restaurants. When I made strawberry risotto for my mother, her skepticism turned to raves. Wild strawberries work best, but local in-season berries are fine, too. I have also made this with blueberries.*   **Serves 4**

**M**elt 4 tablespoons of butter over medium heat in a heavy saucepan. Add the leeks and cook until they are soft and translucent. Add the rice and stir until it is well coated with the butter.

Add the wine, a little at a time, and cook, stirring continuously, over medium heat until the wine has been absorbed. Add ½ cup of the broth and cook, stirring, until it is absorbed. Continue adding the broth, cooking and stirring continuously for 20 to 25 minutes, or until the rice is still firm but cooked through.

Remove the risotto from the heat, stir in the berries, and add the remaining butter and the grated cheese. Serve immediately, garnished with the whole berries.

**6 tablespoons (¾ stick) unsalted butter**

**¼ cup finely chopped leeks**

**1½ cups Arborio rice**

**⅔ cup dry white wine**

**4 cups hot chicken broth**

**1 cup chopped strawberries or blueberries, plus several whole berries for garnish**

**½ cup grated Parmigiano-Reggiano cheese**

# Neapolitan Rice, Pork, and Vegetable Mold

## Sartù

### MOLD

3 tablespoons butter for greasing mold

1 cup toasted bread crumbs

### FILLING

1 pound ground pork

¼ cup fresh bread crumbs

1½ teaspoons fine sea salt

2 tablespoons grated pecorino cheese

1 large egg

1 tablespoon extra-virgin olive oil

3 tablespoons un-salted butter

½ cup diced onion

1 ounce dried porcini mushrooms, rehydrated in hot water

1 cup peas

Freshly ground black pepper

*Even though Nonna Galasso never heard of sartù, her native Naples lays claim to its invention. I was first introduced to this impressive-looking rice mold with a meat and vegetable filling in Sorrento. Sartù has had many adaptations and has been simplified from the richer versions made for the nobility of the past, which contained such exotics as chicken livers, sausages, cheeses, and assorted vegetables. The most important thing to remember when making the sartù is to prepare the mold well by coating it with butter and bread crumbs, and then chilling it well in the refrigerator. The preparation, which can be done in stages, begins with making a risotto in which short-grain, starchy Arborio rice is cooked slowly with the addition of hot broth. The entire dish can be held in the refrigerator for several hours or even overnight before baking. For best results, use a 10-cup ring mold or charlotte mold.* **Serves 8 to 10**

generously butter the mold and coat it with the bread crumbs, pressing the bread crumbs into the butter if necessary. Cover and chill the mold.

To make the filling, in a bowl, combine the pork, bread crumbs, 1 teaspoon salt, cheese, and egg. Mix gently with your hands to combine. With wet hands form small meatballs the size of a gumball.

Heat the olive oil in a sauté pan and when it is hot, brown the meatballs in batches, if necessary, until they are golden brown. With a slotted spoon remove the meatballs to a bowl and set aside. (At this point the meatballs can be refrigerated 2 days in advance of assembling the dish.)

In the same sauté pan, melt 2 tablespoons of the butter, stir in the onions and cook them until they begin to soften. Add more butter if needed. Stir in the mush-rooms and cook a minute or two. Stir in the peas and cook 1 minute. Add ½ tea-spoon of salt and a grinding of black pepper. Combine the mixture with the meatballs.

To make the rice mixture, melt the 3 tablespoons of butter in a heavy-bottomed, 3-quart saucepan, add the rice and cook it over medium heat, stirring constantly, until all the grains of rice are coated in the butter. Add the broth, 1 cup at a time, and continue to cook until the rice has absorbed the broth before adding more. You may not need all the broth. The rice should still be firm but cooked through. Stir in the cheese and remove the saucepan from the heat. Let the rice cool slightly, stir in the parsley and eggs.

Preheat the oven to 325°F.

Remove the mold from the refrigerator. Line the bottom of the mold and the sides with about two-thirds of the rice mixture. Make sure there are no bare spots. Spoon the meatball mixture into the rice-lined mold. Cover the top with the remaining rice, patting it down tightly and making sure the edges are sealed with rice.

Cover the mold with aluminum foil and bake it for 30 minutes. Remove the aluminum foil and bake 10 minutes more. Remove the mold from the oven and let stand about 5 minutes. Have a serving dish or platter ready. Place the dish on top of the mold. Using potholders to hold onto the mold, gently turn the mold over and out onto the serving dish. Do not remove the mold immediately. Let it sit for a few minutes, then shake the mold to make sure that the rice has been released. Lift the mold off and serve the *sartù* immediately.

**Variation:** Serve a homemade tomato sauce to pass on the side.

## RICE MIXTURE

3 tablespoons unsalted butter

2 cups Arborio rice

4 to 5 cups hot beef, chicken, or vegetable broth

¾ cup grated pecorino cheese

2 tablespoons chopped flat-leaf parsley

2 large eggs

# Rice Omelet

## Frittata di Riso

¼ cup pine nuts

4 large eggs, at room temperature

½ cup cooked Arborio rice

2 tablespoons minced flat-leaf parsley

½ teaspoon salt

¼ cup minced boiled ham or prosciutto

½ cup mozzarella, Italian fontina, Swiss, or provolone cheese, cut into bits

1 tablespoon extra-virgin olive oil

1 tablespoon unsalted butter

*A frittata made with Arborio rice can be a very nice, easy supper, especially if you have leftover risotto. This delicious frittata is made even more flavorful with the addition of ham or salame. Pine nuts add another layer of texture.* **Serves 4**

Toast the pine nuts over medium heat in a medium, nonstick frying pan until they are fragrant; watch carefully as they burn easily. Transfer the nuts to a small bowl and set aside.

Whisk the eggs in a medium bowl. Stir in the rice, parsley, salt, ham, cheese, and nuts. Set aside.

In the same pan used to toast the nuts, heat the oil and butter over medium-high heat.

Pour the egg mixture into the pan and pat it evenly with a rubber spatula to an even thickness.

As the frittata cooks on the underside, use the spatula to push any uncooked egg mixture from the top to the edges of the pan and lift the edges of the frittata to allow the egg mixture to run underneath.

When the top no longer looks runny, place a plate larger than the diameter of the pan over the top and flip the frittata over. Slide it back into the pan to cook the other side.

Flip the frittata out onto a serving dish and cut into wedges to serve.

# Barley and Mushroom "Risotto"
## Orzotto ai Funghi

*You can make an interesting "risotto" using pearled barley. Barley (orzo in Italian) is a grain that was known in ancient times and used to make bread and porridge. In this recipe it is a substitute for Arborio rice, but cooked following the technique for making risotto.* **Serves 4**

In a heavy-bottomed, 2-quart pot, heat the olive oil over medium-high heat. Stir in the leeks and cook them until wilted. Stir in the barley and cook to coat the barley in the oil; do not let it brown. Stir in the mushrooms and cook 1 minute.

Add the wine and cook, stirring continuously until most of it has evaporated. Start adding the broth, a little at a time, and allow the barley to absorb the liquid before adding more. Cook, stirring, until the barley is tender. Off the heat, stir in the butter and cheese. Add the parsley and serve hot.

¼ cup extra-virgin olive oil

2 cups finely chopped leeks

1¾ cups pearled barley

1½ cups chopped button mushrooms

½ cup dry white wine

4 cups hot vegetable or chicken broth

3 tablespoons unsalted butter

½ cup grated Parmigiano-Reggiano cheese

2 tablespoons minced flat-leaf parsley

# Fish

Baked Fish and Potatoes

Baked Haddock with Olives, Tomatoes,
and Potatoes

Baked Scallops

Roasted Sea Bass with Fennel, Oranges,
and Olives

Stuffed Baked Fish Bundles

Fish Cakes

Stew with Fish Croquettes

Large Shrimp, Amalfi Style

Christmas Eve Clams

Halibut in Lemon Sauce

Pan-Cooked Shrimp in Garlic
and Wine

Salmon, Peas, and Pasta

Sea Bass with Orange Sauce

Sole in Galliano Butter Sauce

Spaghetti with Tuna, Capers,
and Lemon

Tuna with Caponata

Sweet-and-Sour Tuna

Scallops in Viniagrette

# if it's friday

i always knew what we were having for supper on Friday nights at home. Fish. Most likely some form of baccalà, that stiff-as-a-board stinky codfish that Nonna Galasso loved to cook. Because we were Catholic, we observed the rules of the church. No meat on Fridays, and when Lent rolled around we ate so much fish that it seemed like we swam with them. My father went along reluctantly with these rules because he really did not like fish unless it was fried. I always found that odd since his mother, Nonna Saporito, was from Sicily where fish was king, and she liked to cook everything from sardines to sea urchins. I never asked Dad if he ate this stuff.

Dad loved to take my five brothers fishing and once took me, but after I saw how I had to put a squishy worm on the line, I decided that roller skating was much more fun. Dad would proudly bring the catch of the day home to my mother in some muddy bucket. She would lay out layers of newspaper on the counter and scale the fish; then she cut the head off just below the gills and saved it to make fish stock. She saved the fins, too. She slit the belly of the fish and cleaned out the guts. Then she removed the skeletal bones. All this work made me think why on earth couldn't she just buy frozen breaded fish sticks like everybody else?

Mom would flour and fry the fish to a golden brown and serve it with french fries and tartar sauce. Dad would gulp it down. I would gingerly move it around on my plate and when no one was looking, dump it into my napkin and head for the bathroom. And so it would go, every Friday.

But the greatest test of my aversion to fish as a kid was the *vigilia*, the meatless feast on Christmas Eve. What a way to spoil a holiday! Platters of stuffed squid, marinated sardines, fried fish, and baccalà cooked in tomato sauce, were some of the dishes that I had to endure, and I ate them because the thought of Santa Claus leaving me a lump of coal would have been far worse than eating fish.

I don't know exactly when I started to embrace fish but I can honestly say that I cook and eat more fish than meat. I keep up with all the dietary trends that tell us that eating more fish and less meat will not only improve our health because of the omega 3s, but our memory as well. I have become very discerning, too, when I purchase fish and shellfish, always looking for wild-caught fish as opposed to farm-raised, and I look for what is local in my area because I know that it is the freshest. And truth be told, if it's Friday, I'm usually cooking fish.

## Purchasing Fish

It is getting harder and harder to find wild fish anymore. Most of what is available is farm-raised. By law, fish must be labeled as to where it is from. Try to buy what is local and wild when you can, and avoid those fish that are super high in mercury. Some fish like sole, arctic char, black cod, striped bass, and pollock are lower in mercury than tuna, swordfish, grouper, and bluefish.

# Baked Fish and Potatoes

## Pesce e Patate al Forno

*Flounder fillets or fillet of sole are perfect for this quick-baked casserole because they are thin and cook fast. Other types of fish that work well in this recipe include sea bass, cod, and haddock.*   *Serves 4*

2 large baking
   potatoes, peeled

4 tablespoons extra-
   virgin olive oil

Salt and black pepper

4 tablespoons minced
   thyme leaves, plus
   4 whole sprigs

8 pieces fillet of sole
   (about 1 pound)

1 lemon, cut into 4
   wedges

Put the potatoes in a pot, cover with cold water, and bring to a boil. Parboil the potatoes for 5 minutes. Drain, cool, and cut into thin round slices. Set aside.

Preheat the oven to 425 °F. Lightly brush a 12 ½ × 9 ½ × 2-inch baking dish with 1 tablespoon of the olive oil.

Cover the bottom of the dish with a layer of the potatoes and sprinkle them with salt, pepper, and 1 tablespoon of the thyme leaves. Drizzle 1 tablespoon of olive oil over the thyme.

Arrange the fish fillets in a single layer on top of the potatoes. Sprinkle the fish with salt and pepper and 1 tablespoon of the olive oil. Sprinkle 1 tablespoon of the thyme over the fillets.

Cover the fish with the remaining potato slices, and season with salt and pepper. Sprinkle with the remaining thyme and drizzle with the remaining tablespoon of olive oil.

Bake, uncovered, until the fish turns milky white and the potatoes are cooked through.

Use a wide spatula to transfer the fish from the baking dish to individual dinner plates.

Garnish with a sprig of thyme and a lemon wedge.

# Baked Haddock with Olives, Tomatoes, and Potatoes

## Pesce al Forno con Olive, Pomodori, e Patate

*This quick-baked haddock dish is a favorite for company. Not only is it fast and tasty, but it's also impressive to look at! Add a green salad, fresh rolls, and fresh pears for a healthy and easy menu and the time to enjoy your guests!* **Serves 4**

3 medium red potatoes, scrubbed

2 tablespoons extra-virgin olive oil

1 small onion, peeled and thinly sliced

1½ pounds fresh haddock fillets, or other firm baking fish

½ cup pitted black, oil-cured olives, halved

4 ripe beefsteak tomatoes, cut into ¼-inch-thick rounds

1 teaspoon coarse sea salt or more as needed

Freshly ground black pepper

2 tablespoons fresh thyme leaves

**m**icrowave the potatoes as for baked potatoes. Cool, peel, and thinly slice them.

Preheat the oven to 450°F.

Brush a 12 × 9-inch casserole dish with 1 tablespoon of the olive oil. Sprinkle the onions in a layer over the oil. Layer half of the potatoes over the onions.

Lay the fish over the potatoes and sprinkle the olives and tomato slices around the fish.

Place the remaining potato slices over the fish. Season with salt and pepper.

Drizzle on the remaining tablespoon of olive oil and sprinkle the thyme leaves over the top.

Bake for 10 to 12 minutes, or just until the fish has turned milky white and flakes easily when poked with a fork. Serve the fish cut into serving pieces with some of the potatoes, olives, tomatoes, and pan juices.

*CHEF'S SECRET: Fresh fish waits for no one; that is my rule. Cook it the day you purchase it for maximum flavor and because it is very perishable.*

# Baked Scallops

## Cappesante al Forno

3 tablespoons extra-
virgin olive oil

¼ cup minced
flat-leaf parsley

1 teaspoon salt

¼ teaspoon coarsely
ground black
pepper

16 large dry sea
scallops (about
1 pound)

½ cup dry plain
bread crumbs

2 lemons, cut into
wedges

*Here is a really simple and fast way to have scallops on the table in no time. Add a baked potato, some steamed spinach, and a healthy dinner is ready!*

*Be aware that when purchasing sea scallops to make sure they are dry, meaning they are not water injected.*   ***Serves 4***

Preheat oven to 350°F. Brush an 8- or 9-inch casserole dish with 1 tablespoon of the olive oil and set aside.

Pour 2 tablespoons of the olive oil in a medium bowl. Stir in the parsley, salt, and pepper and mix well. Add the scallops and toss to coat them in the mixture.

Place the bread crumbs in a brown paper bag. Add the scallops, close the bag, and shake to coat the scallops with the crumbs. Transfer the scallops to the prepared casserole dish, arranging them in a single layer.

Bake until the scallops are nicely browned, about 20 minutes. Serve hot accompanied by lemon wedges.

**Variation:** Instead of baking the scallops, cut them in half crosswise before tossing them in the oil mixture and then shake them in the bread crumbs and coat well. Pour ⅓ cup canola oil into a large sauté pan and place over medium-high heat. Add the scallops and fry until golden brown on each side.

# Roasted Sea Bass with Fennel, Oranges, and Olives

## Orata con Finocchio, Arance, e Olivi

*Sea bass is called* orata *in Italian (from* oro, *meaning gold) because of a golden band behind the fish's eyes. It is a delicate fish usually served grilled, but is also delicious slow-cooked in the oven with wine, fennel, olives, and oranges. This recipe and the one on page 238 are variations on technique, cooking the fish stovetop or oven-roasting it. Try them both.* **Serves 6**

Preheat the oven to 325°F.

Heat the olive oil over medium heat in a 12- to 14-inch, oven-to-table sauté pan or casserole dish. Stir in the fennel and cook just until it begins to soften and turn translucent. Add the garlic and cook a couple of minutes. Stir in the wine and cook for 1 minute over high heat. Reduce the heat to a simmer and pour in the orange juice. Stir in the lemon zest. Cook 2 minutes. Season with salt and pepper to taste and set aside.

Gently rub salt and pepper all over the fillets and lay them on top of the fennel. Cover the fish with the orange slices and sprinkle with the olives.

Roast, uncovered, for 25 to 30 minutes, spooning some of the liquid over the fish as it cooks. The fish is done when it flakes easily with a fork.

Serve the fish as is with some of the sauce or, equally as good, serve over a creamy bed of polenta (page 252).

1/4 cup extra-virgin olive oil

2 fennel bulbs, thinly sliced lengthwise into strips

3 garlic cloves, thinly sliced

1/2 cup white wine

1/2 cup fresh blood orange or navel orange juice

Grated zest of 2 lemons

Sea salt

Freshly ground black pepper

Six 8-ounce sea bass fillets

2 blood or navel oranges, peeled and cut into 1/4-inch slices

4 green Cerignola olives, pitted

4 oil-cured black olives, pitted

# Stuffed Baked Fish Bundles

## Involtini di Pesce al Forno

One 16-ounce bag fresh spinach, washed and stemmed

3 tablespoons extra-virgin olive oil

1 medium onion, peeled and minced

2 tablespoons salt-packed capers, well rinsed and minced

4 sun-dried tomatoes packed in olive oil, drained and chopped

Salt and black pepper

8 flounder fillets

*Fresh fish, Italian style, is best enjoyed in Italy because it would be impossible to re-create the flavor here since we have different species of fish. So the best we can do is to use as many authentic ingredients as possible to approximate the Mediterranean flavors. Let's take flounder as an example. This flatfish is thin and bland on its own. It is the kind of fish that cries out for creative preparation. That means stuffing it with a sassy mixture of chopped spinach, capers, onions, sun-dried tomatoes, and olive oil and then rolling it up into a bundle known as* involtino. *Delicious! Flounder works well in this recipe because it is thin enough to roll and holds its shape.*  Serves 4

Place the spinach in a pot, cover, and wilt down over medium heat. Drain in a colander, pressing on the leaves to release their water. Transfer the spinach to a cutting board and chop. Set aside.

Pour 2 tablespoons of the oil in a sauté pan and place over medium heat. Add the onions and cook until they soften and begin to take on some color. Stir in the capers and sun-dried tomatoes. Add the spinach and mix well. Season to taste with salt and pepper.

Preheat the oven to 350°F. Brush a 12 × 9-inch casserole dish with the remaining tablespoon of olive oil.

Divide and spread the filling mixture evenly on top of each of the flounder fillets, then starting at one end, roll each fillet up like a jelly roll and place in the prepared casserole dish.

Bake for 8 to 10 minutes, or just until the fish turns white and flakes easily when poked with a fork.

Serve the involtini hot with the pan juices spooned over the top.

*NOTE: A telltale sign of less than fresh fish fillets is an ammonia smell.*

# Fish Cakes

## Polpette di Pesce

1½ cups soft fresh bread crumbs

¼ cup milk

3 large eggs

Salt

¼ teaspoon coarsely ground black pepper

2 tablespoons minced flat-leaf parsley

1 pound fresh monk-fish, haddock, flounder, or cod fillets, cut into 4-inch pieces

3 cups water

¼ teaspoon coarse salt

1 small carrot, peeled and halved

1 small onion, peeled and quartered

¼ to ⅓ cup un-bleached all-purpose flour

¾ cup dry bread crumbs

2 to 3 cups vegetable oil for frying

Lemon wedges for serving

*My mother was a firm believer in fish, serving it too often for my taste as a child. That was one reason why I dreaded the season of Lent, a time when every Friday meant some sort of fish would be on my plate when all I really wanted was a hamburger and french fries. And as if that were not enough, Mom also made my siblings and I swallow a table-spoon of fish oil every night after supper, Lent or no Lent. Now, when I look back on those days, I can see that Mom was way ahead of her time if you consider all the prod-ding we get these days about how good fish and fish oil are for our health. One of Mom's standby recipes for Lent was fish cakes, formed like meatballs, and then flattened slightly so that they resembled round disks.* **Serves 4**

Combine the fresh bread crumbs, milk, 1 egg, salt, pepper, and parsley in a small bowl. Set aside.

Place the fish in a shallow pan with the water, coarse salt, carrot, and onion. Sim-mer until the fish flakes easily, about 8 to 10 minutes, depending on the type and thickness of the fish.

Carefully lift the fish out of the water with a slotted wide spatula or skimmer and place in a bowl to cool to room temperature. Dice the carrot and add it to the bread crumb mixture. Discard the cooking water and onion. Flake the fish with a fork. Add it to the bread crumb mixture, season with salt and pepper to taste, and combine well.

Have ready a plate with the flour, and one with the dry bread crumbs. In a small bowl, beat the remaining eggs lightly with a fork.

With wet hands, divide the fish mixture evenly into 8 balls. Roll each ball in the flour and shake off the excess. Dip the ball in the beaten egg, then roll in the bread crumbs, and coat evenly. Place the ball on a plate and press down slightly with your hand to flatten into a fish cake. Repeat with the remaining balls.

In a deep pot or deep fryer, heat the vegetable oil to 375°F. Fry the fish cakes in the oil until golden brown, about 4 to 5 minutes. Drain on brown paper or paper towels and serve hot, accompanied by lemon wedges.

# Stew with Fish Croquettes

## Aghoitta a la Novello

*If I could write down all the televised experiences that I have had with professional and amateur cooks, I could fill a large book. I recall very well an episode filmed in Glouces-ter, Massachusetts, a town with a serious fishing-industry history that has been the mainstay of the economy for generations, and is now in jeopardy of disappearing as commercial fisheries die out. There is no question that fishermen live a dangerous life and their families live in peril whenever they put out to sea. This was made very clear when I met and cooked with Angela Sanfilippo, president of the Fishermen's Wives of Gloucester. Like many in her community, her heritage was Sicilian. Angela held regu-lar neighborhood prayers at a shrine in her house for the safe journey of the fishermen of Gloucester. In her neat kitchen we talked about fishing in general, and made a deli-cious fish stew called* Aghoitta a la Novello *given to her by her friend Lena Novello. Below is Lena's recipe with a few tweaks. I used fresh or frozen peas instead of canned, and wine and clam juice as well as water. This is a very tasty and visually beautiful stew.* **Serves 8**

1 pound sole, skate, haddock, flounder, or other white fish fillet cut into chunks

1 cup plain dry bread crumbs

¼ cup grated pecorino Romano cheese

2 garlic cloves, finely minced

1 tablespoon minced flat-leaf parsley

3 large eggs, well beaten

1 teaspoon salt

½ teaspoon freshly ground black pepper, plus more to taste

6 tablespoons extra-virgin olive oil

½ cup chopped onion

3 large red potatoes, peeled and cut into 1-inch cubes

2 cans stewed toma-toes

1 cup dry white wine

1½ cups clam juice

1 cup peas

Place the fish in a food processor and pulse two or three times just until the fish is coarsely chopped. Do not make a smooth paste out of it. Transfer the fish to a me-dium bowl and gently mix in the bread crumbs, cheese, garlic, parsley, eggs, salt, and pepper. Mix well and shape into 1-inch oval croquettes or balls with wet hands. Set aside.

Heat 3 tablespoons of the oil in a 12- to 14-inch nonstick skillet and fry the cro-quettes until they are brown. Transfer them to a dish.

Heat the remaining 3 tablespoons olive oil in a Dutch oven or heavy-bottomed pot. Add the onion and cook until soft; then add the potatoes. Cook, covered, over medium heat for 5 minutes. Add the tomatoes, wine, and clam juice. Cover and cook until the potatoes are tender, about 8 minutes. Add the croquettes and enough water just to cover everything. Cook for 5 minutes over medium-low heat. Add the peas during the last 2 minutes of cooking. Season with salt and pepper to taste. Ladle the stew into bowls and serve with hot crusty bread and a green salad.

# Large Shrimp, Amalfi Style

## Gamberoni all'Amalfitana

20 large shrimp

2 tablespoons extra-virgin olive oil

1 large garlic clove, minced

2 anchovies packed in olive oil, chopped

1 teaspoon hot red pepper flakes

5 large fresh plum tomatoes, seeded and diced

1½ cups dry white wine

¼ cup minced flat-leaf parsley

Salt

*One of the most beloved vacation destinations within Italy is the Amalfi coast. Breathtakingly beautiful with jagged cliffs, the bluest water, the most stupendous lemon trees, and a coastline whose roads are a challenge for even an Indy 500 driver. I come for the fish: tender baby squid, sweet clams, grilled San Pietro, and of course the gamberoni—large shrimp. When I am home I prepare them Amalfitana style and when I do, I am transported back to that heavenly paradise that only divine intervention could have invented.* *Serves 4*

Remove the heads, outer shell, and intestinal tract of the shrimp. (Use a small knife and make a slit along the curved side of each shrimp and use the tip of the knife to scrape out the intestine.) Rinse the shrimp well and set aside.

In a 12- to 14-inch sauté pan, warm the oil over medium heat. Stir in the garlic, anchovies, and red pepper flakes and cook, stirring with a wooden spoon, until the anchovies dissolve in the oil.

Add the shrimp, tomatoes, and wine and cook, covered, over low heat for 15 minutes, or just until the shrimp are opaque and cooked through. Do not overcook the shrimp or they will be tough.

Stir in the parsley. Season to taste with salt.

Serve in bowls and accompany with slices of good bread to mop up the juices.

# Christmas Eve Clams

## Vongole Oreganate per La Vigilia

2 dozen Littleneck clams

2 garlic cloves, finely minced

Fine sea salt

Freshly ground black pepper

3 tablespoons extra-virgin olive oil

¼ cup fresh lemon juice

½ cup diced cherry tomatoes

1 tablespoon dried oregano

*On Christmas Eve, known as the* vigilia, *or vigil, a huge platter of* vongole oreganate *made its ceremonial way along the dining room table. Littleneck clams with dried oregano were not my favorite but I ate them in deference to tradition and the steely stare of Nonna Galasso. Now I make them, and when I do, I say a silent prayer to Nonna. Serves 4*

Preheat the broiler.

Discard any clams that are open or have cracked or broken shells.

Place the clams in a bowl of warm water. When the shells begin to open carefully slide a small knife into the clam to open and separate it. Carefully rotate your knife tip around the inside of the clam to release it entirely from the shell. Place the shell halves on a baking sheet.

In a bowl, combine the garlic, salt, pepper, oil, lemon juice, and tomatoes. Place about ½ teaspoon of the mixture on top of each clam. Place the clams on a broiler pan.

Broil on the lowest rack of the oven for about 4 minutes, or just until the clam juices begin to bubble. Remove from the oven, sprinkle on the oregano, and serve with lots of crusty bread to mop up the juices.

# Halibut in Lemon Sauce

## Ippoglosso al Limone

*Halibut is a beautiful firm fish that is good grilled or pan-fried. I love to serve it with a classic lemon sauce.* **Serves 4**

Combine the lemon zest, lemon juice, and salt in a rectangular dish large enough to hold the fillets in one layer. Add the fish and turn once in the marinade. Cover and refrigerate for at least 2 hours.

Add the olive oil to a 12- to 14-inch nonstick sauté pan and place over medium-high heat. Drain the halibut, reserving the marinade, and add to the pan. Cook the steaks in a single layer (or in batches if need be) for about 4 minutes on each side. The steaks should turn opaque and be easily pierced with a fork.

Transfer the halibut to a platter, cover, and keep warm.

Add the wine to the pan juices and cook over medium-high heat, scraping up any bits in the bottom of the pan with a wooden spoon. When the wine has reduced by half, add the reserved marinade and bring to a boil. Stir in the butter and swirl it around in the pan. Taste for seasoning. Season with additional salt and pepper if needed. Stir in the parsley and serve the sauce spooned over the fish.

**CHEF'S SECRET:** *You can vary this sauce by adding capers and shallots or chopped tomatoes.*

---

**2 tablespoons grated lemon zest**

**Juice of 4 lemons**

**1 teaspoon fine sea salt**

**Four 8-ounce halibut steaks**

**½ cup dry white wine**

**Extra-virgin olive oil**

**4 tablespoons (½ stick) unsalted butter, cut into chunks**

**Freshly ground black pepper**

**2 tablespoons minced flat-leaf parsley**

# Pan-Cooked Shrimp in Garlic and Wine

## Gamberoni in Padella

4 tablespoons extra-
virgin olive oil

4 pounds shelled and
deveined large
shrimp

3 garlic cloves,
minced

1 cup dry white wine

⅓ cup minced
flat-leaf parsley

1 teaspoon fine sea
salt

Juice of 1 large lemon

*Scampi are prawns, not shrimp, that have claws and look like small lobsters. Often the words are used interchangeably but they have different gill structures and unless you are a fisherman, you wouldn't know it. I order them in Italy whenever I can because they are unlike anything we get here, with a very sweet taste. Minimal cooking keeps their flavor fresh. They are usually cooked very quickly in a sauté pan. To approximate the Italian dish, use this recipe and substitute large, 4-count shrimp, meaning there are four to a pound.* Serve 4

divide the olive oil between 2 sauté pans. Heat the oil over medium heat and add half the shrimp to each pan along with the garlic. Sauté very quickly over high heat until the shrimp turn pink, then add ½ cup of the wine to each pan and lower the heat to medium. Cook for 2 minutes, or just until the shrimp are cooked through. Divide and stir in the parsley. Season the shrimp in each pan with salt.

Transfer the shrimp to a serving dish and sprinkle with lemon juice. Serve hot.

# Salmon, Peas, and Pasta

## Salmone, Piselli, e Pasta

*This dish has it all. The delicate combination of salmon poached in fish broth and served with a medley of peas, leeks, peppers, and pasta is refreshing with a subtle flavor of orange zest. Poaching is a cooking method in which barely simmering liquid is used to cook and keep ingredients moist. To save time, poach the salmon up to 2 days in advance.* **Serves 4 to 6**

3 cups fresh (page 70) or canned low-sodium fish broth

1 pound salmon fillets, any remaining pinbones removed

3 tablespoons extra-virgin olive oil

½ pound leeks, white and light green part only, washed and ends trimmed

1 medium ripe, red bell pepper, seeded and diced

2 cups peas

1 teaspoon fine sea salt

1½ tablespoons grated orange zest

1 pound linguine or spaghetti

**P**our the fish broth into a sauté pan just large enough to hold the salmon in a single layer, or use a salmon poacher. Bring the broth to a simmer. Poach the salmon, covered, keeping the broth at a simmer; tiny bubbles should just be visible at the edges of the pan.

The salmon is cooked when it is uniformly light pink in color and flakes easily when pierced with a fork. Do not overcook it; it should remain moist in the center.

Using a slotted spatula, transfer the fillets to a dish and let cool.

Discard all but ½ cup of the broth.

Heat the olive oil over medium heat in a sauté pan large enough to hold the cooked pasta and salmon mixture.

Cook the leeks and peppers, stirring often, until they begin to soften. Add the peas and cook for 1 minute. Remove the pan from the heat and stir in salt to taste. Stir in the orange zest. Set aside.

Remove the skin from the underside of the salmon fillets with a knife. Cut the fillets into bite-size pieces and add them to the leek mixture. Set aside.

In a large pot, bring 4 quarts of water to a rapid boil and add 1 tablespoon of salt.

Cook the linguine until al dente, still firm but cooked through. Drain the linguine in a colander and add it to the leek mixture along with the reserved fish broth.

Reheat the mixture slowly and transfer to a serving dish. Serve immediately.

# Sea Bass with Orange Sauce
## Il Branzino Con La Salsa di Arancia

3 tablespoons golden raisins

2 tablespoons pine nuts

3 tablespoons extra-virgin olive oil

4 sea bass fillets (each weighing about 8 ounces)

½ cup unbleached all-purpose flour

Juice of 2 blood oranges

Fine sea salt

Finely ground black pepper

4 tablespoons heavy cream

1 tablespoon cracked red peppercorns

2 additional oranges peeled and segmented (or substitute navel oranges if blood oranges are not available)

¼ cup minced flat-leaf parsley

*My travels to Italy land me in a variety of restaurants, some featuring basic home cooking while others are* alta cucina *establishments. I am open to trying new things like the sea bass with oranges that left a memorable taste on my palate. Here is my re-creation of the dish.*   *Serves 4*

Soak the raisins in warm water for 10 minutes. Drain and set on a cutting board.

Toast the pine nuts in a small sauté pan until golden brown. Transfer them to the cutting board with the raisins and, with a knife, mince them together. Set aside.

Heat 2 tablespoons of the oil in a sauté pan large enough to hold the fish in a single layer.

Lightly coat the fish fillets in flour and cook them over medium-high heat, turning them once. Pour the orange juice over the fish and continue to cook for 2 minutes. Season the fillets with salt and pepper. Using a slotted spatula, transfer the fish to a platter and keep warm. Add the cream to the pan along with the peppercorns and stir well to form a nice sauce; if the sauce is too thick, thin it down with a little milk. Place the fillets on each of 4 dinner plates and nap each one with some of the sauce.

Sprinkle the raisin and pine nut mixture evenly over the fish. Add a few orange segments to each dish and sprinkle with a little parsley.

# Sole in Galliano Butter Sauce

## Sogliola alla Salsa di Galliano

*I am sure you have seen or tasted Galliano, that sunny yellow liquor in a tall-necked bottle. I remember Mom keeping Galliano hidden away in the dining room china cabinet. It was always served to unexpected guests in shot glasses or used to spike a cup of coffee! There is not too much known about this liquor. It was the invention of brandy producer Arturo Vaccari in 1896. He boasted that it was made with over thirty herbs, spices, and flavorings like anise, licorice, and vanilla. He named his liquor after Maggiore Galliano, the hero of East African wars in the nineteenth century. In this unusual recipe courtesy of the Fishermen's Wives of Gloucester, Massachusetts, Galliano is used to create a tasty sauce for the fish.* **Serves 6**

8 tablespoons (1 stick) unsalted butter

⅔ cup blanched sliced almonds

¼ cup Galliano

¼ cup fresh lemon juice

¼ cup chopped flat-leaf parsley

Salt

2 pounds fillet of sole or flounder

**M**elt 2 tablespoons of the butter in a 12- to 14-inch sauté pan over medium heat. Add the almonds and sauté until fragrant and slightly browned. Add the remaining 6 tablespoons of butter and allow it to melt and begin to brown. Pour in the Galliano, lemon juice, parsley, and salt to taste. Add the fillets. Cover and cook over medium heat for 7 to 10 minutes, or until the fish easily flakes. Spoon the Galliano butter sauce over the fish frequently as it cooks. Serve the fillets napped with some of the sauce.

# Spaghetti with Tuna, Capers, and Lemon

## Spaghetti Al Tonno, Capperi, e Limone

1 medium onion, peeled and quartered

2 garlic cloves, peeled

3 tablespoons capers packed in brine or salt, well rinsed

1 teaspoon hot red pepper flakes, or more to taste

Two 6-ounce cans solid tuna packed in olive oil or one 10.5-ounce jar Marinella brand tuna in olive oil

1 cup peas

1½ teaspoons dried oregano

1 teaspoon fine sea salt

Coarsely ground black pepper

¼ cup fresh lemon juice

1 tablespoon salt

1 pound plain or whole wheat spaghetti

2 tablespoons minced flat-leaf parsley

*A good-quality canned tuna in olive oil teamed with peas, onions, capers, and fresh lemon juice is a sauce that explodes with flavor and is a must-have favorite teamed with pasta for a quick supper. Inspiration for this dish came from my stay in the fishing village of Mondello, Sicily, where the life of a fisherman is always on display. Walking along the shore reveals a chorus line of colorful tuna and swordfish boats painted in brilliant red, green, and blue stripes. As they bob up and down to the rhythm of the waves, fishermen sell their catch, singing out in a wild dialectic cadence while they mend their long expanses of intricately woven fishnets. The success of this recipe depends on using the best canned tuna in olive oil. I prefer the Marinella or Wild Planet brands.* **Serves 4 to 6**

Let your food processor do the work of mincing together the onion, garlic, and capers. The mixture should be very fine. No processor? Mince everything together by hand using a chef's knife.

Pour 1 tablespoon of the olive oil from the jar or can of tuna into a large sauté pan. Reserve the rest. Heat the oil, stir in the minced mixture, and cook until the onion softens. Stir in the red pepper flakes and the tuna with all of the oil. Flake the tuna with a fork and continue to cook over medium heat for 2 minutes. Stir in the peas, oregano, salt, black pepper, and lemon juice. Cover, set aside, and keep warm.

In a large pot, bring 4 quarts of water to a rapid boil and add 1 tablespoon of salt. Cook the spaghetti until it is al dente, cooked through but still firm. Reserve 2 tablespoons of the cooking water. Drain the spaghetti and transfer it and the reserved water to the sauté pan. Raise the heat to medium-high, stir everything together, and cook until heated through. Sprinkle on the parsley and serve.

# Tuna with Caponata

## Tonno Con Caponata

*Bluefin tuna, the pride of Sicily, is one of the most popular fish at the outdoor markets of the Capo and Ballaro in Palermo, but most of it is sent to Japan for exquisite sushi. During May and June the ritual of the* mattanza, *literally the capture of these giant fish (they can weigh up to 1,800 pounds) in nets and then the harpooning takes place. The Italian word for tuna (tonno) comes from* tonnara *for fishing nets. Breaded, fried tuna steaks are a traditional Sicilian specialty but in this recipe caponata, Sicilian eggplant salad, accompanies the mighty fish.*   ***Serves 4***

½ cup natural shelled
   pistachio nuts

Olive oil for frying

12 whole basil leaves,
   stemmed

½ cup unbleached
   all-purpose flour

Fine sea salt

4 tuna steaks (each
   about 8 ounces)

1 cup prepared
   caponata
   (page 305)

To prepare the tuna, toast the nuts in a 12-inch nonstick sauté pan until fragrant and slightly browned. Set aside.

Heat ⅓ cup olive oil in the same sauté pan and when hot, add the basil leaves and cook them until they look translucent. Drain on paper towels and set aside.

Place the flour and salt in a bag; shake well. Dredge each tuna steak in the flour. Shake off excess and place the tuna steaks on a plate.

Add the remaining olive oil to the pan and when it is hot add the steaks in a single layer, not crowding them, and cook them no more than 2 minutes on each side. Transfer the steaks to individual dinner plates and top each with ¼ cup of the caponata.

Serve with fresh basil leaves on the side and scatter the nuts on the plates.

# Sweet-and-Sour Tuna

## Tonno all'Agrodolce

½ cup unbleached all-purpose flour

1 teaspoon sea salt

¼ teaspoon freshly ground black pepper

1¼ pounds tuna steak, cut into 1-inch chunks

½ cup extra-virgin olive oil, plus extra if needed

2 large white onions, cut in thin slices

Salt and black pepper

1 tablespoon sugar

½ cup good red wine vinegar

⅓ cup minced mint leaves, plus whole leaves for garnish

Tonno, *tuna, along with* pesce spada, *swordfish, has defined the fishing industry of Sicily, now somewhat diminished from its glory days. Tuna, when it is fresh, needs very little embellishment, but one delicious holdover from the days of Arabic influence in Sicily is* tonno all'agrodolce, *or sweet-and-sour sauce. Different and refreshing, the balance of sweet and savory is just right in this preparation.*   *Serves 4*

Combine the flour, salt, and pepper in a paper bag. Add the tuna chunks and coat in the mixture.

Heat ½ cup of olive oil in a sauté pan. When it is hot, add the tuna and brown the chunks quickly. As they brown, transfer them to a paper towel–lined dish and keep warm.

Add the onions to the pan, and more oil if the pan seems dry. Cook the onions over medium heat until they soften and begin to brown. Sprinkle the sugar over the onions and continue to cook for 2 to 3 minutes. Raise the heat to high, add the vinegar, and stir and cook until the vinegar evaporates. Season the onions with salt and pepper to taste. Mix in the minced mint.

Spread the onion mixture out on a serving platter. Place the tuna chunks on top and garnish with the fresh mint leaves. Serve with extra-virgin olive oil on the side for drizzling.

**Variation:** Mix the cooked onions with one 14.5-can of drained and rinsed cannellini or chickpeas, then top with the tuna.

# Scallops in Vinaigrette

## Cappesante in Vinaigrette

Cappesante *(holy cape)* means sea scallops in Italian but are also called ventaglio *(fan)* or canestrelli *(little scallop)*. It just depends on where you are in Italy. Once, while watching a scallop boat come in, I asked a fisherman how to he liked to prepare them. He plucked a plump and pinkish-looking scallop from its shell and popped it right into his mouth! If it's fresh, I guess there is not much you have to do to enhance its flavor. Buy dry scallops, meaning those that have not been injected with water. This recipe is a great starter for a fish-themed dinner, but is equally good as a light summer lunch or even an antipasto. *Serves 4*

4 tablespoons good-quality rice, sherry, or champagne vinegar

4 tablespoons honey

Fine sea salt

¼ teaspoon dry mustard

5 tablespoons extra-virgin olive oil

1 tablespoon fresh thyme leaves

1 pound large sea scallops

1 cup sunflower oil

1 cup shaved fennel, white part only

Whisk the vinegar, honey, salt, and dry mustard together in a medium bowl. Slowly whisk in the olive oil until you achieve a creamy consistency. Stir in the thyme leaves and set aside.

Cut each scallop horizontally into 4 rounds. Add the scallop rounds to the dressing and toss gently. Divide the scallops evenly among 4 salad plates and spoon some of the sauce over each one. Set aside.

Heat the sunflower oil in a small saucepan to 375°F. Add the shaved fennel and fry until golden brown. Drain on paper towels. Divide evenly and top each salad with the fried fennel. Serve immediately.

—

# Meats

Steak Neapolitan Style

Beef Stew Val d'Aosta Style

Beef Stew with Roasted Vegetables

Italian-Style Pot Roast

Chuck Shoulder, Spinach, and Carrot
   Casserole

Sicilian Meatballs

Sicilian Meatballs in Sweet-and-Sour Sauce

Sicilian Meatballs (Variation #2)

Mom's Meat Loaf Perfected

Veal Cutlet, Sorrento Style

Oven-Roasted Pork Tenderloin with
   Pomegranate Sauce

Pork Sausage with Bitter Greens

Homemade Italian Sweet Sausage

Pork Sausage with Potatoes and Zucchini

Chicken Cutlets with Marsala Wine
   and Mushrooms

Chicken Cutlets French Style

Chicken Livers and Onions

Lemon-Flavored Chicken Cutlets with
   Orzo and Spinach

Nonna Saporito's Chicken in Wine

Nonna Galasso's Stewed Chicken

Rabbit in Balsamic Vinegar

Roast Capon

Stuffed and Rolled Turkey Breast

Lamb Stew in Lemon and Egg Sauce

Marinated Lamb Shoulder Chops
   with Fresh Mint Sauce

Luigi's Lamb Chops

# meaty matters
· · · · · · · · · · · · · · · · ·

**W**hether it's the *maccelleria* (butcher shop), the *norcineria* (pork sausage shop), the *salumeria* (cured meat shop), or the *rosticerria* (grilled meat and chicken shop), they all mean attention to quality and that is why meats and poultry taste so good in Italy.

Hardly ever will you see meat and poultry packed in plastic unless you are in a *supermercato* (supermarket). You want a chicken? You get the whole thing, head and feet attached. You want porchetta? The bronze-colored roasted pig will have an apple in its mouth and a wreath of bay leaves on its head.

One of my favorite food markets is San Lorenzo in Florence. It is a cavernous place with floors of food items that will leave you dizzy, not to mention hungry. Besides all the great food, it is watching what the Italians buy that is so fascinating. They are determined shoppers who look for seasonal foods, asking questions of purveyors on everything from the best melon to choose to which piece of *trippa* (tripe) would be best for a *sugo* (sauce).

It is a treat to travel to the markets of Italy and just about every day there is an outdoor market somewhere and I am just a little more than envious of the selection and quality available. One day in Camucia, a large town near Cortona in Tuscany, I spotted a huge line of people waiting near one of those fold up and go trucks on wheels that go from town to town. I smelled something good, too. As I inched closer, I could see a mahogany-colored porchetta (baby pig) resting on a lawn of parsley, looking like a polished piece of antique furniture. It sported a lemon in its mouth, a bay leaf crown on its head, and the vendor was cutting thin slices of meat perfumed with rosemary from its trunk area and layering them in crusty rolls. It was only mid-morning but those porchetta panini were being devoured!

Back in the States, unless you raise your own meat and poultry, you are buying them in plastic-wrapped packages from the supermarket. When I buy meat or poultry, I look for organic, and when the farmers' markets are in full swing, I buy from them. Italians have always understood the need to raise animals in the most natural way. Until the day that we have the same regard and respect for how animals are raised, fed, and slaughtered, what we put on the table will never compare in taste or quality to that of Italy.

The recipes in this chapter do not reflect expensive cuts of meat like filet mignon simply because that is not what we prepared at home. Meats were usually in the form of pot roasts, braised shoulder roasts, ground meats, and stews, which all have great flavor and were economical and easy to prepare.

Today's home cook has a real challenge in trying to get meat and poultry to taste the way it did years ago. I, for one, miss the rich, juicy, and intense flavor of good beef and pork. Why? Because when you remove fat, you remove flavor. It is as simple as that. And when you control the feed of animals with mainly corn, instead of grass, you get a product that is bland.

Instead of quantity, we should strive for quality and become very choosy as consumers in the foods we purchase. Only then, when we raise our voices, will we be able to have the same artisan food products that are found in Italy.

# Steak Neapolitan Style

## Bistecchine alla Napoletana

*Quick, easy, and expensive,* bistecchine alla Napoletana *calls for thin slices of tender boneless beef or veal, and is the perfect company dish when splurging is necessary.*
**Serves 4**

**P**reheat the oven to 350°F.

Heat 2 tablespoons of the oil in an ovenproof sauté pan. Cook the ham and mushrooms until the mushrooms have given off their liquid. Stir in the parsley and add salt and pepper to taste.

Salt and pepper the beef slices and arrange them in a single layer on top of the mushroom mixture.

Drizzle the remaining 2 tablespoons of olive oil over the meat and sprinkle the lemon juice over them.

Bake for 15 minutes, then turn the meat and continue cooking for 5 minutes, basting the meat with the juices in the pan.

Bake for another 15 minutes, then turn the fillets and sprinkle them with the lemon juice. Continue baking for 5 minutes.

Serve with sautéed spinach or broccoli rabe.

4 tablespoons extra-virgin olive oil

½ cup chopped boiled ham or prosciutto di Parma

2½ cups fresh mushrooms, thinly sliced, or 1 ounce dried porcini, rehydrated and chopped

⅓ cup minced flat-leaf parsley

Salt and black pepper

8 slices beef filet (each weighing 2 ounces)

Juice of 1 large lemon

# Beef Stew Val d'Aosta Style
## Carbonade all'Val d'Aosta

**MARINADE**

2 cups dry red wine

1 whole bay leaf

10 whole cloves

¼ teaspoon freshly grated nutmeg

½ teaspoon ground cinnamon

1 teaspoon fine sea salt

Freshly ground black pepper

**STEW**

2 pounds stew beef, cut into 1-inch cubes

¼ cup unbleached all-purpose flour

4 tablespoons (½ stick) unsalted butter

2 medium onions, chopped

4 to 6 cups hot beef broth

**SOFT POLENTA**

2 cups whole milk

1 cup heavy cream

½ cup white or yellow stone-ground cornmeal

*My stays in Italy reveal so many "new" old recipes like* Carbonade. *It is one of the classic stews from the smallest and quite mountainous region of northern Italy, the Val D'Aosta. The original recipe called for salt-cured beef that was very dark, like the color of carbon* (carbone) *and from where this recipe takes its name. This hearty but simple baked beef stew was the mainstay of a mountain diet and is spicy, permeated with the flavor of nutmeg, cloves, and cinnamon, which may seem strange as seasonings for a stew but which impart a delicious flavor to the sauce. Start the day before by marinating the meat overnight. This dish is traditionally served over polenta.*   ***Serves 4 to 6***

To make the marinade, in a bowl, combine the wine with the bay leaf, cloves, nutmeg, cinnamon, salt, and pepper. Place the meat in a rectangular glass dish and pour the wine mixture over the meat. Cover and refrigerate overnight.

When ready to make the stew, drain the meat; dry the pieces on paper towels, and toss them in the flour.

Heat the butter in a Dutch oven or a heavy-bottomed, 2-quart pot. Brown the meat pieces well then transfer them with a slotted spoon to a dish. Add the onions to the pot and cook until they wilt.

Return the meat to the pot and season with salt and pepper. Pour in enough beef broth just to cover the meat, and cook over medium-low heat until the meat is fork-tender.

To make the polenta, in a heavy bottomed, 2-quart saucepan, combine the milk and cream off the heat. Whisk in the cornmeal until it is smooth. Place the saucepan over medium-low heat and cook the mixture, stirring often, until it is smooth and bubbly, 8 to 10 minutes. Remove the pan from the heat and stir in the butter, cheese, parsley, and nutmeg.

When the stew is ready, scoop some of the polenta into each soup bowl and top with some of the stew and its juices.

**TIP:** *Mince fresh parsley, divide and wrap tightly in quantities of 4 tablespoons in a paper towel. Fold the paper towel, like an envelope. Place in small sandwich bags and freeze. That way it is always on hand.*

3 tablespoons unsalted butter

1 cup Italian fontina cheese, cut into bits

¼ cup minced flat-leaf parsley

Freshly grated nutmeg

# Beef Stew with Roasted Vegetables

## Stufatino di Manzo Con Le Verdure Arrostite

*Nonna Saporito knew her cuts of meat because she was a butcher, so when she trimmed large carcasses, she knew to save the toughest pieces for* stufatino *(stew). She just threw the pieces into her large stockpot, added what was on hand, and cooked it in Grandpa's red wine, which she said was more like vinegar. When I make stew I start by browning the meat cubes in pancetta, Italian unsmoked bacon, which gives great flavor. Instead of tossing in cut-up vegetables, I roast them in the oven and then add them to the stew when the meat is tender. This makes a huge difference in flavor because roasting the vegetables allows caramelization to occur, making the vegetables sweeter in taste.* **Serves 6 to 8**

3 tablespoons extra-virgin olive oil, plus extra if necessary

¼ pound pancetta, diced

2 pounds stew beef, cut into 1-inch cubes

⅓ cup unbleached all-purpose flour

Salt and black pepper

1 large onion, diced

3 garlic cloves, minced

2 sprigs fresh rosemary

3 cups dry red wine

6 carrots, peeled and cut into thirds

4 red potatoes, scrubbed and quartered

4 celery stalks, cut into 2-inch chunks

**t**o brown the meat, heat the 1 tablespoon olive oil in a large heavy Dutch oven or similar pot. Add the pancetta, and cook it over medium heat until the pancetta begins to melt and render its fat. Place the meat in a brown paper bag and add the flour, salt, and pepper. Close the bag and shake it to coat the meat in the flour mixture. Add the meat to the pan and brown the pieces well on all sides. As the pieces brown, transfer them to a bowl.

Stir the onion and garlic into the pan; if the pan seems dry, add a little olive oil. Cook until the onion softens. Return the meat to the pan along with the rosemary, raise the heat to high, and pour in just enough wine to cover the meat. Reduce the heat to a simmer, cover the pan, and cook until the meat is fork-tender, 45 minutes to 1 hour.

Meanwhile, toss the vegetables with the 2 tablespoons olive oil and place them on a baking sheet. Bake them at 350°F until tender, about 45 minutes. When the stew meat is cooked, add the vegetables to the stew pot and toss and reheat gently. Serve in bowls.

**NOTE:** *Save leftover wine to use for making stews and sauces.*

# Italian-Style Pot Roast

## Braciato

*Cold days call for hearty food; that's when I drag out my slow cooker to make Italian-inspired pot roast like Mom used to make. No slow cooker? Cook the roast in a Dutch oven or heavy-bottomed pot in a 300°F oven for several hours until fork-tender.*
**Serves 6**

**M**ix the salt, pepper, and oregano together and rub all over the roast. Set aside.

Heat the oil in a large skillet and brown the roast well on all sides. This is a really important step because it locks in juices and flavor.

Transfer the roast to the slow cooker or heavy-duty oven roaster. In the same skillet used to brown the roast, cook the onion, carrot, and garlic until the mixture is soft, then add them to the slow cooker or Dutch oven.

Combine the wine and tomatoes in a bowl and add to the slow cooker or Dutch oven.

Tie the rosemary, basil, and parsley together with kitchen twine and add to the slow cooker or Dutch oven. Mix the ingredients well. Cover and cook in slow cooker for 4 to 5 hours on high or 6 to 8 hours on low. For the Dutch oven, cover with heavy-duty aluminum foil and cook 3 to 4 hours, or until fork-tender.

When cooked, transfer the meat to a cutting board, cover, and allow to rest for 20 minutes. Cut the meat into slices and return them to the slow cooker or Dutch oven just to reheat. Serve hot with some of the sauce.

The sauce is also good over pasta or rice.

2½ teaspoons salt

1 teaspoon coarsely ground black pepper

2 teaspoons dried oregano

One 2½-pound boneless chuck roast

2 tablespoons extra-virgin olive oil

1 medium onion, coarsely chopped

1 large carrot, coarsely chopped

2 garlic cloves, minced

1 cup dry red wine

One 28-ounce can crushed plum tomatoes

1 sprig rosemary

2 sprigs basil

2 sprigs flat-leaf parsley

# Chuck Shoulder, Spinach, and Carrot Casserole

## La Spalla di Manzo con Spinaci e Carote

⅓ cup extra-virgin olive oil

2 pounds bone-in shoulder chops cut 1 inch thick

Salt and black pepper

1 large onion, finely minced

3 garlic cloves, finely minced

1 teaspoon hot red pepper flakes

4 cups prepared tomato sauce

1 cup cooked carrots or peas

1 pound fresh spinach, washed, stemmed, and drained

6 or 7 basil leaves, torn into pieces

½ pound paccheri, or large-size rigatoni, cooked and kept warm

Grated pecorino cheese for sprinkling

*This tasty and inexpensive casserole evolved from some leftover cooked carrots, a bag of forgotten spinach in the far recesses of the refrigerator, a half a bag of paccheri (a large rigatoni-shaped pasta without lines), leftover tomato sauce, and some chuck shoulder chops that I had just purchased. Since shoulder chops are tough and not suited for dry heat cooking, I got to work and made this braised casserole dish, which surprised and evoked great satisfaction from my husband who deemed it lip-smacking good.* **Serves 4**

Preheat the oven to 325°F.

Heat the olive oil in a large (12 × 2 ½-inch) oven-to-table casserole dish over medium-high heat. Season the shoulder chops with salt and pepper and brown them quickly on both sides. Transfer them to a plate. Stir in the onion and cook it until it begins to soften. Stir in the garlic and red pepper flakes. Cook until the garlic softens. Return the chops to the pan with any juices that have collected on the plate.

Cover the chops with the tomato sauce. Cover the casserole dish with a lid or aluminum foil and place in the oven.

Bake 45 minutes to 1 hour, or until the meat is fork-tender. Remove the pan from the oven. Transfer the chops to a cutting board, and trim the meat away from the bones. Discard the bones and return the meat to the pan.

Add the carrots and spinach on top of the meat. Return the pan, covered, to the oven and cook 2 or 3 minutes longer, or just until the spinach has wilted.

Remove the casserole from the oven. Stir in the basil and the cooked pasta and serve immediately. Pass the cheese.

**TIP:** *Use a Microplane grater to finely mince unpeeled cloves of garlic; this technique works well with fresh ginger as well.*

# The Mighty Meatball

Let me tell you the story of how meatballs (polpette) came to be part of Italian cuisine. And for that we need to place ourselves around 1 A.D. when the Roman gourmand, Apicus, was writing his **De Re Coquina**, or **Things Concerning Cooking**. In his cookbook he describes how to "grind chopped meat with the center of fine white bread that has been soaked in wine. Grind together pepper, garum [which was fish sauce] and pitted myrtle berries. Form small patties, put in pine nuts and pepper." And the meat that Apicus preferred for making these patties? Peacock, followed by pheasant, rabbit, chicken, and pig.

Since that time the meatball has undergone worldwide change and who can say for certain what the true Italian meatball should be when there are many versions to be found in Italy from north to south. For example, in Modena, in the region of Emilia-Romagna, meatballs called polpette are made with cooked, not raw, meat and combined with nutmeg, egg, and sometimes mashed potatoes. In Sicily, meatballs are called purpetti and are made with pine nuts, raisins, and raw meat and often served with a sweet-and-sour tomato sauce.

The meatball is a transcultural food found in some form around the world, and we recognize it here as an Italian American invention because during the nineteenth century, when Italian immigrants arrived, the meat grinder became available and changed the look and taste of the meatball since inexpensive cuts of meat could be ground and mixed with a variety of ingredients. You could ask any Italian nonna how to make meatballs and a plethora of answers would ensue. This remains true today. There just isn't a "recipe" but that is no surprise when we think of the regionality of Italian foods.

And what is this fascination we have with meatballs? We serve them in mini size for a buffet, we cloak them in buns for a meatball sub, we hide them in casseroles, and most important, we cook them in tomato sauce and serve them with spaghetti. Suffice it to say that meatballs, like meatloaf, lasagne, and macaroni and cheese, are close-to-the-chest comfort foods no matter what their origin.

# Sicilian Meatballs

## Purpetti Siciliani

*These Sicilian meatballs (purpetti in dialect) are moist and delicious and usually made with pork or veal or a combination of both. The ingredients are different from the recipe for sweet-and-sour meatballs on page 263 and most approximates what the Italian American versions of meatballs has come to be. Meatballs were originally fried in lard so they were nice and crusty but I prefer olive oil for a healthier choice. For a really authentic look, form the meatballs into disks.* **Makes 8**

½ **pound ground pork**

½ **pound ground veal**

2 **large eggs, lightly beaten**

½ **cup grated caciocavallo cheese**

1 **cup soft bread crumbs**

¼ **cup minced flat-leaf parsley**

1 **teaspoon fine sea salt**

¼ **teaspoon coarsely ground black pepper**

¼ **cup olive oil**

In a medium bowl, mix the pork and veal with the eggs, cheese, bread crumbs, parsley, salt, and pepper. Form flat patties with the mixture about 2 inches in diameter.

Heat the olive oil in a large sauté pan, and when the oil begins to shimmer, add the patties, being careful not to crowd them in the pan. Cook until browned on each side, frying in batches if necessary, and keep the meatball patties warm as you cook them.

Alternatively, bake them in a preheated 350°F oven on a lightly oiled baking sheet until an instant-read thermometer registers 160°F.

Serve the meatballs hot as a second course.

# Sicilian Meatballs in Sweet-and-Sour Sauce

## Purpetti agruduci

At one time all beef was imported into Sicily from the mainland because the island was too arid to support pasturing of cows. There are as many variations of the meatball theme as there are towns in Sicily and I provide two below. These meatballs were originally fried in lard so they were nice and crusty but olive oil is a healthier choice. Caciocavallo (literally translated, means "cheese on horseback") is used to flavor the meatballs and is said to date back to the fourteenth century, and believed to have originally been made from mare's milk. Today's caciocavallo comes from cow's milk and has a mild, slightly salty flavor and firm, smooth texture when young (about 2 months). As it ages, the flavor becomes more pungent and the texture more granular, making it ideal for grating. Caciocavallo is one of the pasta filata *types of cheeses (like provolone and mozzarella), which means it has been stretched and shaped by hand. It may be purchased plain or smoked and comes in string-tied gourd or spindle shapes.*
***Makes 8***

**MEATBALLS**

1 pound ground veal

2 large eggs

1 cup caciocavallo cheese, grated

2⁄3 cup dry bread crumbs

1⁄4 cup minced flat-leaf parsley

Salt and black pepper

Oil for frying

**SAUCE**

2 cups prepared tomato sauce

1⁄4 cup white vinegar

2 tablespoons sugar

**t**o make the meatballs, mix the veal with the eggs, cheese, bread crumbs, parsley, salt, and pepper. Form flat patties with the mixture about 2 inches in diameter. Fry the patties in oil or bake them on a lightly oiled baking sheet.

To make the sauce, in a sauté pan combine the tomato sauce, vinegar, and sugar. Cook over medium heat for 3 or 4 minutes. Transfer the meatball patties to the tomato sauce and cook 5 minute longer just to heat through.

# Sicilian Meatballs (Variation #2)

⅔ cup fresh bread crumbs

3 tablespoons whole milk

⅓ cup freshly grated pecorino cheese with peppercorns

¼ cup finely chopped onion

3 tablespoons minced flat-leaf parsley

1 large egg

1 garlic clove, minced

Salt

¼ teaspoon freshly ground black pepper

½ pound ground pork sausage

½ pound ground veal

2 tablespoons pine nuts, toasted

2 tablespoons currants

**P**reheat oven to 350°F. Lightly oil baking sheet.

Mix the bread crumbs and milk in medium bowl; let stand 5 minutes. Mix in cheese, onion, parsley, egg, garlic, salt, and pepper. Add the sausage, veal, pine nuts, and currants and blend well. Using wet hands, form the mixture into 1¼-inch balls. Place on an oiled baking sheet. Bake until the meatballs are light brown and cooked through, about 30 minutes. Serve as a second course. *Makes 8*

# Mom's Meat Loaf Perfected

## Polpettone alla Mamma

*Is there such a thing as Italian meat loaf? Yes, but not cloaked in ketchup, oozing ched-dar cheese, and accompanied by mashed potatoes. Italian meat loaf,* polpettone *means meat roll or meatball, recipes vary by region. In Emilia-Romagna ground beef, pan-cetta, cinnamon, and nutmeg are typical ingredients. In Tuscany, ground veal, carrots, and onions are frequent ingredients, and in Rome, lamb, eggs, white wine, and celery are popular. My mother insisted that beef, veal, and pork gave the best flavor, and I have taken a little liberty with her recipe and started my own meat loaf tradition.* **Serves 8**

**P**reheat the oven to 350°F.

In a bowl, combine the beef, pork, potatoes, eggs, garlic, salt, parsley, Parmigiano-Reggiano cheese, and carrots. Do not overmix or the texture will be tough.

Transfer the mixture to a large sheet of parchment paper and flatten the meat into a 14 × 10-inch rectangle with wet hands, or lay a sheet of wax paper over the meat and flatten with a rolling pin. Transfer the meat to a rimmed baking sheet or roasting pan.

Lay the prosciutto slices over the surface of the meat and sprinkle the Asiago cheese evenly over the top.

Starting at the shortest side, roll the meat up like a jelly roll using the parchment paper as a guide, and shape it into a loaf. Be sure no cheese or ham is exposed at the ends.

Pat the bread crumbs evenly on top of the loaf and drizzle with the olive oil.

Bake for 35 minutes.

Combine the wine and broth and slowly pour it into the pan along the sides. Return the meat to the oven and continue cooking until the internal temperature reaches 155°F to 160°F.

Using a large metal spatula, transfer the meat to a serving platter. Cut the meat loaf crosswise into thick slices and serve with some of the pan juices.

1 pound ground beef

1 pound ground pork

2 medium baking potatoes, peeled, cooked, and riced

2 large eggs, lightly beaten

2 garlic cloves, minced

1 teaspoon salt

¼ cup minced flat-leaf parsley

1 cup grated Parmigiano-Reggiano cheese

1 cup grated carrots

8 thin slices pro-sciutto di Parma or boiled ham

1 cup grated Asiago cheese

Bread crumbs

2 tablespoons extra-virgin olive oil

1 cup dry white wine

½ cup chicken broth

# Veal Cutlet, Sorrento Style

## Scaloppe di Vitello alla Sorrentina

¾ cup unbleached
all-purpose flour

2 teaspoons salt

¼ teaspoon freshly
ground black
pepper

2 pounds veal cutlet,
thinly sliced and
cut into 5- or
6-inch-long pieces

4 to 6 tablespoons
(½ to ¾ stick)
unsalted butter,
plus extra for
greasing casserole

2 tablespoons extra-
virgin olive oil

8 fresh, ripe plum
tomatoes, peeled
and diced

1 cup dry white wine

1 tablespoon dried
oregano

2 tablespoons minced
flat-leaf parsley

⅓ pound salame,
finely chopped

One 4-ounce ball
fresh mozzarella,
cut into bits

½ cup grated
Parmigiano-
Reggiano cheese

*Scallope are thin slices of boneless meat, usually veal, that have many regional varia-tions and I love this version from Sorrento that gets added flavor from salame. Use a good imported one if you can find it. Since veal is expensive, I sometimes substitute pork or chicken cutlet. This is a company dish that goes together quickly.*   **Serves 6**

Preheat the oven to 375°F.

Put the flour, salt, and pepper in a bag and shake to combine. Add the veal, a few pieces at a time, and shake to evenly coat them with the seasoned flour. Place them on a plate.

Melt 4 tablespoons of the butter in a large sauté pan and add the olive oil. Raise the heat to medium-high and brown the slices quickly in batches on each side; this should take no more than a minute for each slice. Use additional butter, if neces-sary. As they brown transfer them to a dish. Do not overcrowd the pan or the slices will steam instead of brown.

To the same pan, add the tomatoes, wine, oregano, and parsley. Cook the mix-ture quickly for about 4 minutes over medium-high heat. Season with salt to taste. Set aside.

Lightly grease a large casserole dish with butter. Lay the veal slices in the dish. Scatter the salame on top of the veal. Top the salame with the mozzarella cheese. Cover the mozzarella cheese with the sauce and sprinkle the grated cheese over the sauce.

Bake no longer than 5 minutes, or just until the cheese melts. Serve immediately.

**NOTE:** *Whenever you see a recipe that has the words "alla Sorrentina," it most likely means that tomatoes and fresh buffalo mozzarella cheese are part of the dish.*

# Oven-Roasted Pork Tenderloin with Pomegranate Sauce

## Maiale al Forno con La Salsa di Melagrana

*Pomegranates (melagrane) are dearly beloved in Italy where they grow beautifully suspended from stems on low-growing bushes. They are best eaten out of hand but I like to experiment with them in cooking and use them for sauces and desserts. This oven-roasted pork tenderloin gets its superb flavor from a quick sauce made from a combination of pomegranate juice and orange marmalade.* **Serves 4**

3 to 4 pomegranates to yield ¾ cup pomegranate juice

½ cup pomegranate seeds

1 teaspoon kosher salt

½ teaspoon whole peppercorns or ¼ teaspoon ground black pepper

1 tablespoon fresh rosemary leaves

1 garlic clove, peeled

One 1¼-pound pork tenderloin

1 tablespoon extra-virgin olive oil

½ cup orange marmalade or apricot jam

**U**sing a sharp knife cut off the crown of one pomegranate about ½ inch from the top. Slice the sections through the white membrane. (Do this part in a bowl of water to avoid staining your clothes or cooking surface.) Use your fingers to separate the seeds in the water. The white honeycomb-looking membrane will float to the top as the seeds, or arils, will sink to the bottom of the bowl.

Strain the seeds removing any remaining membrane pieces and set side.

Cut the remaining pomegranates in half and juice them; you will need ¾ cup for the recipe. Strain the juice and set aside.

Preheat the oven to 350°F.

Grind the salt, peppercorns, rosemary, and garlic together or mince them finely with a chef's knife. Spread the mixture out on a large sheet of wax paper.

Dry the pork well with paper towels. Lay the pork over the salt mixture and use the paper to roll the meat in the seasonings; be sure it is evenly coated.

Heat the olive oil in an ovenproof sauté pan to just below the smoking point. Add the pork and sear it quickly on all sides. Transfer the pan to the oven and cook until a meat thermometer inserted into the thickest part of the meat registers between 155°F and 165°F, depending on how you like it cooked. This should take only 7 to 10 minutes.

Transfer the meat to a cutting board and cover loosely with aluminum foil while you prepare the sauce.

Heat the jam with the pomegranate juice until a smooth sauce is obtained, and

cook the mixture over low heat for about 4 minutes. Stir in the pomegranate seeds, cover, and keep the sauce warm.

Cut the pork on the diagonal into medallions about 1 inch thick. Place on a serving platter. Spoon some of the sauce over top and serve. Pass additional sauce on the side.

*Pomegranates are* the new darling of the antioxidant world. Ruby red with a thick leathery skin, the pomegranate grows on low bushes in California and Arizona. The season for them is September through January. In studies by the University of Oklahoma it was found that pomegranates decreased the oxidative damage associated with cancer, diabetes, and heart disease. One to two glasses a day of pomegranate juice can lower blood pressure and the risk of clogged arteries. That should give cause for including them in your diet! Besides being a healthful drink, the juice can also be used to make jellies and sauces, and the seeds are great sprinkled on salads and as a garnish for poultry or pork.

# Pork Sausage with Bitter Greens

## Salsicce con Friarielli

2 pounds good pork
sausage links, in
their casing

2 tablespoons extra-
virgin olive oil

2 garlic cloves, peeled
and cut in half
lengthwise

1 small dried peper-
oncino, seeded
and diced

1 pound turnip tops
or broccoli rabe,
washed and
coarsely chopped

*One of the classic southern Italian dishes is pork sausage served with bitter greens, and in Naples, this means* friarielli, *which are unavailable here but if I had to describe their flavor I would say that they taste similar to broccoli rabe or turnip tops.* **Serves 4**

Place the sausage in a sauté pan and add ½ cup of water. Cover the pan and cook over medium-high heat just until the sausage turns gray. Drain off the water and continue to cook the sausage in its own fat until it is nicely browned. If the pan seems dry, add a little olive oil.

Transfer the sausage to a cutting board and slice into 2-inch pieces and cover with a sheet of aluminum foil. Add the garlic and chili pepper to the pan and cook until the garlic has softened and is beginning to brown. Discard the garlic and add the turnip tops or broccoli rabe.

Place a lid, slightly ajar, over the pan and cook until the greens wilt. Push the greens aside and return the sausage to the pan. Heat through and serve hot.

# Homemade Italian Sweet Sausage

## Salsiccia Casalinga

1 package hog casings, packed in salt

8 pounds ground pork butt

3 tablespoons coarse sea salt

2 or more tablespoons hot red pepper flakes

2 tablespoons coarsely ground black pepper

3 tablespoons fennel seeds

1 tablespoon fennel pollen

*Every summer, my mother and father turned tubs and tubs of ground pork butt into delicious homemade Italian sausage. They would not think of buying sausage in the supermarket. Dad even made his own sausage funnels; no machine was ever used. Nonna Galasso's job was to rinse out the hog casings. These slippery, super long, white casings came packed in salt; they needed to be well rinsed before the meat could be stuffed into them. Mom added the seasonings, hot red pepper flakes, salt, pepper, and fennel seeds. Dad mixed it all in with his hands. Mom fried a bit of it to make sure the seasonings were just right. Dad slipped the casings over the funnel nozzle, tied a knot in the end and started to fill them with the pork. Faster than lightning, coils of sausage appeared, Nonna Galasso poking them here and there with a toothpick to let out any air. Most of it was packed away in the freezer for winter use, but the rest went right to the grill. Mom and Dad were right. It was the best sausage ever and you will think so, too. Your butcher will grind pork butt for you, and casings are available in grocery stores or from sausage-making companies on the Internet.* **Makes 8 pounds**

**m**ake sure to have everything ready before plunging your hands into the meat mixture. Rinse and cut the casings to the desired lengths; I usually cut them into 18-inch-long pieces. Using a hand sausage funnel, slip the casing all the way up the neck of the funnel but leave about 2 inches at the bottom and tie a knot. Set aside.

In a large pot or basin, combine the ground pork butt, sea salt, red pepper flakes, ground pepper, fennel seeds, and fennel pollen. Mix to combine well. Take a small piece of the mixture and fry it to test for seasoning; adjust to your taste.

Starting with small handfuls, fill the mouth of the funnel with the mixture and push with your thumb into the casing. Leave about 2 inches at the top. Slip the casing off the funnel and tie a knot. Poke the sausage with a toothpick here and there to let out any air. Continue making sausage until all the meat is used up.

Coil the sausage and place into plastic bags. Label and freeze.

To cook, place the desired amount of sausage in a sauté pan with a little olive oil and fry gently until nicely browned. Or place on the grill. Either way, it is terrific!

# Pork Sausage with Potatoes and Zucchini

## Salssicia con Patate e Zucchine

*This success of this casserole depends on the quality of the pork sausage; I usually make my own, but when you are in a hurry, good-quality store-bought sweet or spicy sausage will do. Everything goes into a heavy heatproof stovetop-to-oven casserole and cooks, covered, at a low temperature for 40 to 45 minutes, creating a delicious sauce. Vary the vegetables using carrot chunks or brussels sprouts.* **Serves 3 to 4**

1 pound good-quality Italian sweet or spicy sausage

1 medium onion, thinly sliced

1 large red potato, cut into ¼-inch-thick slices

2 medium zucchini, trimmed and cut into ½-inch chunks

Salt and black pepper

**P**reheat the oven to 325°F.

Put the sausage an ovenproof casserole at least 12 inches in diameter. Pour in ½ cup of water and place over medium-high heat. Cover the casserole and cook the sausage for 2 minutes on each side, or until it just turns gray. Discard any water. Move the sausage to the center of the casserole, scatter the onions around the sausage, layer the potatoes over the onions, and then the zucchini over the potatoes. Sprinkle everything with salt and pepper to taste.

Bake, covered, 40 to 45 minutes, or until the sausage is cooked and the vegetables are tender. Serve with some of the pan juices.

# Chicken Cutlets with Marsala Wine and Mushrooms

## Scaloppine alla Marsala e Funghi

Scaloppine alla Marsala *is a popular company dish in my home and is a cinch to make if you have all the ingredients on hand. I always buy boneless chicken breasts and keep them in the freezer because there are so many ways to use them from stir-frying to stuffing them. When I make this dish, I cut the breasts horizontally in half while partially frozen because it is easier to make thin slices.*   **Serves 4**

6 tablespoons extra-virgin olive oil

½ pound sliced button mushrooms

1 teaspoon salt

Freshly ground black pepper

3 boneless chicken breasts (about 1½ pounds) sliced ⅛ inch thick

½ cup unbleached all-purpose flour

4 tablespoons (½ stick) unsalted butter

⅔ cup dry Marsala wine

Juice of 2 lemons

¼ cup minced flat-leaf parsley

**h**eat 4 tablespoons of the oil in a 12- to 14-inch sauté pan. Add the mushrooms and sauté until they give off their liquid and the pan is dry. Season them to taste with salt and pepper and transfer to a bowl.

On a plastic cutting board remove any visible fat from the chicken breasts and place them between two sheets of wax paper. Using a meat pounder, thin them to an even thickness of ⅛ inch, or ask your butcher to do this for you.

Place the flour in a large paper bag; season with salt and pepper to taste.

Dredge each cutlet in the flour mixture, coating them well and shaking off the excess flour. Place them on a baking sheet.

Heat the remaining 2 tablespoons olive oil and the butter in the same sauté pan used to cook the mushrooms. Over medium-high heat, brown the cutlets in batches on both sides. Transfer them as they brown to a dish.

If the pan is dry add a little more butter. Raise the heat to high and pour in the wine. Stir, scraping up any bits in the pan, and reduce the wine to half its volume. Stir in the lemon juice. Return the chicken and any collected juices to the pan along with the mushrooms.

Reheat until hot, add the parsley, and serve immediately.

# Chicken Cutlets French Style

## Pollo Francese

1 pound chicken
cutlets

1 cup unbleached
all-purpose flour

Salt and black pepper

3 large eggs

¼ cup minced
flat-leaf parsley

½ cup sunflower oil

½ cup fresh lemon
juice

¼ cup extra-virgin
olive oil

4 tablespoons (½
stick) unsalted
butter

1 garlic clove, minced

½ pound
mushrooms,
brushed clean,
stems discarded,
and caps thinly
sliced

¼ cup dry white wine

¼ cup chicken stock

6 lemon slices

*For years I have tried to find the origins of various recipes for chicken cutlets and have concluded that it is a global dish. Every time I see* Pollo Francese *offered on an Italian American menu, I am reminded of this. Here is my take on this very popular dish.* **Serves 4**

If the cutlets are thick, place them between two sheets of wax paper and flatten them with a meat pounder until they are about ¼ inch thick. Place the flour in a clean paper bag and season with the salt and pepper. Slightly beat the eggs and 1 tablespoon parsley together in a shallow bowl.

Add the cutlets to the bag and shake to coat them evenly on both sides with the flour. Shake off the excess flour. Set the cutlets aside. Coat the cutlets on both sides in the egg mixture and then a second time in the flour. Heat the sunflower oil in a 12- to 14-inch sauté pan and fry the cutlets for 2 to 3 minutes per side. Sprinkle with lemon juice and continue cooking them for 1 to 2 minutes, or until golden brown. Transfer the cutlets to a serving platter and keep warm.

Drain any excess oil from the pan and return it to the stovetop. Add the olive oil and butter and, over medium heat, stir any browned bits in the pan until sizzling. Add the mushrooms, 2 tablespoons of parsley, and garlic and cook until the mushrooms soften and give off most of their liquid.

Raise the heat to high and add the wine, allowing it to evaporate. Pour in the stock, reduce the heat to medium, and let the mixture reduce until it starts to thicken. Add the lemon juice and cutlets to the sauce, two at a time, and cook for 20 to 30 seconds per side just to coat with the sauce and to reheat them. Transfer them to a serving dish. Pour the sauce over the chicken, garnish with lemon slices and remaining parsley, and serve immediately.

# Chicken Livers and Onions

## Fegatini con Cipolle

*Our refrigerator had geographic boundaries—some shelves dedicated to Italian foods, and others to "American" food. Chicken livers were always on those shelves, too, the standard fare for Saturday night supper. As a child I was commanded to eat them, and I choked down every mouthful. Mom would say that liver and onions provided a good source of iron and today, some say that they are a delicacy. I can honestly say that I don't go out of my way to have them even today, but they are a tried-and-true standby in Italian cooking. Here is the recipe that has survived from my mom's kitchen.* **Serves 4**

4 tablespoons extra-virgin olive oil

3 tablespoons unsalted butter

2 yellow onions, thinly sliced

1½ pounds chicken livers, washed and patted dry

2 tablespoons chopped flat-leaf parsley

⅓ cup red wine

Salt and black pepper

**h**eat the olive oil and butter in a 12- to 14-inch sauté pan over medium heat. Add the onions and cook slowly until the onions are very soft and glazed. Transfer the onions to a bowl.

Raise the heat to high and add the chicken livers. Cook about 2 minutes, turning them frequently. Return the onions to the pan and sprinkle on the parsley. Add the wine and stir well. Cover the pan, lower the heat to medium, and cook about 4 minutes longer.

Transfer the chicken livers and onions to a serving dish and season to taste with salt and pepper.

# Lemon-Flavored Chicken Cutlets with Orzo and Spinach

## Scalloppine Piccate con Orzo e Spinaci

**1½ cups orzo (tiny soup pasta)**

**¾ cup extra-virgin olive oil**

**½ cup fresh lemon juice (about 3 large lemons)**

**One 10-ounce package frozen chopped spinach, thawed and squeezed dry**

**1 cup grated Parmigiano-Reggiano cheese**

**½ teaspoon fine sea salt**

**Coarsely ground black pepper**

**1 pound chicken cutlets**

**¼ cup unbleached all-purpose flour**

**2 tablespoons un-salted butter**

**1 small onion, peeled and minced**

**2 tablespoons salt-packed capers, well rinsed and minced**

*An Italian American concoction to be sure, and a favorite found on many Italian American restaurant menus, chicken piccata is a zesty-tasting lemon-flavored dish that is often made with scalloppine, very thin slices of tender veal cutlet, which is expensive. So if you want to make this dish without breaking the bank, use chicken or pork cutlets. Add interest to this all-in-one main dish and serve the dish with orzo and spinach.* **Serves 4**

**b**ring 4 cups of boiling water to a rapid boil and add 1 teaspoon of salt. Add the orzo and cook until it is no longer hard but cooked through, about 12 minutes. Drain the orzo and place in a medium bowl. Stir in ¼ cup of the olive oil and ¼ cup of the lemon juice. Stir in the spinach and ½ cup of the cheese. Season with salt and pepper to taste. Cover and keep warm.

Pound the cutlets between two sheets of wax paper with the flat side of a meat pounder until they are about ⅛ inch thick; take care not to tear the meat while pounding.

Combine the flour, salt, and pepper together on a dish and coat each cutlet in the flour mixture. Set aside on a plate in a single layer.

Heat the remaining ¼ cup olive oil in a large, nonstick sauté pan and brown the cutlets on each side; add more oil to the pan if it seems dry. Transfer the cooked cutlets to a dish as they brown.

Add the butter to the pan, stir in the onions, and cook them about 3 minutes. Stir in the capers and cook 1 minute. Stir in the wine, raise the heat to high, and cook 3 minutes. Stir in the lemon zest and the remaining ¼ cup lemon juice and cook over medium heat just until the sauce begins to thicken.

Return the cutlets to the pan and reheat just until hot.

Make a bed of the orzo mixture on a serving platter. Place the cutlets over the orzo and pour the sauce over the top. Sprinkle with the parsley and remaining ½ cup cheese and serve.

**Variation:** You can substitute orzo with rice. This dish is also delicious with broccoli rabe instead of spinach.

½ cup dry white wine

2 tablespoons grated lemon zest

¼ cup minced flat-leaf parsley

# Nonna Saporito's Chicken in Wine

## Pollo al Vino alla Nonna Saporito

3 pounds cut up chicken pieces (free-range or organic is best)

4 tablespoons extra-virgin olive oil

1 large onion, peeled and finely chopped

2 garlic cloves, thinly sliced

2 teaspoons fine sea salt

½ teaspoon coarsely ground black pepper

1 whole bay leaf

2 sprigs rosemary

2½ cups dry red wine

¼ cup balsamic vinegar

1 tablespoon tomato paste

*I have never been able to really duplicate Nonna Saporito's chicken in wine. It was a dish so succulent with tender pieces of glazed chicken deeply flavored with a rich wine sauce that whenever she served it, I would literally chew on the bones. No amount of my nostalgic recollecting or toying with ingredients has ever come close to that taste from childhood. Maybe it was because she butchered her own chickens and made her own wine that it had such a unique flavor. Here is my version of that memorable dish.*
**Serves 4**

Preheat the oven to 325°F.

Wash and dry the chicken pieces. Set aside.

Heat 2 tablespoons of the olive oil in a heatproof stovetop-to-oven casserole, or a sauté pan. When the oil is hot, brown the chicken pieces a few at a time and transfer them to a dish. Add more oil as needed to the pan while browning.

Drain off all but 2 tablespoons of the drippings. Add the onions and cook over medium heat until they begin to soften. Add the garlic and continue cooking until the garlic is soft. Return the chicken to the pan and season it generously with salt and pepper to taste.

Tie the bay leaf and rosemary together with kitchen twine and add to the casserole or pan.

In a small bowl, combine the wine and balsamic vinegar with the tomato paste. Lower the heat and pour it over the chicken pieces. Turn the chicken in the wine mixture several times.

Turn off the heat. Cover the pan and transfer it to the oven. Bake for 45 minutes to 1 hour, or until the chicken has an internal temperature of 165°F.

Discard the bay leaf and rosemary sprigs.

Serve the chicken with some of the pan juices.

# Nonna Galasso's Stewed Chicken

## La Gallina in Umido alla Nonna Galasso

*"Una gallina vecchia fa buon brodo." That's what Nonna Galasso used to say and she was right: an old hen makes good broth because it has more fat. But it also has tough muscles and needs to be stewed, not roasted, so its meat will be tender. Since chicken is pretty much uniformly processed in this country, it might be harder to find an old hen unless you have access to a chicken farmer. Whole chicken from your favorite grocery store will work just fine.* **Serves 4**

**m**icrowave the potatoes until tender. Cool, then peel and dice them and set aside.

In a soup pot, warm the olive oil over medium heat. Add the chicken and brown on all sides. Stud the onion with the cloves and add to the pot. Add the bay leaf, parsley, carrots, celery, and tomatoes. Pour in cold water just to cover all the ingredients. Bring the ingredients to a boil, lower the heat, and simmer until the chicken is fork-tender and falling off the bone.

Using a wide slotted spoon, transfer the chicken to a cutting board. Remove the onion, bay leaf, and parsley and discard.

Remove the celery and carrots, cut them into small pieces, and return them to the broth.

Remove the chicken meat from the bones, cut the meat into chunks, and return it to the broth.

Add the diced potatoes. Season to taste with salt and pepper. Reheat the stew gently and serve hot in soup bowls.

2 large all-purpose potatoes, well scrubbed

2 tablespoons extra-virgin olive oil

One 3½-pound whole chicken, rinsed well and patted dry

1 onion, peeled

10 whole cloves

1 whole bay leaf

1 small bunch flat-leaf parsley, tied with kitchen twine

2 carrots, peeled and cut into quarters

2 celery stalks, cut into quarters

2 cups peeled and diced plum tomatoes or one 16-ounce can diced tomatoes

Fine sea salt

Freshly ground black pepper

# Rabbit in Balsamic Vinegar

## Coniglio all'Aceto Balsamico

1 tablespoon un-
salted butter

1 red onion (about 4
ounces) peeled
and thinly sliced

¼ cup balsamic
vinegar

1 tablespoon extra-
virgin olive oil

¼ pound pancetta,
thinly sliced

Fine sea salt

Freshly ground black
pepper

2 pounds rabbit
pieces, washed and
dried

2 garlic cloves,
minced

2 large shallots,
peeled and minced

1¼ cups dry red wine

1 tablespoon minced
fresh rosemary
needles

*Some say it has healing properties, others regard it as highly as a fine Port. I am drawn to the wonderful taste that aged balsamic vinegar imparts to game and poultry. Osteria di Rubbiara, in Modena, near Parma and Reggio Emilia, is the place to go to enjoy the finest rabbit cooked with wine and balsamic vinegar. The food is straightforward and is proudly prepared and served by owner Italo Pedroni, along with his wife and daughter. This rustic-looking inn with low-beamed ceilings and wooden tables and chairs was originally a place where only men went to drink wine. Displays of award-winning bottles of balsamic vinegar line the walls, and the smells coming from the kitchen immediately tell you that the prized vinegar is a key ingredient in the cooking. Don't expect a menu here; just follow the suggestions of Italo who will whet your appetite with offerings of the classic tortellini in brodo, or penne in a rich salsa Bolognese to start. For the second course the choices are even harder; roast pork and chicken or rabbit cooked in wine with balsamic vinegar were my favorites. When I asked Italo about the preparation of the rabbit, he smiled but would not divulge the recipe. What follows is my adaptation. For best results use fresh domestic rabbit or chicken and cook the meat slowly to ensure tenderness without dryness. Because rabbit is so lean and bony, allow 1 pound per person for a serving.* **Serves 2**

In a 12- to 14-inch sauté pan melt the butter over medium heat. Stir in the onions and cook them, stirring occasionally, until soft and glazed. Stir in the vinegar and cook until most of the vinegar has evaporated. Transfer the onions and any juices to a bowl.

Add the olive oil and pancetta to the pan and cook until the pancetta is crisp. Remove the pancetta with a slotted spoon to the bowl with the onions.

Rub salt and pepper all over the rabbit pieces. Add the rabbit to the pan along with the garlic and shallots and cook over medium heat, browning the rabbit evenly on all sides. Add ½ cup of the wine and continue cooking for 3 to 4 minutes. Return the onion mixture to the pan, add the remaining ¾ cup of wine, and cook, uncovered, over low heat for 20 to 30 minutes, turning the rabbit pieces occasionally.

The rabbit is done when a knife is easily inserted into the meat. Sprinkle the rosemary over the rabbit and serve immediately.

*Did you know* that the production of balsamic vinegar has a long history and that it is made from the unfermented Trebbiano grape must? The best aged aceto balsamico is at least twelve years old, and some a hundred years old. They never leave Modena and there is a contest each year in the town of Spilamberto to determine who has made the best. Do not be fooled by imitations, of which there are many. Most vinegars bought here are young vinegars, no more than five years old. Look on the label to see if the product comes from Modena or Reggio Emilia; the label will have the abbreviations Mo for Modena or RE for Reggio Emilia.

# Roast Capon

## Capone al Forno

*Except for the occasional stuffed turkey breast (page 289), a roast turkey was a rare sight on the dinner table at holiday time. Mom stuck pretty much to Italian tradition and always served capon (capone), which to be blunt, is a castrated male chicken that is very flavorful and moist. And to this day, that is what I serve on Thanksgiving and Christmas, too. But I do something very nontraditional with the bird, I brine it first. Since capons are small in size, anywhere from 6 to 11 pounds, this recipe is perfect when you don't want a large turkey.* **Serves 8**

**BRINE**

10 whole cloves

4 whole bay leaves

10 whole black peppercorns

2 quarts apple cider or apple juice

2½ cups firmly packed light-brown sugar

¾ cup kosher salt

3 oranges, quartered

2 large lemons, quartered

One 10- to 11-pound capon, rinsed and dried

Olive oil for roasting

Place the cloves, bay leaves, and peppercorns in a small piece of cheesecloth and tie into a small bundle with kitchen twine. Set aside.

Pour the apple cider into a large soup pot and stir in the sugar and salt. Add the oranges and lemons and bring the mixture to a boil. Cook for 2 minutes to dissolve the sugar and salt. Remove from the heat and let the mixture come to room temperature. (This can be made several days ahead and refrigerated.)

Place the capon in a large, clean, food-safe plastic bag. Carefully pour the apple cider mixture in the bag. Tie the bag tightly.

Place the bag in a large roasting or disposable aluminum roasting pan and refrigerate for 2 days, turning the bag often to evenly brine the capon.

When ready to roast the capon, preheat the oven to 425°F.

Drain the capon from the brine and pat dry with paper towels. Discard the brine. Place the capon, breast side up, on a rack in a roasting pan and brush the skin all over with olive oil.

Roast the capon for 1½ hours, or until an instant-read thermometer inserted in the thickest part of the bird registers 165°F and the juices run clear.

Allow the capon to sit, loosely tented, with aluminum foil for about 20 minutes before carving.

## Royal Guests for Christmas Dinner

*I hated going into the attic of the big old fourteen-room house where I grew up. It was dark, musty, the stairs creaked, and I was always afraid that some night creature like a bat or worse, a monster, would latch onto me! I never let my parents know how scared I was.*

*Mom kept all her Christmas lights, ornaments, and other holiday stuff in the attic, and it was my job to lug things down the stairs on December 6th, the feast of Saint Nicholas, and the date that signaled the "start of the season."*

*It was my job to decorate the house because Mom was just too busy with all the holiday baking that needed to be done. And I loved it. As I unwrapped the glass ornaments, the star for the tree, and the miniature Santa sleigh, Mom would yell out to me to be careful with the nativity set. Those ceramic figures in pastel colors and made in Italy were her pride and joy and each one stood well over two feet tall, too tall to be set under the tree. Instead, Mom wanted them on the conference-size dining room table, right in the middle. Thank God the baby Jesus was lying on a bed of straw because Mary, Joseph, the three Kings, a donkey, and a camel not only towered over the table but took up just about the entire space!*

*We always had a houseful for Christmas and Mom insisted that we would all fit around the table even with the almost human-size nativity set in place. For her, the nativity figures were the most important royal guests and she would not have them banished to some obscure place where their impact on the day would be lost.*

*On Christmas Day, we all crammed ourselves in around the table elbow to elbow. The problem as I saw it was that there was no room on the table for the homemade pork sausage, the roast capon, deep-dish lasagne, or the multitude of vegetable dishes that came with it, not to mention where to put the jugs of wine!*

*Mom always had a solution, and Dad just went along with whatever she suggested because it was easier that way. So he carved the capon in the kitchen and he and I went around to each person balancing platters like professional waitstaff so that everybody could help himself or herself. By the time the roast chestnuts and spumoni were served as part of dessert, the table looked like a war zone with chestnut shells, bread crumbs, and splatters of tomato sauce and red wine blotches all too visible at the feet of the nativity figures. And that just* wouldn't do. So right after dinner, the table was cleared, the nativity moved carefully like antique furniture and with great ceremony, and a clean tablecloth waved its way down into place. The figures were returned to their rightful place and all was well again with the world.

On January 6, feast of the Three Kings, Mom once again worked her magic in the kitchen, only this time it was just our family who paid homage to the royal guests. Cheese ravioli, lentils and sausage, and Befana cake were her classic standbys.

On January 7, all the Christmas decorations came down and each nativity figure was well wrapped in layers of towels and laid in boxes for their journey back to the dreaded attic. Once I hauled them back up those creaky stairs and put them away, I rushed back down the stairs, closed the door, and breathed a sigh of relief. Jesus, Mary, and Joseph, I wouldn't have to do this again for a whole year!

# Stuffed and Rolled Turkey Breast

## Rotolo di Tacchino

*Finding whole turkeys in Italy is not easy, but finding turkey breast is. It is sold more and more in supermercati. Honestly, I have never been a fan of turkey but when I watched my friend, chef Mario Ragni from Perugia, make this stuffed, butterflied turkey breast, I was hooked. It was moist and flavorful and is perfect when you want to have a turkey dinner with just white meat.* **Serves 8**

Preheat the oven to 450°F.

With a small sharp knife, make an X in the top of each chestnut. Place them on a rimmed baking sheet and roast them for 25 minutes, or until the skins split open. Let the chestnuts cool, then crack them open with a nutcracker. Remove the nutmeats and place in a large bowl.

Reduce oven temperature to 400°F.

Heat ¼ cup of the olive oil in a small sauté pan and brown the bread crumbs over low heat. Transfer the crumbs to the bowl with the chestnuts.

Add 1 tablespoon of the olive oil to the pan add the prosciutto and cook until it is brown and crispy. Add the prosciutto to the chestnut mixture. Stir in the rosemary, parsley, garlic, cheese, and 1 tablespoon of the olive oil and mix everything well. (The stuffing can be made and refrigerated up to 3 days ahead.)

Lay the butterflied turkey breast out on a cutting board. Place a large piece of wax paper over the turkey and pound it with a meat pounder to flatten it to an even thickness of about ½ inch.

Rub the turkey with salt and pepper. Spread the stuffing mixture evenly over the turkey to within ½ inch of the sides. If you have some stuffing left over, save it for the top after the meat is rolled.

Starting at one long side, roll the turkey up on itself like a jelly roll and tie it with kitchen string every 2 inches or so. If some of the stuffing falls out while rolling, shove it back in with your fingers.

In a sauté pan large enough to hold the turkey roll, heat the remaining 2 tablespoons of olive oil over medium heat. Brown the turkey roll on all sides.

½ pound whole chestnuts

½ cup extra-virgin olive oil

1½ cups fresh bread crumbs

¼ pound prosciutto, diced

¼ cup fresh rosemary needles

4 tablespoons minced flat-leaf parsley

2 large garlic cloves, minced

⅓ cup freshly grated Parmigiano-Reggiano cheese

One 4-pound skin-on turkey breast, butterflied

Salt and black pepper

1½ cups dry white wine

Transfer it to a rack in a roasting pan and add any juices from the pan. Sprinkle the turkey with salt and pepper and pat on any remaining stuffing over the top.

Add ½ cup of the wine to the pan. Roast the turkey for 1 hour and 10 minutes, basting the meat occasionally with the pan juices, and adding the remaining 1 cup wine to the pan halfway through the cooking time.

When the internal temperature registers 170°F on an instant-read thermometer, remove the turkey roll from the oven. Let it rest, loosely covered with aluminum foil, for 15 minutes. Cut the roll into ½-inch-thick slices and arrange them on a platter. Pour the pan juices over the meat and serve.

**NOTE:** *The term butterflied means to slice a piece of meat vertically almost cutting it in half but stopping ½ inch from the edge so the meat remains in one piece but can be opened like a book. You can do this yourself or ask your butcher to do it for you.*

# Lamb Stew in Lemon and Egg Sauce

## Abbacchio Brodettato

*Abbacchio Brodettato is an old Roman lamb stew dish, which is served with lemon and egg sauce. It is quite delicious. The trick is not to scramble the eggs when making the sauce.* **Serves 6**

heat the oil in a Dutch oven or heavy-bottomed pot over medium-high heat. Add the onion and prosciutto and cook until the onions begin to soften. Combine the lamb pieces in a paper bag with the flour and shake to coat the pieces evenly. Add the lamb to the pan with the onions and brown on all sides over medium heat being careful not to let the onions burn. Season to taste with salt and pepper.

Add the wine to the pan, and cook until most of it has evaporated. Add enough boiling water to almost cover the meat. Cover and simmer about 45 minutes, adding more water as necessary to keep it from evaporating; the sauce should be thick.

When the meat is fork-tender, beat the egg yolks with the minced herbs and the lemon juice. With the stew just at a simmer, pour the yolk mixture over the meat and mix well until the yolks thicken and the sauce is velvety. Be careful not to scramble the eggs.

¼ cup extra-virgin olive oil

1 medium onion, thinly sliced

¼ pound prosciutto, diced

2 pounds lamb stew meat, cut into 1-inch pieces and dried with paper towels

2 tablespoons unbleached all-purpose flour

Fine sea salt

Coarsely ground black pepper

½ cup dry white wine

Boiling water

3 large egg yolks, beaten

¼ cup minced flat-leaf parsley

2 tablespoons minced marjoram

Juice of 1 lemon

# Marinated Lamb Shoulder Chops with Fresh Mint Sauce

## La Spalla Marinata di Agnello con La Salsa di Menta

**MINT SAUCE**

2 cups packed whole mint leaves

1 cup water

2 tablespoons honey

Pinch of salt

**MARINADE**

1 large garlic clove, minced

Juice of 2 large lemons

1 tablespoon honey

⅓ cup minced mint leaves

¼ teaspoon coarsely ground black pepper

1 tablespoon extra-virgin olive oil

4 blade cut lamb chops

*Lamb blade shoulder chops are far tastier than their more expensive center-cut cousins and that's because they have more marbling. Marinate them first, then broil or grill them and serve with fresh mint sauce.* **Serves 4**

To make the sauce, combine the whole mint leaves with the water and honey in a small saucepan and bring to a boil. Reduce the heat and simmer, uncovered, until the liquid is reduced by half. Strain the mixture through a fine sieve into a bowl. Add salt to taste. Set aside and keep warm, or make several days ahead and refrigerate. Reheat when ready to use.

To make the marinade, in a shallow bowl large enough to hold the chops in a single layer, mix the garlic, lemon juice, honey, mint, pepper, and olive oil. Place the chops in the marinade, cover with plastic wrap, and refrigerate for at least 2 hours or overnight. Turn the chops over once or twice while they are marinating.

To cook the lamb, prepare a gas grill or preheat the broiler.

Drain the chops from the marinade and grill or broil them. Use an instant-read thermometer for gauging when they are done: 145°F for rare, 160°F for medium, and 170°F for well done.

Serve immediately with some of the mint sauce.

# Luigi's Lamb Chops

## Costolette d'Agnello alla Luigi

1 rack of lamb (7 to 8 chops), cut into chops, or pre-cut chops from the butcher

3 tablespoons melted lamb fat, lard, or butter

⅓ cup extra-virgin olive oil

2 red onions, coarsely chopped

1 small dried peper-oncino, seeded and finely chopped

2 teaspoons fine sea salt

1 cup dry red wine

2 bay leaves

4 to 6 large plum tomatoes, peeled, seeded, and quartered, or one 16-ounce can of plum tomatoes

*Whenever I am in Italy I take the opportunity to learn from native cooks and such was the case at the Di Majo Norante winery in Molise where owner Luigi di Majo shared his favorite recipe for rack of lamb. They were more than finger-licking good!* **Serves 4**

**I**f you plan to use rendered lamb fat, cut the fat off the chops and sauté in a large pan to get the required amount of 3 tablespoons liquid fat. Set aside, leaving just a coating of fat in the pan and turn the heat up to high. Brown the lamb chops on both sides. Set the meat aside.

In a Dutch oven or deep sauté pan, combine the liquid fat with the olive oil and place over medium heat. Add the chopped onion, hot pepper, and salt and mix well. Cook the mixture for 5 minutes and then add ½ cup of the wine. Cook for 5 more minutes, or until the vegetables have absorbed just about all of the liquid. Return the lamb chops to the pan, add the remaining ½ cup wine, cover, and simmer for 1 hour. Check the pan after about 20 minutes; if the mixture looks dry add more wine, stock, or water.

After 1 hour of cooking, remove the cover and add the bay leaves and tomatoes. Simmer until the tomatoes soften, about 10 to 12 minutes. Transfer the lamb chops to a platter and keep warm for the second course. Remove and discard the bay leaves and serve the sauce immediately over the pasta of your choice.

# Vegetables

Artichokes Stuffed with Pork Sausage

Cubanelle Peppers Stuffed with Farro

Eggplant Bundles with Nuts

Caponata

Nonna Saporito's Eggplant Rolls

Nonna Saporito's Stuffed Artichokes

Stuffed Baked Cabbage Leaves

Stuffed Swiss Chard

Creamy Cauliflower Baked in a Mold

Stuffed Escarole

Baked Leeks in White Sauce

Potato Fritters

Grandma Galasso's Potato Croquettes

Squash Fritters

Batter-fried Radicchio Wedges

Devilish Broccoli

Carrots in Vermouth

Mushrooms in Green Sauce

Pan-cooked Bitter Greens

Roman-Style Artichokes

Spinach with Garlic and Oil

Nonna Galasso's Twice-Cooked
     Cardoons

Chunky Vegetarian Vegetable Stew

Stewed Peppers

Asparagus Molds

Venetian Tart

Potato, Zucchini, and
     Parmigiano-Reggiano Cheese Tart

Grilled Asparagus

Asparagus with Browned Butter

# talking vegetables

**O**pen any refrigerator in Italy and I'll bet that you will be greeted with shelves of *le verdure fresche* (fresh vegetables). It is no secret that vegetables make up the bulk of what Italians eat. And to further substantiate this, walk through any outdoor *mercato* (market) in any Italian town and you will see a vast and vivid carpet of glorious vegetables that look so perfect, it is hard to believe that they are real without touching them!

Italians are picky and discerning cooks who will think long and hard about which eggplant or artichoke to choose, and the vendors who sell them often get into the conversation, asking how one plans to use the vegetables, then makes a recommendation as to what to buy. This is quintessentially Italian! (We have something like this in America—it's the farmers' market—and I am a huge supporter of buying fresh, local vegetables as much as possible, if I do not grow them in my home garden.)

When Italians cook vegetables they take a very Sherlock Holmes approach, looking for clues that tell how fresh things are. For instance, did you know that vegetables talk? I'll explain. How would you know if an artichoke is fresh? If you roll it back and forth under the palm of your hands on a cutting board, it will squeak and the leaves will open a bit! That's fresh! What would you look for in a head of cauliflower? Florets that make a snapping sound when detached from the stem. Ditto on green beans. No snapping sound means they are not fresh. Lettuce is another good indicator of freshness. It should have a crunching sound when torn into pieces. Cucumbers should make a crisp sound when cut into rounds.

Now let me tell you about the best way to cook them Italian style. There is such a fondness for grilling and roasting them. The best vegetables for grilling are sweet peppers, hot peppers, eggplant, zucchini, radicchio, fennel, and onions because they have some structure and will hold up well. Just a brushing of olive oil is all that is needed and when they are cooked, a spray of coarse sea salt, a dash of red wine vinegar, and a sprinkling of fresh herbs keeps the integrity and the flavor fresh.

Roasting vegetables is an easy method that brings out the natural sugars and intensifies the flavor. It is a favorite winter method. Beets, leeks, artichokes, broccoli, carrots, cauliflower, asparagus, and tomatoes are all terrific done this way and the preparation is a breeze. Sautéing, which means cooking ingredients quickly on the stovetop in a drizzle of olive oil, is another classic method. Potatoes, mushrooms, spinach, Swiss chard, celery, and peas are good for this. Boiling vegetables to death is never done. Even in soups, vegetables retain their shape. Boiling benefits bitter greens like broccoli rabe, tough leaf vegetables like kale, and cardoons and fava beans.

So next time you choose to cook vegetables the Italian way, listen first.

# Artichokes Stuffed with Pork Sausage

## Carciofi Ripieni con Salsicce

*I'm not saying that cooking artichokes is easy. They are time-consuming to prepare, but for me it is worth it, especially when I stuff them with a tangy pork sausage mixture and bake them. Think of this recipe as a complete meal in an edible container. Buy artichokes with tightly closed leaves, an indication of freshness. Artichokes are in season in the spring and fall.* **Serves 4**

3 tablespoons extra-virgin olive oil

1 small onion, peeled and minced

1 garlic clove, minced

1 teaspoon hot red pepper flakes or hot red pepper paste

1 pound sweet pork sausage, casings removed

½ cup dry white wine

1 teaspoon fennel seeds, ground

Salt and black pepper

4 large Globe artichokes

½ cup chicken broth

heat 1 tablespoon of the olive oil in a sauté pan over medium heat. Add the onion and cook until soft. Stir in the garlic and red pepper flakes and cook until the garlic softens. Add the pork sausage and cook until browned. Raise the heat to high, add the wine, and cook until almost evaporated. Turn off the heat and stir in the fennel, and season with salt and pepper to taste. Set aside.

Preheat the oven to 350°F.

Cut the stems off even with the base of the artichokes and discard them.

Remove the tough outer base leaves of the artichokes and discard them. Use scissors to trim the tips of the rest of the leaves to remove the thorns. Using a chef's knife, cut off ¼ inch from the top of the artichokes.

Roll each artichoke around on a work surface to loosen the leaves.

With a small spoon or melon baller, spread open the center of the artichoke and remove the yellow leaves. Scrape out the hairy choke at the base and discard.

Rinse the artichokes well and turn them upside down on a cutting board to drain.

Divide and stuff the pork mixture in the center of each artichoke.

Place them standing upright in a Dutch oven or similar type oven casserole.

Drizzle the remaining 2 tablespoons olive oil over the surface of each artichoke and pour the chicken broth into the Dutch oven or casserole. Cover with a lid or aluminium foil. Bake for 35 to 40 minutes, or until you can detach a leaf easily.

Serve the artichokes hot with any pan juices poured over.

# Cubanelle Peppers Stuffed with Farro

## Peperoni Ripieni

*Cubanelle peppers (banana peppers), sometimes referred to as Italian frying peppers, are a must grow in my garden because I love to fill their cavities with everything from sausage and onions to rice and whole grains like farro, which is an old wheat berry enjoying renewed interest today for its wonderful health properties. Substitute rice or pearled barley for the farro.* **Serves 4**

1 cup farro, rice, or pearled barley

3 cups vegetable or chicken broth (or water)

1 large egg

2/3 cup grated Parmigiano-Reggiano cheese

3 tablespoons minced flat-leaf parsley

2 tablespoons extra-virgin olive oil

4 banana peppers

**C**over the farro, rice, or barley with the broth or water in a 1-quart saucepan. Bring to a boil, lower the heat to simmer, cover the pan, and let the farro cook until most of the broth is absorbed and the farro is tender.

Drain the farro in a colander and transfer it to a medium bowl. Stir in the egg, ½ cup of the cheese, the parsley, and 1 tablespoon of the olive oil. Set aside.

Cut ½ inch off the stem tops of the peppers and set aside. Tap out the seeds in the peppers or use a small spoon to remove and discard them.

Fill the peppers with some of the farro mixture but do not pack them too tightly, or they may split while baking. Make a small incision on the side of each pepper with a small paring knife to allow steam to escape while baking.

Brush a medium casserole dish with the remaining tablespoon of olive oil and place the peppers in a single layer in the dish.

Cover the dish with aluminum foil and bake the peppers for 30 minutes. Uncover, sprinkle the remaining cheese over the peppers, and bake 5 minutes longer.

Serve hot.

## What Vegetables Need

Even if you lived in an urban area, a vegetable garden was part of growing up Italian. That was a given. As a child, I cared not for vegetables of any sort but my nonna Galasso did. Outside the backdoor to the kitchen was her precious little garden, which she could not live without because it was a lasting connection to her home in Naples. And what she did not have in the garden, she combed the roadways for in search of wild cardoons and dandelion greens. I still see her loaded down with mint, beans, mustard greens, and other vegetables bulging out of the folds of her flowered apron.

On one of my first trips to Italy, I was amazed at how many home gardens I saw squeezed into thimble-size backyards, or along the sides of railroad tracks, and even on rooftop terraces in many small towns. No matter how confining the space is in Italian neighborhoods, there will always be a spot for tomatoes growing in pots, or herbs in hanging planters. And amazingly, given a fair amount of sunlight, one could grow the basics: basil, parsley, tomatoes, lettuce, beans, and zucchini.

There are many Italians who will tell you that no matter how big or small a garden, it needs certain things and not just good soil and fertilizer. As one seasoned Italian gardener I know put it, "A vegetable garden needs a dead man." Startled by this comment, I asked him what he meant. Translation: someone needs to be in the garden at all times. In other words, vegetables need constant care. And this same gardener cautions that one should never plant a garden until the first full moon appears. That is when the amount of moisture in the soil is at its peak to encourage the germination of seeds. That would mean waiting until all danger of frost has passed, which varies from place to place depending on what zone you live in.

Why are Italians so passionate about their gardens? Because they come from a farm-to-fork tradition, an agrarian culture that is inbred in them and because the older generation of Italians remembers the endless days of hunger during wartime when there were scarce amounts of food available. Survival meant self-sufficiency. This they passed on to family members who carried on the traditions even into urban centers. Just look up in any busy Italian city today and there you will see olive trees growing on rooftops, herbs in clay pots snuggled together on balconies, and beans climbing up building sides on strings.

To say that Italians are fussy about their produce would be an understatement, so it is no surprise that the Slow Food movement started in Bra, Italy, and its message of locally grown and sustainable agriculture has taken hold worldwide. There is a viable movement in the states, too, for more locally grown fruits and vegetables as evidenced by the number of farmers' markets that are springing up all over the country. We are beginning to realize that our well-being depends on knowing where our food comes from and what kind of safe farming practices are in place. We are beginning to demand that our children be educated about good eating habits; plant a vegetable garden at home or in the schoolyard and a whole new world opens. Vegetables and fruits, locally grown without pesticides, are something we should all demand, and if we do, the corporate agribusinesses that control most of what we buy in our local grocery store will get the message. What vegetables need are tender loving care for generations to come.

# Eggplant Bundles with Nuts

## Involtini di Melanzane Con Le Noci

1 large eggplant (at least 7 inches long), stem trimmed, eggplant cut into 8 lengthwise ¼-inch-thick slices

4 ounces shelled walnuts, hazelnuts, or pistachio nuts

2 garlic cloves, peeled

1 small bunch flat-leaf parsley

½ cup unbleached all-purpose flour

2 large eggs

Peanut oil for frying

¼ pound feta cheese, crumbled

Coarsely ground black pepper

Coarse sea salt

⅓ cup extra-virgin olive oil

¼ cup fresh lemon juice

*The word* involtino *has many meanings; it could mean thinly sliced pieces of meat like veal, beef, and pork or thin slices of fish or thinly sliced vegetables such as eggplant, that have a savory filling and are rolled up into bundles. It is more likely that you will see and hear the word* involtino *used in the north of Italy for stuffed and rolled bundles because in the south they are called* braciole. *(See page 306 for Nonna Saporito's Eggplant Rolls.)* **Serves 4**

Place eggplant slices in a colander and salt the slices. Let stand for 1 hour, then rinse the slices and pat dry. Set aside.

Chop the nuts, garlic, and parsley together to make a mixture with a fine breadcrumb consistency. Transfer the mixture to a shallow dish. Set aside.

Place the flour in a paper bag.

Lightly beat the eggs and pour into a shallow dish.

Dredge the eggplant slices, a few at a time, in the flour and dip each one into the egg, coating the slices well on both sides. Press each slice into the nut mixture, coating each side well.

Roll the slices up and insert a couple of toothpicks in each one to hold them closed. Set aside.

Heat 1 cup of the peanut oil in a deep sauté pan and when the oil is hot, fry the involtini a few at a time until they are nicely browned. Use more oil as needed. Transfer them as they brown to paper towels to drain, then place them on a platter and keep them warm in the oven while you fry the remainder.

When ready to serve, sprinkle the cheese over them and season generously with salt and coarsely ground pepper.

In a small bowl, whisk the olive oil and lemon juice together and drizzle it over the involtini.

# Caponata

*Unless you are of Sicilian descent, you might not recognize the word* caponata. *There is no firm translation of the word other than to say that it is a sweet-and-sour eggplant relish of sorts. When my garden is overflowing with the purple beauties, I make jars of it and freeze it for future use. Caponata can be used for many things. Top a fried tuna steak (page 243) or swordfish with it. Use it on bruschetta, or for a sauce for pasta. It is a pleasant surprise topping for pizza or focaccia. Come the snows of January, opening a jar of homemade caponata can banish those winter blues in a flash.* **Makes about 9½ cups**

Place eggplant cubes in a colander, salt them, and let them sweat in the sink for 1 hour, then rinse and dry them.

In a small saucepan, add the celery to the boiling water and cook for 3 or 4 minutes. Drain the celery, saving the water, and set aside.

In a large skillet or electric frying pan, heat half the peanut oil. Add half of the eggplant pieces and fry until softened and lightly browned, 12 to 15 minutes. Drain the pieces on brown paper and continue with the remaining eggplant and peanut oil.

In the same skillet, heat the olive oil, add the onions, and sauté until soft and glazed-looking, about 10 minutes. Lower the heat and mix in tomato paste, reserved celery water, olives, capers, sugar, vinegar, and cocoa. Mix well and let the mixture simmer about 5 minutes.

Add the eggplant and the celery pieces to the skillet, and mix well to coat the pieces with the sauce. Simmer the mixture uncovered for about 10 minutes. Add salt and pepper to taste.

Because this recipe makes a lot, I spoon the mixture into jars, cover, and store some in the refrigerator and freeze the rest. Use as needed.

**Variation:** Serve the caponata in an eggplant that has been cut in half lengthwise and scooped out. Surround the eggplant with slices of semolina bread, lightly fried in a fruity olive oil.

---

8 young eggplant (4 to 5 inches long), washed, trimmed, and cut in 1-inch cubes

Coarse sea salt

1¼ cups thinly sliced celery (about 2 ribs)

1½ cups boiling water

1½ cups peanut oil

½ cup extra-virgin olive oil

4 onions, thinly sliced (about 3½ cups)

1 cup tomato paste

1 cup drained and chopped green or black olives in brine

½ cup capers in wine vinegar, drained

½ cup sugar

⅔ cup red wine vinegar

2 teaspoons baking cocoa

Freshly ground pepper to taste

# Nonna Saporito's Eggplant Rolls

## Braciole di Milinciani alla Nonna Saporito

1 large eggplant (7 to
  8 inches long),
  stem removed, cut
  into 8 ¼-inch-thick
  lengthwise slices

Extra-virgin olive oil

⅔ cup minced mint
  or oregano

1 teaspoon fine sea
  salt

½ teaspoon coarsely
  ground black
  pepper

½ cup pine nuts

1½ cups prepared
  tomato sauce

1 cup toasted bread
  crumbs, made
  from stale bread

*Eggplant* (melanzane) *has occupied star status in the southern Italian kitchen, especially in Sicily where it was first introduced by the Arabs and over the centuries has undergone many changes in preparation and taste. We are all familiar with numerous versions of eggplant Parmigiana, fried, baked, or grilled slices that are sandwiched between cheese and tomato sauce. But Nonna Saporito would never have recognized those versions. Her* milinciani (eggplant) *would have been stuffed and rolled and flavored with tomatoes and bread crumbs, not cheese, which was just too expensive even for many Sicilians. And if by chance she had a handful of pignoli, they would be added, too.* **Serves 8**

Prepare the eggplant slices as on page 304.

Preheat the oven to 350°F, or fire up the grill.

Brush the eggplant slices on both sides with olive oil and place them in single layers on lightly oiled rimmed baking sheets. Bake them for about 10 minutes, or just until they are soft. Set them aside to cool. Or grill them on both sides until they soften and grill marks appear.

Mix the oregano, salt, pepper, and pine nuts together in a bowl. Spread a couple of tablespoons of the mixture along the length of each eggplant slice, and then roll the slices up into bundles.

Spread ½ cup of the tomato sauce in the base of a 12 × 9-inch casserole dish. Place the eggplant bundles in single rows in the dish and spread the remaining sauce evenly over the top.

Cover the dish with aluminum foil and bake for 30 minutes. Uncover, and bake 5 minutes longer. Serve hot and pass the bread crumbs in a small bowl to be sprinkled on top.

**CHEF'S SECRET:** *Purchase eggplants that are very shiny, have intact stem tops, show no bruising or soft spots, and feel heavy.*

# Nonna Saporito's Stuffed Artichokes

## Carciofi Ripieni alla Nonna Saporito

4 large Globe artichokes, washed

2 tablespoons plus ¼ cup extra-virgin olive oil

2½ cups soft bread crumbs

3 garlic cloves, peeled

½ cup mint leaves

½ cup flat-leaf parsley leaves

1 cup grated pecorino cheese

Fine sea salt

Freshly ground black pepper

1 cup chicken broth or water

Juice of 2 lemons

8 tablespoons (1 stick) salted butter, melted

*Since Sicily is one of the major suppliers of artichokes in Italy, there are numerous ways they are prepared but my fondest memory of cooking artichokes in Sicily was at the Regaleali winery in the central area where whole artichokes were roasted on the ground on top of burning embers. Served with olive oil and coarse salt, they were memorable.*  **Serves 4**

Cut the stems off even with the base and discard. Cut off ¼ inch of the top of each artichoke and discard. Remove the tough outer base leaves and discard. Using scissors, cut the thorns off of the remaining leaves.

Roll the artichokes around on your cutting board to loosen the leaves.

Fill a large pot of water, add the artichokes, and parboil them for 5 minutes. Drain them upside down in a colander. When cool, use a spoon to remove the yellow leaves and hairy choke in the center. Set the artichokes aside while you make the filling.

Preheat the oven to 350°F.

Heat 2 tablespoons of the olive oil in a skillet and brown the bread crumbs. Transfer the crumbs to a bowl.

Mince the garlic, mint, and parsley together and add to the bowl with the bread crumbs. Stir in the cheese, salt, and pepper.

Stuff the center cavity of each artichoke with about ⅓ cup of the mixture. Spread the rest of the bread crumb mixture in between the leaves of the artichokes.

Place them in a 12 × 9 × 2-inch casserole dish in a single layer. Divide and drizzle the remaining ¼ cup oil over the artichokes.

Pour the broth or water along the sides of the dish to coat the bottom. Cover the dish with aluminium foil and bake the artichokes for 25 to 30 minutes. Uncover and bake an additional 5 minutes, or until a leaf easily pulls away from the artichoke.

Combine the lemon juice and butter and pour evenly over the artichokes. Serve hot.

The all powerful God of Gods, Zeus had a really bad crush on the Goddess Cynara, but she cared not a wit for him. So he did what any angry God would do, he hurled a thunderbolt towards earth where she was headed to meet up with her mother, and turned Cynara into an artichoke! If he could not have her, nobody could. Well, when you eat artichokes you will notice that there is a slight sweet aftertaste due to cynarin, a component found in them and derived from the word cynara.

# The Art of the Artichoke

Artichokes are one of the glories of the Italian table. In spring and fall, they are piled high in outdoor and indoor markets all over Italy, mainly coming from Puglia, Sicily, and around Tuscany. Their color hues range from delightful purples to all shades of green, and watching market vendors effortlessly peel them like magicians to get to the heart, the best part of the artichoke, is mesmerizing. The hearts are tossed into large tubs of lemon juice and water to prevent discoloration and sold to happy Italians who know just what to do next. Italian varieties are thornless and small varieties are so tender and chokeless (the nasty inside hairy part), that they can be thinly sliced and eaten raw as part of an antipasto or in a salad.

Artichokes are members of the thistle family and there are many varieties. The most common variety for us is the Globe artichoke, big, meaty, and thorny. Artichokes were introduced to America by way of California and Italian immigrant farmers who settled there and planted the first commercial crop. Today Castroville, California, is the artichoke capital and main source for artichokes sold nationwide.

Here's what to look for when buying artichokes. The leaves should be closed, not fanned open; tight leaves indicates freshness. They should feel heavy in your hand and the stem end should not be soft or bendable. They should have a uniform color but most aficionados agree that artichokes that have been nipped by frost and have tinges of brown on their leaves taste even better.

Preparation takes many forms, including stuffing them whole, or using only the hearts and stuffing their cavities, or marinating them as part of a salad, or cutting them in wedges and stewing them. My favorite? Stuffed alla Nonna Saporito. Nonna used to tell me about how artichokes were roasted right on the ground in her native Sicily. Right after the harvest, a really hot charcoal fire was built and in the glow of burning embers, artichokes would be roasting! Many years later when I was in Sicily, I saw this very method in use at the Count Tasca estate at Regaleali. Of course Nonna could never cook them that way in her Rochester, New York, kitchen. So she adapted to how things were done in "L'America." She would dig out and discard the choke, parboil the artichokes whole, drain them, make a mixture of bread crumbs, mint, garlic, parsley, and pecorino cheese, if she had any, and stuffed this mixture in the center of and in-between the leaves.

*She put them in a baking pan, poured oil over them, and baked them, covered, until tender, which she said was when the outer leaves could easily be pulled away.*

*I rediscovered my love for artichokes after I got married. Sometimes I made them like Nonna's, other times I served them plain with melted butter. When I want to wow company, I stuff them with spicy Italian sausage, and stew them with tomatoes and wine for cold weather eating. Still, I like them best straight up, unpretentious.*

*Getting to the most tender part of the artichoke requires the fortitude of an archaeologist, scraping away layers of leaves and removing that hairy choke at the very bottom before the big payoff, the tender heart. There is an easier way. Strip away the tough outer leaves (and this could mean a couple of layers) with your fingers by bending the leaves backwards, or use scissors and cut them off. A good way to know if you have taken off enough tough leaves is to stop when the color of the leaves turns from dark to pale green. Cut off about ¼ inch down from the top with a sharp knife and cut off the stem. Trim any remaining thorns with a kitchen scissors, then submerge the artichokes in a nonreactive pot of boiling water and cook them until tender. But don't use aluminum or iron pans because they will impart a tinny taste and give an off color to the artichokes. Drain them and let them cool. Cut them in half lengthwise and use a spoon or a melon baller to remove the hairy choke. Presented this way, they become edible containers that can be filled with cheese, cooked rice, diced vegetables, or just melted butter, which is my favorite way to have them. Nutty and mild with a slightly sweet taste, the artichoke is art itself.*

# Stuffed Baked Cabbage Leaves

## Verza Ripiena al Forno

¼ cup farro

1 head cabbage (about 2¼ pounds), washed

1 small onion, minced

1 large garlic clove, minced

1 pound ground beef or half ground beef and half pork

1 egg, slightly beaten

½ cup grated Grana Padano, plus extra for sprinkling

¼ cup minced flat-leaf parsley

½ teaspoon paprika

1½ teaspoons salt

½ teaspoon freshly ground black pepper

2 tablespoons minced sage

¼ pound Prosciutto di Parma or San Daniele, thinly sliced and cut in half crosswise

2½ cups prepared tomato sauce

*Eggplant* (melanzane) *is to southern Italy what cabbage* (verza) *is to northern Italy, especially in the region of Friuli Venezia Giulia in the far northeast corner of the boot. There they make savory casseroles and soups out of the Savoy variety with its dark green crinkly leaves. It is called Savoy because the Savoy dynasty ruled this part of Italy. Savoy cabbage is more tender and sweeter than its paler green cousin.*   **Serves 4**

**S**oak the farro in 1 cup of water for a couple of hours or overnight. When ready to use, drain off the water.

Cook the farro in 1½ cups of boiling water until it is tender. Drain and transfer it to a medium-size bowl.

Core the cabbage, leaving it whole. Carefully remove 10 large leaves. Reserve the rest of the cabbage for another use, such as soup.

Fill a large soup pot with water and bring it to a boil. Add 1 tablespoon of salt and the cabbage leaves. Cook for 2 to 3 minutes or just until the leaves wilt.

Remove the leaves with a slotted spoon and let them cool.

Meanwhile add the onion, garlic, ground meat, egg, grated cheese, parsley, paprika, salt, pepper, and sage to the bowl with the farro. Combine all the ingredients just until mixed.

Lay out each cabbage leaf on a cutting board and with a small knife remove the lower 1 inch or so tough part of the central core because it makes it difficult to roll up the leaves into bundles.

Place a couple of slices of the prosciutto on each leaf and top with a generous ⅓ cup of the meat mixture in the center and then roll the leaf up, folding in the sides to form a bundle.

After making all the bundles, spread a thin layer of tomato sauce in the base of a 9 × 13 × 2-inch casserole dish.

Place the bundles seam-side down in the casserole dish and top with the remaining tomato sauce. Sprinkle the tops with additional cheese.

Cover the dish with foil and bake for 35 minutes. Uncover and bake 5 minutes longer. Serve hot with some of the sauce.

# Stuffed Swiss Chard

## Bietola Ripiena

*Swiss chard is one of those vegetables that mystifies people. What to do with it? Short of steaming or boiling it and serving it like spinach, it doesn't seem to get the same kind of innovative treatment that other vegetables get. Why not stuff it with ricotta cheese? Light and airy, this makes a good side to meats and fish and is a vegetarian's dream.*
*Serves 4*

One 15-ounce container ricotta cheese (skim or whole milk)

1 large egg

½ cup grated Parmigiano-Reggiano cheese

Salt

2 tablespoons chopped flat-leaf parsley

8 large whole Swiss chard leaves with stems, washed

2 tablespoons extra-virgin olive oil

1 small onion, diced

1 cup tomato sauce

Preheat the oven to 350°F.

In a bowl combine the ricotta cheese, egg, ¼ cup of the grated cheese, salt to taste, and parsley. Set aside.

Cut away the stems from the Swiss chard and thinly slice them. Set aside.

Bring a large pot of water to boil and add 1 teaspoon salt. Add the whole leaves and blanch for 10 seconds. Carefully remove the leaves with a slotted spoon or skimmer and allow them to cool.

Meanwhile heat the olive oil in a sauté pan. When the oil is hot, add the onion and sliced stems and cook them over medium heat until the stems soften. Cool the mixture slightly, then add to the bowl with the ricotta cheese mixture.

Lay each Swiss chard leaf flat and spread ¼ cup of the cheese mixture down the center of each. Starting from the end nearest you roll each leave up to encase the filling, folding in the sides as you go.

Spread ½ cup of the tomato sauce in the base of the casserole.

Place the Swiss chard rolls in a single layer in the casserole and spread the remaining tomato sauce over the tops of each.

Sprinkle the tops with the remaining ¼ cup of cheese.

Cover the dish tightly with aluminium foil and bake for 35 minutes. Uncover, and serve immediately.

# Creamy Cauliflower Baked in a Mold

## Sformato di Cavolfiore

**BREAD CRUMB COATING**

2 tablespoons unsalted butter, melted

¼ cup plain fine bread crumbs

**FILLING**

1 head (2 pounds) cauliflower, core and outer leaves removed and florets cut into small ¼-inch pieces

3 large eggs

3 tablespoons minced parsley

1 cup grated Parmigiano Reggiano or Grana Padano cheese

½ cup Montasio cheese, grated

1 teaspoon fine sea salt

Freshly ground black pepper

**WHITE SAUCE**

3 tablespoons unsalted butter

*A sformato (from* sformare, *to unmold) is usually an impressive vegetable mold made in a soufflé-type casserole or springform pan. A sformato can give a whole new look and taste to many vegetables, especially those vegetables like cauliflower that often never get a second glance unless it is transformed into this rich, creamy, and smooth sformato. Serve it as a delectable side dish or main entree. Choose cauliflower with a tight head and vibrant green stem. Brown spots on the floret are a sign of old cauliflower.*
***Serves 8***

**b**rush a 9 ½ × 2 ½-inch springform pan or soufflé-type pan with the melted butter and coat the pan with the bread crumbs. Shake out any loose crumbs and refrigerate the mold until ready to fill.

Fill a large pot with 3 cups of water and bring to a boil. Add the florets, cover the pot, and cook until the florets are very tender, about 6 minutes.

Drain the cauliflower, reserving 1 cup of the cooking water.

Transfer the cauliflower to a food processor and pulse several times until smooth. You can also use an immersion blender to smooth out the cauliflower.

Transfer the cauliflower to a large bowl and whisk in the eggs, parsley, cheeses, salt, and pepper.

Cover and refrigerate while you make the sauce.

In a medium-size pan over medium heat, melt the butter and whisk in the flour to make a smooth paste. Whisk in the half-and-half and reserved water. Whisk in the salt and nutmeg and cook until the mixture thickens.

Preheat the oven to 375°F.

Transfer the sauce to the bowl with the cauliflower and combine well.

Pour the mixture into the prepared pan and smooth the top.

Bake for 40 to 45 minutes or until the sformato sets and is lightly browned.

Remove the sformato from the oven and scoop from the pan to serve. If using a springform pan, wait 5 minutes, then unlatch the sides and lift off. Cut into wedges to serve.

Serve warm or at room temperature.

**TIP:** *To help temper the smell of cauliflower, try adding a ½ cup of milk and one whole bay leaf to the pot in which the cauliflower is cooking.*

3 tablespoons unbleached all-purpose flour

1 cup half-and-half

1 teaspoon fine sea salt

½ teaspoon freshly ground nutmeg

# Stuffed Escarole

## Scarola Ripiena

*Next to our children and me, I think my husband Guy loves escarole the best. He craves it raw in salads, loving it for its bitter taste and crunch. But I've convinced him that it is equally as good as a stuffed vegetable and to prove it, I made him Nonna Galasso's version with walnut and raisin stuffing.* ***Serves 4***

Preheat the oven to 400°F. Cut the escarole lengthwise in half, then in lengthwise half again, leaving the stem end attached. Place the quarters in a 12- to 14-inch sauté pan. Add 2 cups of the broth or water and bring to a boil. Lower the heat to medium and cook just until the leaves wilt. Lift the quarters out of the water with a slotted spoon and drain and cool. Reserve the liquid.

Pour the remaining 1½ cups chicken broth or water into a medium saucepan. Bring to a boil and stir in the rice. Add salt to taste and parboil the rice, uncovered, for 10 minutes; the rice will not be cooked through. Drain the rice, reserving the liquid, and transfer it to a bowl.

Wipe out the pan used to cook the escarole and add the olive oil. Over medium heat sauté the nuts, garlic, thyme, raisins, and capers together until the mixture softens. Season to taste with salt and pepper. Remove from heat and add the mixture to the rice. Mix well. Stir in the egg and ¼ cup of the cheese.

Cut and discard the base from one escarole quarter. Gently spread the leaves to create a 4-inch-wide area. With the base nearest you, pack one-fourth of the rice mixture in the center of the bottom half of the escarole. Fold the base of the leaves over the rice, then fold in sides and roll up the rice mixture, encasing it in the escarole. Place the bundle, seam side down, in a 2-quart flameproof shallow baking dish. Repeat making bundles with the remaining escarole and rice.

Drizzle the bundles with ½ cup of the reserved cooking liquid and sprinkle with the remaining ½ cup cheese.

Cover the baking dish tightly with aluminum foil or a lid and bake 30 minutes.

Remove the foil or lid and turn on broiler. Broil the bundles for 4 to 7 minutes, or until the cheese is browned. Serve hot.

1 large head of escarole (about 1¼ pounds), well washed but left whole

3½ cups canned, low-sodium chicken broth, or water

½ cup brown rice

Salt and black pepper

¼ cup extra-virgin olive oil

½ cup chopped walnuts

2 cloves garlic, finely chopped

2 tablespoons fresh thyme leaves, finely chopped

⅓ cup raisins, chopped

3 tablespoons salt-packed capers, well rinsed and chopped

1 large egg, lightly beaten

¾ cup grated Parmigiano-Reggiano cheese

# Baked Leeks in White Sauce

## Porri in Bianco

2 tablespoons
unsalted butter

2 tablespoons
unbleached
all-purpose flour

¾ cup milk or half-
and-half

1 teaspoon dry
mustard

Salt

¼ teaspoon coarse
ground black
pepper

2 tablespoons minced
tarragon

6 medium-size leeks,
leaves trimmed
down to the
lightest shade of
green, and cut
crosswise into
¾-inch long pieces
and then length-
wise in half

One 6-ounce ball
fresh mozzarella
cheese, cut into
small pieces

4 tablespoons grated
Parmigiano-
Reggiano cheese

*Leeks are often thought of as a gourmet ingredient, and many people bypass this vegetable because they are unsure what to do with it. Leeks are the mild members of the onion family and are impressive looking with their sturdy bright long green leaves and white bulbs. They have many uses, including as a key ingredient in leek and potato soup, or chopped and sautéed like onions. I grow a lot of leeks in my garden and am always experimenting with new ways to use them. One day as I was washing the dirt from just harvested leeks, I decided to make a casserole with them. I was more than pleasantly surprised by the results.* **Serves 6**

Preheat the oven to 375°F.

Brush a 9 × 13-inch casserole dish with one tablespoon of the butter and set aside.

In a medium-size saucepan, melt the remaining tablespoon of butter over medium heat and whisk in the flour to create a smooth paste.

Slowly pour in the milk and continue whisking until the mixture thickens enough to coat the back of a spoon. Take the saucepan off the heat and whisk in the dry mustard, salt, pepper, and tarragon.

Place the leeks cut side down close together in a single layer in the casserole dish (use two dishes if need be), and evenly pour the sauce over the leeks.

Dot the top with the mozzarella and sprinkle on the Parmigiano-Reggiano cheese.

Cover with foil and bake 25 minutes. Uncover and bake 10 minutes longer or until the sauce is bubbly and the leeks are tender. Serve hot.

# Potato Fritters

## Frittelle di Patate

There is fried food and then there are frittelle, *delicious, crunchy fritters that are addicting. Get 'em while they are hot!*   **Serves 4**

**I**n a bowl, mix together the eggs, cheese, flour, salt, and pepper. Add the potatoes and fold in.

Heat 3 cups canola oil to 375°F in a deep fryer or heavy-bottomed, deep pot.

Drop spoonfuls of the fritter batter in the oil and fry until golden brown. Remove the fritters with a slotted spoon and drain on paper towels. Sprinkle with salt and serve hot or with a simple tomato sauce on the side.

2 large eggs

2 tablespoons grated pecorino cheese

2 tablespoons unbleached all-purpose flour

1 teaspoon salt, plus extra for sprinkling

Freshly ground black pepper

4 medium potatoes, peeled and finely grated

Canola oil for frying

# Grandma Galasso's Potato Croquettes

## Crocche di Patate alla Nonna Galasso

4 Yukon Gold
   potatoes, well
   scrubbed

½ cup grated
   pecorino cheese

2 large eggs

1 tablespoon
   chopped mint

Salt

1 to 2 cups bread
   crumbs, preferably
   panko

Vegetable oil for
   frying

2 cups tomato sauce,
   kept warm
   (optional)

*Crunchy and beautifully browned potato croquettes affectionately called* crocche di patate *in Neapolitan dialect were a special treat and only Nonna Galasso made the best, in my opinion. I loved watching her take heaping mounds of mashed potatoes, flavored with cheese and her beloved mint, coating in bread crumbs, and sculpting them into smooth orange-size balls. When I make them, I like to serve them with a side of tomato sauce.* **Serves 4**

Place the potatoes in a pot and cover them with cold water. Bring to a boil and cook until the potatoes are fork-tender. Drain and cool. Peel them and cut into chunks and place them in a bowl.

Use a hand masher to mash them, then add the cheese, eggs, mint, and salt to taste. There is salt in the cheese so go easy with it.

Place the bread crumbs in a shallow bowl. (I like to use Panko for that added crunch.)

Using lightly floured hands, scoop up ½ cup portions of the mixture and form into balls. Roll the balls in the bread crumbs to coat them. Place the balls on a baking sheet and place them in the refrigerator, uncovered, for at least an hour.

Heat 4 to 6 cups of vegetable oil in a deep fryer or heavy-bottomed, deep pot. When the oil reaches 375°F, add the balls a few at a time and fry them until golden brown. Remove them with a slotted spoon and drain on paper towels.

Serve hot with a little of the tomato sauce on the side.

**Variation:** Make miniature size balls and serve as part of antipasti. Cook and peel the potatoes, mash them. Combine them with the cheese, eggs, mint, salt, and pepper. Flour your hands and, using small amounts, about ⅓ cup, form the mixture into a small cylinder shape. Roll them in bread crumbs and fry in vegetable oil until nicely browned.

## Potatoes and Oranges

*Nonna Galasso had no formal education, could not read English, and spoke in fractured English, and for all these limitations she had common sense smarts. Everyday was a contest to survive, beat the odds, and overcome the hand that fate had dealt. To me she could do anything because she had such determination. Much of what I came to appreciate about my Italian heritage was because of her. She would tell me stories about her boarding house and the people whom she cooked for. Cooking was her livelihood, her ticket to a better life. Her pudgy hands were always busy making something for boarders or for family.*

*Early in the morning, while I was still in bed, she would make my school lunch, which more often than not was a fried egg sandwich on her dark homemade bread, an apple, and a Hostess cupcake. Later in the morning she would whip up the bread dough and during the day she would busy herself with plans for supper. She knew my favorites like* crocchette di patate, *smooth mashed potatoes flavored with cheese, rolled in bread crumbs, and fried to a crunchy golden brown hue. Depending on how she felt that day, she would make them either in cylindrical or pear shapes. I liked the pear-shaped ones best. Or she might make* arancine, or *rice balls, that were shaped like oranges and filled with whatever was on hand from cheese and peas to ham and parsley or even leftovers.*

*Looking back, I would bet her peasant cooking against any chef with formal training because she understood food from the ground to the table, never compromising it, always respecting it, whether it was potatoes or oranges or fresh killed deer, which often graced the table. Nonna took what she could get and let her magic hands do the rest.*

# Squash Fritters

## Frittelle di Zucca

2 cups grated zuc-
chini (about 3
medium zucchini)

2 large eggs

1 cup whole milk

2/3 cup cornmeal

1/3 cup unbleached
all-purpose flour

Salt and black pepper

1/4 to 1/2 cup canola oil
for frying

*Bake, fry, saute, grill, puree, or shave, there is so much you can do with zucchini. And just when you thought there was nothing else to be done, along comes these delicious grated zucchini fritters. They can stand on their own for lunch or make a great side dish to meat or poultry.* **Serves 4 to 6**

In a large bowl, mix together all the ingredients except the oil.

Heat 1/4 cup of the oil in a 12- to 14-inch nonstick sauté pan over medium-high heat. When the oil starts to shimmer, drop 1/4 cupfuls of the batter into the pan, spacing the batter a couple of inches apart. Fry 3 or 4 fritters at a time. When the fritters begin to brown along the edges, carefully flip them over with a spatula and brown the other side. Transfer them to a dish as you make them and keep them warm in a 200°F oven.

Serve hot as a side dish or simple luncheon dish with a salad.

**TIP:** *Grate the zucchini ahead of time and wrap it in several layers of paper towels. This will absorb the excess water and make for a much crisper tasting fritter.*

# Batter-fried Radicchio Wedges

## Radicchio Fritto

Small heads radicchio, washed and cut into thin wedges, core attached

1 cup unbleached all-purpose flour

1 cup beer

1 large egg, separated

Canola oil for frying

Salt and black pepper

*Radicchio isn't just for salads; try it grilled and sprinkled with coarse salt and a drizzle of olive oil or make these delicious crisp wedges.* **Serves 6**

Cut the radicchio into thin wedges.

Combine the flour, beer, and egg yolk in a bowl and whisk well.

Whip the white to soft peaks and fold it into the batter. Using a heavy duty 2-quart pan or deep fryer, heat 4 cups of oil to 375°F. Dredge the radicchio in the batter, fry it until crisp golden brown. Drain it well on paper towels, season to taste with salt and pepper, and serve hot.

# Devilish Broccoli

## Broccoli al Diavolo

*Broccoli is a much-misunderstood vegetable on the American table but it is revered in Italy. I think it is because the Italians really know the point of no return when cooking it. Overcooking will ruin its flavor but undercooking it will, too. My solution is to forget boiling altogether and simply sauté it. You'll save lots of the nutrients that would otherwise be destroyed by boiling. But the trick is first to look for the freshest tightly closed heads, with no yellow flowers or soft stems. Separating the florets into small bite-size pieces works best for this method. This recipe takes its name,* al diavolo, *from the hot red pepper flakes.*  **Serves 4**

1 medium-size bunch broccoli

¼ cup extra-virgin olive oil

2 garlic cloves, minced

1 teaspoon or more hot red pepper flakes

½ cup dry white wine

Salt

**C**ut off the stem end close to where it meets the florets and discard it or save it for making soup. Turn the head of broccoli upside down on a cutting board and, with a knife, cut the florets into 1-inch pieces. Rinse, dry, and set aside.

Heat the olive oil over medium-high heat in a 12-inch-wide sauté pan. When the oil begins to shimmer, add the garlic and red pepper flakes and swirl them around to flavor the oil. Add the florets and sauté them to evenly coat them with the oil. Raise the heat to high, pour in the wine, and cook 1 minute. Reduce the heat to a simmer, cover the pan, and cook until a knife is easily inserted into the stem end of a floret.

Transfer the florets with a slotted spoon to a bowl and season with salt to taste.

# Carrots in Vermouth

## Carote al Vermouth

*Very rarely have I seen carrots (carote) offered on an Italian menu as a vegetable side dish. They are considered part of* gli odori, *or the the base vegetable along with celery, onions, and garlic that are used to give flavor to many a dish. But I encourage you to try them cooked in vermouth, all on their own.*   **Serves 6 to 8**

6 large carrots
   peeled, quartered,
   and diced

4 tablespoons (½
   stick) unsalted
   butter

1 teaspoon salt

1 tablespoon sugar or
   honey

⅔ cup inexpensive
   white vermouth

¼ cup chopped
   flat-leaf parsley

**P**ut the carrots in a pot with the butter, salt, and sugar. Cook for a few minutes. Add the vermouth and a couple tablespoons water. Cover the pot and stew the carrots until soft, about 10 minutes. Uncover and cook a few minutes more, stirring often until the carrots are glazed. Transfer to a serving bowl and sprinkle with the parsley.

# Mushrooms in Green Sauce

## Funghi al Verde

1 large bunch flat-leaf
   parsley

2 large garlic cloves,
   peeled

2 tablespoons
   unsalted butter

¼ cup extra-virgin
   olive oil

1 pound porcini or
   mixed fresh
   mushrooms,
   stemmed, wiped
   clean with a damp
   cloth, and thinly
   sliced

Salt and black pepper
   to taste

*There I was in the lush forest near St. Helena, California, looking for little earth mounds on the ground—telltale giveaways that porcini mushrooms lurked there. I had just returned from Italy where I had eaten fabulous porcini and I was driven to duplicate the taste at home. It is not often one comes across wild porcini, so any fresh mushroom can be prepared according to this recipe which is called* al verde *because of the use of garlic and parsley.* **Serves 4**

finely mince the parsley with the garlic.

Heat the butter and olive oil in a sauté pan over medium heat. Add the garlic and parsley and cook until the mixture softens.

Add the mushrooms and season with salt and pepper to taste. Stir to combine the ingredients, then cover the pan and allow the mushrooms to cook over low heat for about 7 minutes. Uncover the pan and cook until no liquid remains in the pan. Serve hot.

*TIP: Do not keep mushrooms in plastic bags or plastic containers from the grocery store; the trapped moisture will make slimy mushrooms. Keep mushrooms in brown paper bags and use within 2 days of purchase.*

# Pan-cooked Bitter Greens

## Le Verdure di Campo in Padella

Le verdure di campo *(wild greens)*, piled high in the kitchen sink, is a mental image that I have kept all these years. When I prepare broccoli rabe, dandelions, or mustard greens, I think of Nonna Galasso. She knew how to cook them in many ways from all'agro *(blanched)* with a little olive oil and lemon, ripassate in padella *(pan-fried with garlic, oil, and hot red pepper flakes)*, or as pancotto *(literally, cooked bread)* where cubed pieces of dried bread were added. She often mixed them with spaghetti or poured beaten eggs over them to make a Saturday frittata. **Serves 4**

2 pounds broccoli rabe, or dandelion greens, well rinsed and drained

¼ cup extra-virgin olive oil

2 garlic cloves, cut into slivers

¼ teaspoon hot red pepper flakes, or more to your liking

¾ cup dry white wine

Salt and black pepper

**b**ring a large pot of water to a boil with 1 tablespoon of salt. Add the greens and cook for about 3 minutes. Drain the greens in a colander, squeezing out as much water as possible. Chop them coarsely and set aside.

Heat the olive oil in a 12-inch sauté pan over medium-high heat. Stir in the garlic slivers, pressing on them with the back of a spoon to release their flavor. Do not let them burn. As soon as they look transparent, stir in the red pepper flakes. Add the greens and wine. Lower the heat to simmer and cover the pan. Cook for 3 or 4 minutes. Uncover the pan, season with salt and black pepper, and serve hot.

# Roman-Style Artichokes

## Carciofi alla Romana

*Clusters of plump, violet-tinged artichokes are a definite sign of spring, and when they are in season, my enthusiasm for them runs deep. But many of my fellow cooks stay away from this vegetable because of the time required to prep them. Rather than struggle in the usual way to get at the hairy choke and remove stubborn and prickly leaves, I offer a simpler, gentler way to approach them.* **Serves 4**

4 tablespoons fresh lemon juice

4 large artichokes, washed and drained

1 cup dry white wine

½ cup extra-virgin olive oil

2 tablespoons minced flat-leaf parsley

3 tablespoons minced mint

2 garlic cloves, minced

Coarse salt

Coarsely ground black pepper

**h**ave ready a large bowl of cold water acidulated with 2 tablespoons of the lemon juice.

Trim ¼ inch off the top of each artichoke and the same off the stem.

Peel the stems with a vegetable peeler to remove the outer layer.

Carefully remove the first two outer rows of leaves and trim the thorns on the remaining leaves with scissors.

With a sharp knife, cut the artichoke in half horizontally and use a spoon or melon baller to remove the yellow center leaves and scoop out the hairy choke. As you prepare them, toss them in the bowl of cold water.

Drain the artichokes from the water and place them, cut side down, in the base of a large saucepan. Add the wine, oil, parsley, mint, remaining lemon juice, garlic, and 1½ cups water. Sprinkle with salt and pepper and bring to a boil.

Reduce the heat to low and cook the artichokes, turning them occasionally, until they are tender, 10 to 12 minutes; it should be easy to just pick off a leaf.

Transfer the artichokes to a serving platter and pour any pan juices over the tops. Serve two halves per person.

# Spinach with Garlic and Oil

## Spinaci Aglio e Olio

1 pound fresh
spinach, well
washed, stemmed,
and drained

2 tablespoons extra-
virgin olive oil

2 large garlic cloves,
peeled and sliced
into thin slivers

Fine sea salt

Freshly ground black
pepper

Juice of 1 lemon

*The old cartoon character Popeye ate spinach to make him strong, and my mother used him as a way to get us to eat our spinach. Today I need no coaxing; I am a fan, especially of young tender leaf spinach. When you buy it, be sure there are no yellow or wilted leaves, a telltale sign of old spinach. I like buying loose bunches but spinach in cellophane bags is fine, too, as long as you check the sell by date on the bag. Spinach is dirty so even if the bag says pre-washed, wash it again by submerging the leaves in a bowl of cold water; lift the leaves out by the handful leaving the dirt behind.*

*Cooking spinach could not be easier so I don't know why anyone would buy canned spinach, a ghastly poor imitation of the real thing that even Popeye would never eat and neither should you! The best way to cook spinach is to sauté it with garlic and olive oil.*
***Serves 4***

**U**se a large sauté pan for this even though the spinach will cook down in a flash and almost into nothing more than a cup and a half when squeezed of its water. Add the spinach to the pan, cover, and allow it to wilt down; it won't take very long, less than 5 minutes. Transfer it to a waiting colander in the sink and press on it with a wooden spoon to get out the excess water.

Return the sauté pan to the stovetop, and pour in the olive oil. Add the garlic slivers and over medium heat, swirling, press on the garlic with a wooden spoon to flavor the oil. When the garlic just begins to take on some color, but is not yet brown, return the spinach to the pan and quickly stir it around for 2 to 3 minutes.

Transfer the spinach to a serving dish, add salt and pepper to taste, and toss with the lemon juice.

**Variation:** Add diced, oil-cured olives, pine nuts, or hot red pepper flakes for a change of taste.

***CHEF'S SECRET:*** *Spinach is over 90 percent water so why boil it to add more? There is enough water clinging to the leaves of just-washed spinach for it to cook just fine.*

# Nonna Galasso's Twice-Cooked Cardoons

## Cardi Rifatti alla Nonna Galasso

*Cardoons were one of Nonna Galasso's favorite vegetables; she had a keen eye for finding them wild on the roadsides. To me they looked like dangerous weapons, curled up long stalks with thorns on them. I remember her cleaning them on sheets of newspaper, cutting off the thorns with a knife, stripping the strings off the stalks, and boiling, boiling, boiling them for hours to get out the bitterness. While they cooked, she simmered her homemade tomato sauce in a pan. She added the cardoons to the sauce and cooked them again just until they were heated through. Sprinkled with pecorino cheese, they made a simple meal that reminded her of her homeland. It was worth watching her enjoy them just for that.* **Serves 4 to 6**

2 pounds young cardoons, washed

Juice of 4 lemons, or equal amount of red wine vinegar

1 tablespoon fine sea salt

2 cups canola oil for frying

Unbleached all-purpose flour

3 cups prepared tomato sauce

½ cup grated pecorino Romano cheese

**U**se a knife to remove any small leaves at the top of the stalk. Peel and remove the strings from the stalks. Cut the stalks into 2-inch-long pieces and immediately place them in a bowl in lemon juice to prevent discoloration.

Bring a large pot of salted water to a boil, add the cardoons, and boil them until tender. Depending on how thick and how fresh the cardoons are, this can take from 15 to 30 minutes.

Drain the cardoons in a colander and quickly rinse in cold water to stop the cooking process. Dry on paper towels.

Heat oil in a large sauté pan.

Coat the cardoons in flour and fry them in the oil until lightly browned. Transfer them to paper towels to absorb excess oil.

Heat the tomato sauce in another sauté pan, add the cardoons, and cook gently in the sauce for 5 minutes. Transfer to a serving dish and sprinkle the cheese over the top. Serve hot.

# Chunky Vegetarian Vegetable Stew

2 tablespoons extra-virgin olive oil

1 medium onion, diced

2 celery stalks, minced

3 garlic cloves, minced

1 teaspoon hot red pepper flakes (optional)

4 small eggplants, cut into 1-inch chunks

2/3 cup water

6 plum tomatoes, cut into 1-inch chunks

2 medium zucchini, cut into 1-inch chunks

1 cup frozen corn kernels

2 teaspoons celery seed

1 teaspoon dried oregano

Salt and black pepper

1/2 cup chopped basil

1/2 cup grated Parmigiano-Reggiano cheese

*Many family members make a choice to be vegetarians. That can sometimes discourage the carnivore cook who does not want to have to make two meals to satisfy everyone's dietary preferences. Why not opt for a vegetable stew that everyone would love? The beauty of this stew is that it can also double as a sauce for chunky pasta like rigatoni. No vegetarian tastes to satisfy? How about adding some tiny meatballs!*
*Serves 6*

Heat the olive oil in a 2-quart saucepan and add the onion and celery. Cook until the vegetables soften. Stir in the garlic and red pepper flakes and cook until the garlic softens.

Add the eggplant and the water, cover the pot, and allow the eggplant to soften. Add the tomatoes and zucchini, cover the pot, and cook until the zucchini softens. Stir in the corn kernels, celery seed, oregano, and salt and pepper to taste. Cover the pot and cook for about 3 minutes. All the vegetables should be soft but not mushy. Just before serving, stir in the basil and cheese.

Serve hot in soup bowls.

# Capers from the Black Pearl

Years ago on my first trip to Sicily, I discovered capers. But not just any capers, capers from the island of Pantelleria, which lies south of the western most tip of Sicily, close to Tunisia. It is often referred to as the "Black Pearl of the Mediterranean" because of its black volcanic appearance. The name Pantelleria comes from the Arabic bint-al-rion, meaning daughter of the wind, because gusts sweep through the Channel of Sicily and blow an average 337 days per year on Pantelleria. Wind is a key factor for the low bush growth of several major food products of the island, including capers, olives, and grapes.

Plant scientists from around the world have come to study the hundreds of plant varieties found on the island, and one of the best sources of revenue is the caper bush growing haphazardly out of rocks and crags. In fact in ancient times capers were used as a form of currency among traveling merchants.

The unopened flower bud of the lily-like plant is harvested, cleaned, sorted according to size, and covered in salt. The salt dissolves because of the moisture in the capers, creating brine. They are kept like this for about a week, then the brine is drained from the capers and they are salted again before being exported. Many agree that the capperi in sale di Pantelleria (capers in salt from Pantelleria) are some of the best in the world.

Yet the culinary debate rages on as to whether capers packed in salt or those packed in vinegar brine are better for cooking. My vote is for salt-packed capers, and preferably those from Pantelleria, which have a subtle pungent flavor that delivers great taste, especially for chicken- and fish-based dishes.

Vinegar-brined capers lose much of their flavor in processing and can only deliver a faint taste.

To use capers in salt in cooking, rinse them well to remove the excess salt (although I know many cooks who do not rinse them and instead prefer to minimize the amount of salt that they add to their cooking).

Capers in salt or in brine should be stored in the refrigerator once opened. They will last a long time and are an essential ingredient in such classic dishes as vitello tonnato, caponata, insalata russa, and scaloppine ai capperi.

# Stewed Peppers

## Peperoni in Umido

*My mother often worked at our church fair and one of the classic dishes that brought out long lines of hungry fair-goers was sausage and peppers. I am reminded of this whenever I am at a sagra (festival) in Italy. There peppers will be roasted, stewed, or marinated. I like them stewed and the best way to coax out their sweet flavor is to cook them at a low simmer until they are soft and velvety in texture. This is a perfect side dish for meat or poultry and is especially good with homemade sausage.* **Serves 4**

⅓ cup extra-virgin olive oil

3 anchovies packed in olive oil, chopped

1 medium red onion, peeled and cut into quarters

1 shallot, peeled

2 garlic cloves, peeled

2 tablespoons green peppercorns packed in brine, drained

2 tablespoons salt-packed capers, well rinsed

2 large red bell peppers, cored, seeded, and cut into 1-inch chunks

2 large yellow bell peppers, stemmed, halved, seeded, and cut into 1-inch chunks

10 oil-cured black olives, pitted and halved

Salt and black pepper

2 tablespoons minced flat-leaf parsley

heat the olive oil in a heavy-bottomed 2-quart saucepan over low heat. Add the anchovies and cook until they have almost dissolved in the oil.

Mince together the onion, shallot, garlic, peppercorns, and capers. Add this to the pan and cook over medium heat until the mixture softens.

Add the peppers and coat them with the mixture. If the pan seems dry, add a little more olive oil. Cover the pan and simmer the peppers for 30 to 35 minutes, or until they are very soft but still hold their shape. Stir in the olives, salt, and pepper to taste, and the parsley.

Serve hot or at room temperature.

# Asparagus Molds

## Budinetti di Asparagi

4 tablespoons (½ stick) unsalted butter, at room temperature

2 tablespoons plain bread crumbs

2 tablespoons whole milk

1 cup chicken broth

2 pounds asparagus, ends trimmed

½ teaspoon salt

Freshly ground black pepper

½ cup heavy cream

¼ cup grated Parmigiano-Reggiano cheese

¼ teaspoon freshly grated nutmeg

2 large eggs

Budinetti di asparagi, *little molds of pureed asparagus, cheese, and eggs, are just the right touch for a do-ahead dinner party. You can even make them the day before.*
***Serves 6***

Preheat the oven to 325°F. Grease six 3×2-inch custard cups or ramekins with 2 tablespoons of the butter and set aside.

Place the bread crumbs in a small bowl and mix with the milk; set aside.

Pour the chicken broth into a 12- to 14-inch sauté pan. Add the asparagus and cook, covered, until the spears are tender. Transfer the asparagus with a slotted spoon or skimmer to a dish, draining off any broth.

Reserve 12 whole asparagus spears and keep warm. Cut the remaining asparagus spears into 1-inch pieces. Add the remaining 2 tablespoons of butter to the sauté pan and melt it over medium heat. Add the asparagus pieces and salt and pepper to taste. Cook 1 minute.

Transfer the asparagus pieces to a blender, food processor, or use an immersion blender and puree them until smooth. Add the heavy cream, cheese, nutmeg, eggs, and reserved bread crumbs. Whirl or pulse again until smooth.

Divide and fill the ramekins with the asparagus puree and place them in a 12×9-inch, or similar, baking pan. Pour boiling water into the bottom of the pan to come halfway up the sides of the ramekins. Be careful not to get water into the puree.

Bake for 35 minutes, or until the puree is set. Remove the ramekins from the baking pan and allow to cool for a few minutes. Run a butter knife along the inside edge of each ramekin to loosen the molds.

Invert each mold onto an individual serving dish. Top each with two of the reserved asparagus spears and serve immediately.

# Venetian Tart

## La Torta Veneziana

*Whenever I traveled to Italy, I wrote in my journal what I ate every day, and sometimes I was very surprised. When I got home I would tell my mother about the trip and give her recipes that I reconstructed from my notes and taste buds. Like this savory Venetian tart, made with Asiago cheese, one of the cheeses of the Veneto region. For a flaky crust, grate the butter on a cheese grater. It will blend more readily with the flour.*
**Serves 8**

**DOUGH**

- 2 cups unbleached all-purpose flour
- Pinch of salt
- 6 tablespoons (¾ stick) unsalted frozen butter
- 2 large egg yolks
- 1 tablespoon extra-virgin olive oil
- ⅓ to ½ cup cold water

**FILLING**

- ½ pound pancetta, diced
- 2 leeks, white part only, washed and chopped
- ½ pound button mushrooms, chopped
- 1½ pounds spinach, washed and stemmed
- Salt and black pepper
- 2 large eggs
- 4 ounces Asiago cheese, grated
- ¼ cup toasted pine nuts
- 1 egg yolk, beaten for egg wash

grate butter on the large holes of a stand grater.

Add the flour and salt to the bowl of a food processor and pulse to combine. Add the butter and pulse to mix into dry ingredients and until the butter is in flecks.

In a separate bowl, whisk together the egg yolks, olive oil, and enough of the water to make a dough. Gather the dough into a ball, wrap, and refrigerate for at least 30 minutes.

Cook the pancetta in a 12- to 14-inch sauté pan, and when it begins to render its fat, add the leeks and cook until they soften and begin to brown. Stir in the mushrooms and cook them until they soften and begin to brown. Stir in the spinach and allow it to wilt. Season the mixture with salt and pepper to taste and set aside. Allow the mixture to cool to room temperature. The filling mixture can be made a day ahead.

In a small bowl, whisk together the 2 whole eggs and set aside.

Preheat the oven to 375°F.

Roll out the dough on a lightly floured surface to fit a 9-inch springform or tart pan. Fit the dough in the pan, allowing the excess dough to overhang the edges. Spread the grated cheese on the bottom of the tart shell. Spread the cooled filling mixture over the cheese, and pour the eggs over the filling.

Sprinkle the pine nuts on top. Fold the overlapping dough towards the center like a galette or free-form pie. Brush the dough with the egg yolk.

Bake the tart for 45 minutes, or until the crust is a deep golden brown. Let cool about 8 minutes; release the pan sides. Place on a serving plate and cut into wedges to serve.

# Potato, Zucchini, and Parmigiano Reggiano Cheese Tart

## Tortino di Patate, Zucchine, e Parmigiano-Reggiano

*When I was growing up I could count on the same lunch every Saturday: chicken livers with onions and fried potatoes and zucchini. That memory of Saturday's main fare has always stayed with me. I have since all but given up eating chicken livers and have given potatoes and zucchini a new lease on taste in this easy to make layered tart, no pastry involved. Just an elegant presentation of simple fare.* **Serves 8**

**C**oat a 9 × 3-inch springform pan with 1 tablespoon of the butter and set aside.

Preheat the oven to 375°F.

Place the potato slices in a bowl and toss them gently with the thyme and season with salt and pepper. Set aside.

Cut four zucchini into ¼-inch-thick slices and sauté in the olive oil until lightly browned. Transfer the zucchini to a bowl and stir in the mint leaves. Season with salt and pepper to taste and set aside.

Make 4 alternating layers of potatoes, zucchini, and cheese, dotting each layer with bits of the remaining 4 tablespoons butter.

Bake the tart for 20 to 25 minutes, or until nicely browned on top.

Transfer the pan to a cooling rack. Remove the sides of the springform pan. Place a sprig of mint on the tart. Cut into wedges to serve.

*TIP: Potatoes should be kept in brown paper bags in a cool, not cold, dark place.*

---

5 tablespoons (½ stick plus 1 tablespoon) unsalted butter

4 to 5 medium-size baking potatoes (Russet or Yukon Gold), cooked, peeled, and cut into thin slices

1 large sprig thyme, leaves picked

Salt and black pepper

4 medium zucchini, plus 1 for garnish

3 tablespoons extra-virgin olive oil

3 whole mint leaves, minced

1 cup grated Parmigiano-Reggiano cheese

# Grilled Asparagus
## Asparagi alla Griglia

2 tablespoons extra-virgin olive oil

Grated zest and juice of 1 large lemon

1 tablespoon coarse sea salt

1 pound fresh asparagus, ends trimmed

*One day in Campobasso in the region of Molise, I walked around a football-size field of asparagus (asparagi) with winemaker Alessio di Majo, and we gathered enough pencil-thin stalks for dinner and headed for the kitchen. Alessio likes to sauté his with olive oil and garlic but I think the best way to cook them is to grill them, so we did both. Unless you have your own asparagus patch, you need to be diligent when purchasing them. Look for bright green spears with tight scales at the tip. Open scales are a dead giveaway that this is old stuff. Bend a spear in half; it should have a natural breaking point at the base and make a snapping sound. This easy cooking method proves that some good things should never be tinkered with too much.* **Serves 4**

Preheat the grill.

Combine the olive oil, lemon zest, and coarse salt in a rectangular dish. Carefully toss the asparagus in the mixture and arrange them in a single layer on a large sheet of aluminum foil. Seal the ends of the foil.

Place the package directly on the grill. Cook about 5 minutes, turning the package once.

Serve hot with lemon juice passed on the side.

# Asparagus with Browned Butter

## Asparagi al Burro

*There's an old Roman expression that goes something like this: To get something done do it in the time it takes to cook asparagus. That meant quickly. That is the trick to cooking asparagus. Depending on the thickness of the spears, asparagus cooks in just a few minutes. It should not be mushy and limp but hold it shape and have a bite. My favorite way to cook them is* asparagi al burro, *asparagus served with browned butter. Usually cooked upright in a deep pot, I just put the asparagus in a sauté pan until the spears are still firm but a knife can easily penetrate them. Guild the lily a little bit and serve them with cheese and fried eggs.* **Serves 4**

1 pound asparagus, rinsed and ends trimmed

6 tablespoons (¾ stick) unsalted butter

4 large eggs

Salt and black pepper

⅓ cup grated pecorino or Parmigiano-Reggiano cheese

Place the asparagus in a sauté pan large enough to hold them in a single layer. Cover them with water and sprinkle with a teaspoon of salt. Bring to a boil and cook them just until firm but a knife easily pierces the spears. Drain and set aside on a dish.

Return the pan to the stovetop and add 5 tablespoons of the butter. Over medium-low heat, melt the butter until it begins to brown. Return the asparagus spears to the pan and gently toss them in the butter. Keep warm.

Melt the remaining tablespoon of butter over medium heat in a nonstick medium sauté pan. Crack each of the eggs into the pan and fry until set. Season them with salt and pepper to taste.

Place the asparagus on a shallow platter, sprinkle them with the cheese, and top with the fried eggs. Serve immediately.

**TIP:** *To keep asparagus bright green after cooking, place them in a large bowl of ice water for a minute or two, then drain and pat dry.*

# Salads

Barley Salad

Bean Salad

Chickpea Salad with Black Olives

Tuna and Chickpea Salad

Marinated Carrot, Caper, and Sweet Red
Pepper Salad

Molded Fava Bean and Parmigiano-
Reggiano Cheese Salad

Mixed Mushroom Salad

Nonna Saporito's Reinforced Salad

Roasted Carrot and Beet Salad

Marinated Basil Beet Salad

Russian Salad

Basil-Infused Grilled Fruit Salad

Fruit and Vegetable Salad

Escarole Salad with Oranges, Pears,
and Walnuts

Peach, Prosciutto, and Radicchio Salad
with Honey-Basil Vinaigrette

Sorrel and Fresh Fruit Salad

Watermelon and Strawberry Salad

Pear and Pecorino Cheese Salad

Mom's Summer Tomato Salad

Cardoon and Raisin Salad

Summer Green Bean Salad

Mozzarella Tomato and Salad
with Sorrel

# saving salad service

Salad (*insalata*) used to be the caboose to an Italian meal and was always served *after* the main course, not before it. This custom is fast disappearing in Italy and it is becoming more common today to see many restaurants serving salad with the main course. Often tourists order it as *the* main course, which raises the eyebrows of many Italians to Gothic heights!

Well, why all the fuss in the first place? As long as salads are included in one's diet what difference does it make when you eat it? Well several medical studies have shown that eating salad after the main course can do much to curb your sweet tooth and lessen that craving for dessert. And while modern medical research revels in this finding, it is not new to the Italians. They have been eating salads after their main course for a very long time, even as far back as the 1600s.

Salads will "lighten the stomach so it is not offended by too much food." These words are from the seventeenth-century author, Salvatore Massonio, who wrote a treatise on edible plants called *Archidipno, Ovvero dell' Insalatae dell' uso di essa*. The book contains sixty-eight chapters devoted to salads, dressings, and the seasons for each. But even before all the information on salads was in book form, Italians were eating wild bitter greens that they foraged for in open lands, plucking such things as dandelion greens, chicories, and mustard greens.

The most familiar of the salad greens served on the Italian table was romaine, originally called *cos* by the ancient Romans who are said to have discovered it on Cos (or Kos), a Greek island. The name romaine probably comes from the Romans. This lettuce is an elongated head with dark green, compact leaves. The best part is the inner leaves, which are lighter shades of green and yellow and very crisp. Romaine has a mild flavor and can be mixed with a variety of other raw vegetables or fruits.

Escarole, known as *scarola,* along with endive and radicchio, are also favored bitter greens in the Italian salad bowl. They all belong to the family of chicories. Escarole has sturdy outer green bitter leaves and a pale yellow white center with a milder flavor.

Wild, bitter greens were the survival food of the poorer classes and became a digestive for the rich who found that eating a salad after the indulgences of the main meal helped to calm their digestion. This practice is still adhered to in many areas of Italy and by many Italian Americans.

# Barley Salad

## Insalata d'Orzo

2 cups water

½ cup uncooked hulled whole or pearled barley

¼ cup minced flat-leaf parsley

½ cup grated carrot

½ cup diced cucumber

½ cup diced provolone cheese

1¼ teaspoons dried oregano

½ cup shredded radicchio

4 tablespoons extra-virgin olive oil

Juice of 1 large lemon

Salt

4 to 6 large beefsteak tomatoes

*The use of barley (orzo) dates to the Stone Age and is possibly the oldest grain in the world. Adaptable and strong, it grows on both frigid mountaintops and in blistering desert heat. Though barley has been used as a staple grain for millions of years, its main use today is for animal feed and for making beer and whiskey.* *Serves 4–6*

bring the water to a boil in a large saucepan and add the barley. Cover, reduce the heat, and simmer until tender. Drain and rinse with cold water. Transfer to a large bowl.

Stir in the parsley, carrot, cucumber, cheese, oregano, radicchio, olive oil, lemon juice, and salt. Mix to combine and set aside.

Cut off the tops of the tomatoes and reserve. Hollow out the pulp, cube it, and add it to the bowl with the barley mixture.

Stuff the tomato cavities with the barley mixture and replace the tops. Serve or refrigerate until needed. Bring to room temperature before serving.

# Bean Salad

## Insalata di Fagioli

*Fresh beans, dried beans, canned beans—they all figure prominently in the Italian diet as a great source of protein and fiber. One of the only concessions made at home to anything canned was chickpeas and cannellini beans, which were impossible to find fresh. If I had a nickle for every time my grandmothers lamented their loss of fava beans, I would have quite a stash of coins. But they made do and, as with so many things they made, original tastes of the old country were altered by what was available to them like this cannellini and chickpea salad which was great on a hot summer's day.*  *Serves 8*

One 15½-ounce can cannellini beans, rinsed and drained

One 15½-ounce can chickpeas, rinsed and drained

1 pint (about 2 cups) cherry tomatoes, halved

1 small red onion, finely chopped

½ cup extra-virgin olive oil

4 tablespoons red wine vinegar

Salt

¼ cup chopped mint

Place all the ingredients except the olive oil, vinegar, salt, and mint in a shallow rectangular glass or ceramic dish.

In a small bowl, whisk together the olive oil, vinegar, salt to taste, and mint. Pour the dressing over the bean mixture and toss well to combine. Cover and allow to marinate at room temperature for several hours before serving.

# Chickpea Salad with Black Olives

## Insalata Marinata di Ceci e Olive Nere

One 15½-ounce can chickpeas, drained and rinsed

1 small red onion, halved and thinly sliced

½ cup pitted and chopped oil-cured black olives

⅓ cup extra-virgin olive oil

¼ cup red wine vinegar

Fine sea salt

Freshly ground black pepper

¼ cup minced mint

*My mother adored chickpeas and had cans of them stacked in her pantry for all kinds of dishes. She always said that if you had a can of chickpeas, you had dinner like the* zuppa di ceci *on page 63. One of her classic dishes was marinated chickpea salad with mint, onions, and black olives. Mom used canned black olives but I prefer oil-cured.*
*Serves 4*

In a salad bowl, toss together the chickpeas, onion, and olives.

In a small bowl, whisk together the olive oil, vinegar, and salt and pepper to taste.

Pour the dressing over the salad and toss well. Taste and correct seasoning, if needed. Sprinkle the mint over the salad and toss again.

# Tuna and Chickpea Salad

## Insalata di Tonno e Ceci

*Tuna and chickpea salad is an amazing and pleasant experience for your taste buds because so many flavors pop at once. And the best part is that this salad can be ready in a flash if all the ingredients are on hand. This is a great summertime salad to serve for a picnic.* **Serves 4 to 6**

Place the tuna in a bowl and flake it with a fork. Add the artichoke hearts, chickpeas, fennel or celery, onion, capers, and parsley.

Toss the ingredients well. Pour the olive oil over the ingredients and toss. Sprinkle the vinegar over the salad and toss again. Taste and add additional salt, if necessary. Serve at room temperature.

Two 6-ounce cans tuna packed in olive oil

1 teaspoon coarse sea salt

1 jar marinated artichoke hearts, drained and cut into small pieces

1 cup canned chickpeas, rinsed and drained

½ cup diced fennel or celery

½ cup diced red onion

2 tablespoons salt-packed capers, well rinsed, dried, and minced

¼ cup minced flat-leaf parsley

⅓ cup extra-virgin olive oil

2 tablespoons white balsamic vinegar

# Marinated Carrot, Caper, and Sweet Red Pepper Salad

## Insalata di Carote, Capperi, e Peperoni

*Carrots are usually utilized in the Italian kitchen as part of a* battuto, *a mince of flavorful vegetables like celery, onion, and garlic that form the base dish. Here is a marinated carrot and red pepper salad that is as refreshing as a breezy summer's day.*
*Serves 4*

Combine all the marinade ingredients in a 12 × 9-inch rectangular glass or ceramic dish. Mix well. Set aside.

Fill a 12- to 14-inch sauté pan three-quarters full with water. Add the carrots and 1 tablespoon salt. Bring to a boil and cook until a knife tip easily pierces the carrots. Drain in a colander and transfer them to the dish with the marinade. Toss well.

Add the bell pepper strips and fennel and toss again. Let stand at room temperature for at least 1 hour, tossing occasionally to meld the flavors. Just before serving toss the salad with the parsley and mint.

Serve at room temperature.

**MARINADE**

⅓ cup extra-virgin olive oil

1¼ teaspoons salt

Freshly ground black pepper

1 tablespoon minced garlic

¼ cup red wine vinegar

2 tablespoons salt-packed capers, well rinsed

**SALAD**

4 large carrots, washed, peeled, and cut into 2-inch-long matchstick pieces

1 tablespoon salt

2 large sweet red bell peppers, cored, seeded, and cut into thin, 2-inch-long strips

1 cup thinly sliced fennel bulb

¼ cup minced flat-leaf parsley

2 tablespoons minced mint

# Molded Fava Bean and Parmigiano-Reggiano Cheese Salad

## Insalata di Fava e Parmigiano Reggiano

1 cup shelled fava beans

2 celery stalks, diced

2 tablespoons diced red onion

1 tablespoon minced scallions

2 tablespoons minced tarragon

3 tablespoons extra-virgin olive oil

1 tablespoon white balsamic vinegar

Salt

2²/₃ cup grated Parmigiano-Reggiano cheese

*Nothing says spring like the arrival of the first crop of fava beans (a.k.a., broad beans) now making their presence known in the produce department. These long sturdy pods hide brilliant green, flat, oval "beans" that resemble lima beans. They have been a staple food worldwide for centuries but do not seem to get their day in the culinary sun here probably because it is a mystery to many as to what to do with them.*

*Fava beans are a great source of iron, magnesium, potassium, zinc, copper, and selenium. I love them raw, but there are so many ways to prepare them from just boiling them and tossing them with olive oil and salt to pureeing them for a nutty tasting spread on good bread to serving them with pasta or marinating them for this dynamite and impressive-looking salad good enough for company.* **Serves 4**

Cook the fava beans in 3 cups of boiling salted water until the outer skin slips off easily. Drain and place in a bowl. Add the celery, onions, tarragon, olive oil, vinegar, and salt to taste. Toss to combine well. Cover and marinate at least 2 hours.

Meanwhile, heat a 10- or 12-inch nonstick sauté pan with sloping sides over medium heat.

Spread ²/₃ cup of the cheese in the pan and shape it into a 9 × 3-inch strip. Cook until the cheese begins to bubble and melt and turns a golden brown. Slip the cheese out of the pan onto a wooden cutting board and while it is still warm, wrap it around a 2-inch diameter juice glass or jar and press the ends together. Place the glass or jar on its side, seam side down, on a cutting board. When cool, slip the cylinder off the glass and set aside. Continue making three more cheese cylinders.

When ready to serve, place each cylinder on an individual salad plate and carefully fill each with some of the fava bean mixture.

# Mixed Mushroom Salad

## Insalata di Funghi Misti

*Mushrooms (funghi) are like gold to the Italians and every fall mushroom hunters go in secret to their favorite gathering places far into the misty woods to pluck such beauties as porcini, ovuli, and gallinaccio mushrooms. I get my fill of them when I am in Italy but at home I imitate the taste of those mushrooms by making an earthy salad with a variety of mushrooms like oyster, shiitake, and cremini. If none of these is available, use all button mushrooms. The success of this salad depends on slicing the mushrooms as paper thin as possible and using a good extra-virgin olive oil.* **Serves 4**

½ pound button or mixed mushrooms, stemmed, caps wiped clean with damp paper towels

1 cup thinly sliced celery

¼ cup minced flat-leaf parsley

Freshly ground black pepper

½ cup extra-virgin olive oil

1 teaspoon coarse sea salt

Shavings of Parmigiano-Reggiano cheese

Place the mushrooms in a salad bowl with the celery, parsley, and black pepper. Pour the olive oil over the mixture and toss again.

Spoon the mushroom mixture onto a serving platter. Sprinkle the salt and the shavings of cheese over the top.

# Nonna Saporito's Reinforced Salad

## Insalata Rinforzata alla Nonna Saporito

1 small head cauliflower, cored, stemmed, and florets cut into uniform small pieces

½ cup pitted and diced green or black oil-cured olives

1 cup coarsely chopped fennel bulb

2 tablespoons minced red onion

½ cup diced sweet red bell pepper

¼ cup chopped flat-leaf parsley

2 tablespoons salt-packed capers, well rinsed

1 cup diced plum tomatoes

1 cup canned chick-peas, drained and rinsed

⅔ cup extra-virgin olive oil

2 garlic cloves, minced

5 tablespoons red wine vinegar

Salt

*Nonna Saporito made the most wonderful "reinforced" vegetable salad, especially at Christmastime. It was called* rinforzata *because once it was served, and if any was left over, more vegetables were added to the bowl to give it new life and it was served the next day . . . and the next . . . It was a salad with no end!*   *Serves 6 to 8*

**b**ring a large pot of water to a boil and add 1 tablespoon of salt. Add the florets and cook for 2 minutes. Drain the florets and transfer them to a large salad bowl.

Add all the other ingredients except the olive oil, garlic, red wine vinegar, and salt.

In a small bowl, whisk together the olive oil, garlic, vinegar, and salt to taste. Pour the dressing over the vegetables and toss well.

Cover the salad and allow it to marinate at room temperature for at least 30 minutes before serving, tossing the ingredients occasionally. Or make the salad and refrigerate it overnight. Bring to room temperature before serving. If any salad is left over, reinforce it by adding new ingredients like cucumbers, celery, radishes, carrots, and broccoli. Refrigerate and serve the next day.

# Salad, Roman Style

I like how the ancient Romans thought when it came to making a salad, and I have posted their advice on my refrigerator. I think you should, too. There are four things needed when making a salad:

1) A wise man (or woman) to add salt (because too much is not a good thing); salt was expensive in ancient Rome and used as a form of payment for Roman legions.
2) A miser to add the vinegar (because you can overdo it on the taste end); vinegar is strong so a little goes a long way.
3) A spendthrift to add the oil. (You need more oil than vinegar usually in a ratio of 3 to 1 in order to balance the overall taste of the dressing.)
4) A madman to mix it all together. (Tossing well is the key to well-coated greens.)

# Roasted Carrot and Beet Salad

## Insalata di Carota e Barbabietola

8 carrots, peeled and sliced diagonally ½-inch-thick and 1-inch-long

⅓ cup plus 2 tablespoons extra-virgin olive oil

Salt and black pepper

2 sprigs thyme

4 medium yellow or red beets, peeled and cut into ¼-inch rounds

2 garlic cloves, minced

Grated zest of 1 orange

2 tablespoons orange juice

1 tablespoon balsamic vinegar

1 medium head arugula or romaine lettuce, washed, dried, and torn into bite-size pieces

*Root vegetables form the basis for this colorful roasted carrot and beet salad.*
*Serves 6 to 8*

Preheat the oven to 400°F.

Toss the carrots in a bowl with 1 tablespoon of the olive oil, salt and pepper to taste, and 1 tablespoon thyme leaves. Transfer them to rimmed baking sheet in a single layer. Cover with a sheet of aluminum foil and set aside.

In the same bowl used to toss the carrots, toss the beets with salt and pepper to taste, 1 tablespoon of the olive oil, and 1 tablespoon thyme leaves. Transfer them to a separate rimmed baking sheet in a single layer. Cover with a sheet of aluminum foil and set aside.

Place the baking sheets in the oven and roast the vegetables until tender, about 30 minutes for the carrots and 45 to 50 minutes for the beets. Uncover and cook 5 minutes longer.

Meanwhile, combine the remaining ⅓ cup olive oil, garlic, orange zest and juice, and balsamic vinegar in a bowl and whisk the ingredients together until well blended. Add salt to taste.

Arrange the carrots and beets on a platter on a bed of arugula or romaine and drizzle the dressing over the top and serve.

# Marinated Basil Beet Salad

## Insalata di Bietole e Basilico

⅓ cup extra-virgin olive oil

3 tablespoons rice wine vinegar or white balsamic vinegar

1 large shallot, peeled and thinly sliced

1 garlic clove, minced

1 teaspoon celery salt

1 tablespoon sugar

8 large beets, cooked, peeled, and cut into thin rounds

½ cup chopped arugula

½ cup torn basil leaves

Fine sea salt

*This refreshing, marinated beet salad will even win over those who do not like beets. Instead of boiling or roasting the beets, cook them in the microwave in half the time.*
*Serves 6*

In a rectangular glass or ceramic dish, whisk together the oil, vinegar, shallot, garlic, celery salt to taste, and sugar.

Add the beets and toss to combine in the marinade. Cover and marinate at least 1 hour at room temperature. Just before serving toss the mixture with the arugula and basil. Add salt if more needed, and serve.

*NOTE: Do not use metal bowls to marinate acidic foods; they could react with the metal and give an off taste.*

# Russian Salad

## Insalata Russa

Insalata Russa, *or Russian salad, is very popular in Italy and in the eighteenth century was known as* Insalata Genovese *because it is said that it was served for the Ligurian aristocracy for gala dinners. Other legends claim that the Piedmont region of Italy invented this salad when Russian aristocracy came to visit. It is composed mainly of vegetables and mayonnaise and can be served as an antipasto as well as a salad. It is often found on Italian tables at Christmastime. There are many variations on this salad.* Serves 4

2 large red or Yukon Gold potatoes, scrubbed

4 medium carrots, scraped and diced

1 cup peas

4 hard-boiled eggs, 2 cut into small pieces and 2 cut into quarters

¼ cup minced flat-leaf parsley

4 sweet cucumber pickles, diced

½ cup diced green or black olives (Cerignola or even small Gaeta)

2 tablespoons salt-packed capers, well rinsed

1 cup low-fat mayonnaise

Salt and black pepper

Cook the potatoes in the microwave on high power until a knife easily pierces them. Cool, peel, and dice. Place the potatoes in a bowl.

Add the carrots to the potatoes along with the peas, eggs, parsley, cucumber pickles, olives, and capers. Gently fold in the mayonnaise and salt and pepper to taste.

Line a 1-quart glass bowl with plastic wrap leaving an overhang. Fill the bowl with the salad, pressing it firmly. Cover the top of the bowl with the overlapped plastic wrap, and refrigerate the salad for at least 2 hours.

When ready to serve, unwrap the salad and invert it onto a round platter. Decorate the top with egg slices and a dollop of mayonnaise.

NOTE: *The salad can also be formed in individual ramekins.*

# Basil-Infused Grilled Fruit Salad

## Frutta Fresche Grigliate

*This lovely-to-look-at and even-better-to-eat grilled fruit salad is just right as the finale to a summer supper. What is unique about it is the infusion of fresh basil syrup.*
*Serves 4*

Combine the water and sugar and salt in a small saucepan and cook until the sugar is completely dissolved and the mixture is clear and syrupy, about 5 minutes. Turn off the heat, add 8 of the fresh basil leaves, and allow them to steep in the syrup for 10 minutes. Strain the liquid and set aside. Discard the basil leaves.

Combine the lime juice and honey and set aside.

Preheat the grill.

Place the fruit halves, cut side down, directly on the grill and brush with the lime-honey mixture. Allow the fruit to cook until a few char marks appear. Transfer the fruit to a cutting board and cut into ¼-inch-thick slices. Combine the slices in a bowl and toss with ¼ cup of the basil-infused syrup.

Transfer the fruit mixture to individual fruit cups. Pour some of the remaining syrup into each cup, and garnish with a fresh basil leaf.

1 cup water

1 cup sugar

Pinch of salt

12 large basil leaves

Juice of 2 limes or lemons

2 tablespoons warm honey

3 large red or purple plums, halved, stone removed

3 nectarines, halved, stone removed

3 apricots, halved, stone removed

## Mix It Up

*They say that variety is the spice of life, and so it is with the daily salad bowl. Italians enjoy a salad every day, combining various salad greens like escarole, radicchio, romaine, and oak leaf lettuce. This keeps the tastes and textures interesting, so why not move away from predictable iceberg lettuce and enjoy these favorites:*

BUTTERHEAD. A creamy green head lettuce with red coloring on tender leaf tips. It is known in Italy as quattro stagione or *four seasons lettuce.*

ENDIVE. The elongated tender white leaves of Belgian endive add a nice crunch to salads. It is also called indivia.

ESCAROLE. A sturdy leafy green with a slightly bitter taste, escarole holds up well to dressing and is known in Italy as scarola. The outer leaves are often steamed or used in soups while the creamy white inner leaves are used for salad.

FRISÉE. A curly lettuce with long, lacey leaves that is also called curly endive. It adds texture to a salad.

MISTICANZA. These mixed cutting lettuces add variety to a salad.

OAK LEAF. A type of butter lettuce that does not keep more than 2 to 3 days, its leaves are tender, curly, and crisp. There are red and green varieties.

RADICCHIO. The starlet of the salad bowl, there are many varieties of this mildly bitter tasting chicory. The red leaves with white veining adds visual appeal as well as delicious taste. The most popular radicchio is the round head Verona variety but there is also the lesser-known elongated radicchio di Treviso variety.

# Fruit and Vegetable Salad

## Insalata di Frutta e Verdure

*Here is an interesting fruit and vegetable salad, not one that my grandmother or mother would recognize but something more in the realm of* alta cucina *these days.*
*Serves 6*

Place all the ingredients, except the grapefruit and orange segments, in a salad bowl and toss well. Add the segments and gently toss again.

1 English cucumber, peeled and thinly sliced into rounds

1 small fennel bulb, thinly sliced

6 large escarole leaves, washed, dried, and torn into small pieces

3 tablespoons extra-virgin olive oil

Fine sea salt

2 grapefruits, peeled and segmented

1 blood or navel orange, peeled and segmented

# Escarole Salad with Oranges, Pears, and Walnuts

## Insalata di Scarola con Arance, Pere, e Noci

*We enjoy a green salad every night at our house after our main course; it's tradition. I try to vary the ingredients to keep it interesting. Escarole (scarola) is one of my husband's favorites. He loves the sturdy leaves and slightly bitter taste. I usually dress it with nothing more than olive oil and vinegar and some grains of coarse salt, but every now and then I depart from tradition, adding blood or navel oranges, pears, and walnuts. Sometimes you just need to mix it up!* **Serves 4 to 6**

In a jar, combine the olive oil, vinegar, and salt to taste and shake well.

Combine the escarole, oranges, and pears in a salad bowl. Toss to combine. Pour the dressing over the salad ingredients and toss well.

Sprinkle the walnut pieces over the top and serve immediately.

*NOTE: Believe it or not tossing the salad for several minutes instead of just a quick toss will yield a much better taste.*

5 tablespoons extra-virgin olive oil

3 tablespoons white balsamic or rice wine vinegar

Salt

1 head escarole, leaves separated, well washed, dried, and torn into bite-size pieces

2 blood or navel oranges, peeled and segmented

2 ripe Bosc pears, cored and cut into thin slices

½ cup walnut pieces

# Watermelon and Strawberry Salad

## Insalata di Cocomero e Fragole

*Italians love to cool off with hunks of juicy watermelon (cocomero), and maybe they would find it just as delicious in this summer salad that I concocted one blazing August day.* *Serves 4*

Combine the watermelon, avocado, strawberries, and red onion in a salad bowl. Sprinkle with salt. Drizzle some olive oil over the top, and toss the ingredients gently. Sprinkle the crumbled feta cheese over the salad and serve immediately.

2 cups cubed watermelon

1 large avocado, cubed

2 cups sliced strawberries

1 sweet red onion, thinly sliced

Fine sea salt

Extra-virgin olive oil

½ cup crumbled feta cheese

# Pear and Pecorino Cheese Salad

## Insalata di Pera e Pecorino

4 tablespoons extra-
virgin olive oil

2 tablespoons white
wine vinegar

Salt

2 cups washed and
dried arugula
leaves

4 ripe Bosc pears,
peeled, cored, and
cut into ½-inch-
thick slices

¼ pound pecorino
cheese with black
peppercorns, cut
into thin slices

¼ cup golden raisins

¼ cup toasted pine
nuts

*This nontraditional Italian salad was inspired by an old Italian saying that goes like this: "Don't tell the farmer how good the cheese is with the pears," referring of course to pecorino cheese. So why not combine them in this simple salad.* **Serves 4**

In a small bowl, whisk together the olive oil, vinegar, and salt to taste and set aside.

Place the arugula in a salad bowl and add the pear slices. Pour the dressing over the salad and toss gently. Add the cheese and toss again. Sprinkle over the raisins and pine nuts.

# Mom's Summer Tomato Salad

## Insalata di Pomodori alla Mamma

*My dad always came home for lunch during the week since his office was close by. I guess you could say that he was spoiled because my mother was such a fantastic cook. She made everything from scratch so why should he brown bag it? I always marveled at the fact that with seven children, Mom never tired of the three-meals-a-day routine. If she did she never said anything. Anyway, when Dad's tomatoes were coming in, she would make him this tomato salad, which I also crave. Not only were the tomatoes the best ever, but the homemade bread that she served them with was her signature triumph in the kitchen. It was a great marriage: homemade bread and homegrown tomatoes. The salad is best made several hours in advance.* **Serves 4**

In a rectangular glass or ceramic dish, combine the olive oil, wine vinegar, sugar, parsley, garlic, oregano, and salt to taste. Stir with a wooden spoon to really mix the ingredients well. Lay the tomatoes over the dressing in a single layer or just slightly overlapping. Cover the dish with plastic wrap and allow to marinate at room temperature for several hours before serving. Occasionally spoon the dressing over the tomatoes as they sit.

Serve with slices of bread and *fare la scarpetta*, which means to use the bread to soak up the tomato juices. Pure heaven!

½ cup extra-virgin olive oil

4 tablespoons red wine vinegar

1 tablespoon sugar

2 tablespoons minced flat-leaf parsley

1 garlic clove, peeled and finely minced

1 teaspoon dried oregano

Salt

4 gorgeous beefsteak-type tomatoes, thinly sliced

Slices of good artisan or homemade bread

# Cardoon and Raisin Salad

## Insalata di Cardi e Uva Passa

1 pound cardoons, washed

2 garlic cloves, minced

6 tablespoons extra-virgin olive oil

4 tablespoons chopped raisins

Pinch of ground cinnamon

Fine sea salt

*Here's a very different salad from Sardinia using cardoons and raisins. It is a favorite of my Sardinian friends, Mario and Giulia Cocco. Cardoons are an old variety vegetable in the artichoke family that seems to have gone out of favor because they are a bit time-consuming to prepare, but I think it is worth bringing them back.* **Serves 4**

Use a knife to remove any small leaves at the top of the cardoon stalk.

Peel and remove the strings from the stalks. Cut the stalks into 2-inch-long pieces and immediately submerge them in a bowl of water and lemon juice to prevent discoloration.

Bring a large pot of water to a boil, add the cardoons, and boil them until tender. Depending on how thick and how fresh the cardoons are, this can take from 15 to 30 minutes.

Drain in a colander and quickly rinse in cold water to stop the cooking process. Dry on paper towels.

In a rectangular glass or ceramic dish, combine the garlic, olive oil, raisins, cinnamon, and salt. Add the cardoons and turn them in the oil mixture. Cover and allow to marinate several hours at room temperature before serving.

# Summer Green Bean Salad

## Insalata di Fagiolini

*I am always thinking of new ways to serve green beans, trying to add a twist to the more classic recipes. In this case, Nonna Galasso always made green beans dressed in a vinaigrette of olive oil, garlic, vinegar, and fresh mint, and I love it. But in this version, I have added roasted cherry tomatoes, hot red peppers, pine nuts, and strips of Parmigiano-Reggiano cheese. Make the salad a couple of hours ahead of time to allow the flavors to develop. Unforgettable! A salad that really sings of the best that summer has to offer.* **Serves 8**

2 tablespoons plus ¼ cup extra-virgin olive oil

1 pint cherry tomatoes, halved horizontally

3 tablespoons balsamic vinegar

1 teaspoon sugar

2 pounds green beans, ends trimmed

1 small red cherry pepper, seeded and diced

2 garlic cloves, minced

Salt and black pepper

⅓ cup toasted pine nuts or walnut pieces

¼ cup minced mint

Shavings of Parmigiano-Reggiano cheese

Preheat oven to 350°F.

Brush a baking sheet with 2 tablespoons of the olive oil and add the cherry tomatoes, cut side down. Sprinkle them with the balsamic vinegar and the sugar and bake for about 7 minutes, or until they soften and begin to caramelize. Remove them from the oven and transfer them to a serving platter.

Meanwhile, cook the beans in plenty of salted boiling water in a large pot until fork-tender. Drain well and add to the platter with the tomatoes. Add the minced cherry pepper, garlic, and salt and pepper to taste. Toss well. Drizzle the salad with the remaining ¼ cup olive oil and toss again.

Sprinkle the salad with the nuts and mint and top with the cheese shavings. Serve at room temperature.

*TIP: Want to keep the green color in green beans? Then use plenty of water to cook them in so the acids can leach out, and do not cover the beans while cooking.*

# Mozzarella and Tomato Salad with Sorrel

## Insalata di Bocconcini di Mozzarella, Pomodorini e Acetosella

½ cup extra-virgin olive oil

Salt

1 pound tiny mozzarella balls, drained, halved

1 pint (about 2 cups) best cherry tomatoes like Sweet One Hundreds, halved

1 cup sorrel leaves, shredded

*Sorrel, that perennial lemon-tasting herb with leaves that resemble fresh spinach, is one of my favorite plants in the herb garden. And even though it is not something that Italians use to any great degree in their cooking, I like to use it raw in green salads and also pair it with cherry tomatoes and tiny mozzarella balls for a refreshingly delicious summer salad.* *Serves 4 to 6*

In a salad bowl, combine the olive oil and salt to taste. Gently mix in the mozzarella and tomatoes, coating them well with the oil. Add the sorrel leaves and toss again.

*NOTE: Sorrel plants are available in greenhouses and, once planted, will last for years. It is one of the last herbs to give in to cold weather, lasting long into fall.*

# Desserts

Buttermilk Chocolate Cake

Almond Paste Cheesecake

Dried Prune Cake

Easter Lamb Cake

Fig and Grape Cake

Florentine Flat Cake

Fudgy Chocolate Cake with Walnuts
and Cream Sauce

Mom's Chiffon Cake with Lemon Curd

White Lemon Cake

Vignola's Secret Chocolate Cake

Fresh Plum Tart

Neapolitan Easter Pie

Glazed Strawberry Tart

Upside-down Peach Tart

Pear and Pastry Cream Tart

Almond Paste Cookies

Little Hazelnut Cookies

Mom's Dried Cherry, Cranberry, and
Pistachio Nut Shortbread Cookies

Little Orange-scented Madeleines

Mom's Date Nut Bars

Dried Apricot Bars

Fat Tuesday Puffs

Golden Puffs

Powdered Sugar Strips

Nonna Saporito's Cannoli

Pugliese Sweet Ravioli

Pizzelle

Chocolate-Dipped Figs

# my mother's recipe box
· · · · · · · · · · · · · · · · · · · · · · · · · · ·

In my first book, *Ciao Italia*, I said that my mother never took a shortcut with anything. From cooking to caring for my grandmother and our large extended family, Mom always went the extra mile. Her favorite thing to do though for relaxation (when she could get it), was to bake. And I mean bake everything from fabulous fruit pies to delicate cream puffs and light and fluffy doughnuts, all from scratch! Everyone who knew her declared her the queen of exquisite cakes, master baker of delicate cookies, champion bread maker, and more. Mom was very serious about the ingredients she used for baking even to the point of driving to Canada from Buffalo, New York, to buy Canadian flour because she considered it superior to any other flour. She would purchase fifty-pound sacks that were loaded into the trunk of the car for the trip back home. The sacks were stored in an unheated room to keep them fresh. She would go through them in no time.

One of the things that I am most grateful for are the recipes that she passed on in her faded, dog-eared notebooks and in her old wooden recipe box chock-full of splattered handwritten recipes. When I read through them, vivid memories surface of my mother mixing dough in her old Mixmaster at her butcher-block baking center in one corner of the kitchen and I want to rush into my kitchen and re-create that taste of home and of a time gone by when homemade meant "I really care about you."

When the holidays roll around and it's time to bake cookies, I go through those old notebooks and that recipe box like they were the family jewels to retrieve my favorites. Her date nut bars bring back memories of my lugging boxes of them home on the plane for my husband Guy because he once told her that they were his favorites. Her dried cherry cookies always remind me of how I snatched them out of the gleaming tins she kept them in for Christmas giving. Her dried apricot bars remind me of a family trip that we took to Montreal and how we wound up staying overnight at a complete stranger's home because the hotels were full. In the morning, we shared the apricot bars that Mom had made and packed for us to have on the trip with our new French Canadian friends whose bedrooms we had occupied the night before. Her hazelnut cookies remind me of the bushels of Italian cookies she made for my wedding, making sure that there was enough for each guest to take a plateful home. And so it seems that each recipe in my mother's recipe box had a story connected to it, and that is, for me, a treasure.

# Buttermilk Chocolate Cake

## Torta di Cioccolato al Latticello

7 ounces good-quality semisweet chocolate, broken into pieces

1 cup (2 sticks) unsalted butter, softened

2 cups granulated sugar

4 large eggs

2¼ cups sifted unbleached all-purpose flour

1 teaspoon baking soda

½ teaspoon salt

1 cup buttermilk

1 tablespoon pure vanilla extract

Confectioners' sugar

Half-and-half

A few fresh raspberries

A few mint leaves

*My mother was fascinated with buttermilk; she drank it for health but she also loved to bake with it because it gave richness and moistness to rolls, quick breads, and cakes. This chocolate cake was my favorite and the one Mom always made when my birthday rolled around. It was a big cake that she liked to bake in a decorative Bundt or tube pan.* **Makes 1 cake; serves 8 to 10**

Preheat the oven to 350°F.

Coat a 9¼ × 4½-inch Nordic Ware festive cake pan, Bundt, or tube pan with nonstick cooking spray or butter.

Fill the bottom of a double boiler one-third full with water and bring to a simmer. Turn off the heat. Place the top pan of the double boiler over the bottom and add the chocolate to the pan. If you do not have a double boiler, place a glass bowl over a saucepan of simmering water; the bottom of the bowl should not touch the water.

Let the chocolate sit until it begins to melt, then stir it with a wooden spoon until it is completely melted. Do not allow any water to get in the chocolate or it will seize and clump and you will need to start over.

In a stand mixer fitted with the paddle attachment, cream the butter with the sugar on medium speed until light and lemon colored. Beat in the eggs one at a time until well blended. On low speed blend in the melted chocolate.

In a bowl, sift together the flour, baking soda, and salt. Slowly beat the flour mixture into the egg mixture in three additions, alternating with the buttermilk. Stir in the vanilla.

Pour the batter into the prepared pan and bake for about 1 hour or until a cake tester inserted in the center comes out clean. My Nordic Ware pan took 1 hour.

Cool the cake for 20 minutes in the pan, then unmold it and place on a wire rack to cool completely.

When completely cool, sift confectioners' sugar over the top or make a glaze with confectioners' sugar and a little half-and-half and pour it over the cake. Garnish with raspberries and mint leaves.

**NOTE:** *Pure extracts must be 35 percent alcohol, otherwise they are labled "imitation."*

# What Is Buttermilk?

Buttermilk is actually the liquid left over from the butter-making process. Acidic, and sour in flavor, it often has bits of butter floating in it and that is how it got its name. Old-fashioned buttermilk, much thinner and more acidic than cultured buttermilk, is widely used in many parts of the world but is difficult to find in the states. Instead we have what is called "cultured" buttermilk, made by fermenting milk, which causes the sugars in the milk to become lactic acid. The milk proteins become solid and the result is a thick, milkshake consistency liquid.

Cultured buttermilk is created by fermenting milk so that milk sugars turn into lactic acid, causing milk proteins to become solid, as they are no longer soluble. Cultured buttermilk is more tart than regular milk because of its increased acidity. Buttermilk lasts longer than regular milk, because the acidic conditions keep bacteria from growing.

In a pinch, buttermilk can be made by adding 1 tablespoon white vinegar or fresh lemon juice to 1 cup whole milk; stir and allow to stand for 10 minutes until thickened. Use in recipes calling for buttermilk. There is also a powdered version available in the baking section of most grocery stores.

# Almond Paste Cheesecake

## Torta di Mandorle

16 amaretti cookies,
 or other firm plain
 butter cookie

⅓ cup whole
 almonds

2 tablespoons plus ½
 cup sugar

1 teaspoon grated
 orange zest

⅓ cup unsalted
 butter, melted

1 cup almond paste,
 cut into small bits

1 pound ricotta
 cheese, well
 drained

4 large eggs

1 cup light cream or
 ⅓ cup buttermilk
 and ⅔ cup half-
 and-half

¼ cup unbleached
 all-purpose flour

¼ teaspoon salt

Amarena cherries in
 syrup (see Note)

*My mother never craved desserts unless it was cheesecake, and she was critical of the ones that passed her lips. It had to be a dense New York–style cheesecake or else! But when I made this almond paste version, she gave me two thumbs up. This cake is moist with a nice texture and not too sweet. It's a keeper.* **Makes one 9-inch cake**

Preheat the oven to 350°F.

Lightly coat a 9-inch springform pan with nonstick cooking spray.

Process the cookies and almonds to fine crumbs in a food processor. Transfer the crumbs to a bowl and stir in the 2 tablespoons sugar, orange zest, and butter. Press the mixture into the bottom and up the sides of the prepared springform pan.

Bake the crumb crust for 12 minutes, or just until the edges begin to brown. Remove from the oven and cool for 10 minutes.

Lower the oven temperature to 325°F.

In the bowl of a food processor or stand mixer filled with the paddle attachment, process or beat the almond paste with the ricotta cheese. Add the eggs one at a time, blending well after each addition. Add the ½ cup sugar and the cream, flour, and salt and blend well.

Pour the filling into the cooled crumb crust.

Bake the cake until the filling is set, 45 to 50 minutes. Cool completely.

Cut into wedges and serve with amarena cherries in syrup drizzled over the top, or top with sliced fresh strawberries and whipped cream.

*NOTE: Amarena cherries in syrup are available in Italian speciality food stores or online.*

# Dried Prune Cake

## Torta di Prugna Secca

*Here is an unpretentious but delicious cake that my mother often made for company. She always had dried prunes on hand and could whip this up in no time. She served it plain with a veil of confectioners' sugar dusted over the top, but a dollop of whipped cream would be heavenly, too.* **Makes one 10-inch cake**

**P**reheat the oven to 375°F.

Coat a 10 × 2-inch round cake pan with butter or nonstick cooking spray. Line the pan with a piece of parchment paper cut to fit, and butter or spray again.

Place the prunes in a medium saucepan. Add 2 tablespoons of the granulated sugar, the orange zest, and wine. Stir to combine. Cover the pan and simmer the prunes until all the wine has been absorbed. Set aside.

In a bowl, using an electric mixer, cream the butter and the remaining ½ cup plus 2 tablespoons of the sugar until light and fluffy. Add the egg yolks one at a time and beat until smooth.

In another bowl, sift together the flour, baking powder, and salt. Add the dry ingredients to the yolk mixture and beat gently to combine.

In a separate clean bowl, beat the whites into soft peaks and fold them into the batter.

Pour the batter into the prepared pan. Arrange the prunes on top and bake for 45 minutes to 1 hour, or until the cake is golden brown. The prunes will sink into the batter.

Cool the cake on a wire rack. Dust with confectioners' sugar, or glaze. Or serve with whipped cream.

1 cup dried, pitted prunes

¾ cup granulated sugar

Grated zest of 1 large orange

½ cup dry red wine

6 tablespoons (¾ stick) unsalted butter

3 large eggs, separated

¼ cup heavy cream

1 cup plus 2 tablespoons unbleached all-purpose flour

3¼ teaspoons baking powder

¼ teaspoon salt

Confectioners' sugar for dusting or glaze (optional)

# Easter Lamb Cake

## Torta di Agnello

**CAKE**

2 cups cake flour

¾ teaspoon baking powder

⅛ teaspoon nutmeg

¼ teaspoon salt

1 cup (2 sticks) unsalted butter

1 cup granulated sugar

2 teaspoons grated lemon zest

1 teaspoon grated orange zest

1 tablespoon vanilla extract

1 teaspoon almond extract

4 large eggs

½ cup finely ground almonds

**FROSTING**

½ cup solid vegetable shortening

8 tablespoons (1 stick) unsalted butter, softened

8 cups confectioners' sugar

1 tablespoon almond extract

Currants

Almond confetti

*If you find yourself in Italy at Easter, brace yourself! It has always been a holiday bigger than Christmas and one that is celebrated for days! One of my fondest memories is of the pastry shop windows displaying almond flavored lamb cakes. They are adorable and the centerpiece of the Italian table for* Pasqua *(Easter). At home I carry on the tradition using my mother's lamb cake mold. Molds are available in kitchen and cake supply stores.* **Makes 1 cake**

Preheat the oven to 350°F. Coat a 10×4-inch, two-piece lamb cake mold well with butter and dust it with flour. Set aside.

Sift together the flour, baking powder, nutmeg, and salt in a large bowl.

In the bowl of a stand mixer, beat the butter and sugar until pale yellow. Beat in the zests, and vanilla and almond extracts. Beat in the eggs one at a time. Then gradually beat in the flour mixture. Fold in the nuts.

Spoon the batter into the bottom half of the mold. Place the top half of the mold over the bottom half, making sure the fit is even. Bake for 40 to 45 minutes.

Carefully lift off the top of the mold and test the cake. If it is still soft in the center, bake about 10 to 15 minutes longer, or until firm, without replacing the mold top. A cake tester inserted in the center should come out clean. Transfer the cake to a rack to cool completely.

To make the frosting, in a bowl beat the shortening and butter until smooth. Gradually beat in the sugar. Beat in the almond extract. The frosting should be firm enough to pipe through a pastry bag.

Carefully loosen the cake from the sides of the mold by running a butter knife around the inside edges and carefully remove the cake. Let it cool completely.

Spread a thin layer of frosting on the cake stand base or serving plate. This will "glue" the cake in place. Place the cake on the frosting and make sure it is secure.

Fill a pastry bag fitted with a medium star tip with frosting and squiggle the frosting all over the cake to simulate wool. Use the currants for eyes and sprinkle almond confetti along the lamb's back and at the base of the cake to give it a festive look. Tie a ribbon carefully around the lamb's neck. To serve, cut the cake into thin slices.

## A Day for Lambs and Chocolate

*It all started on Ash Wednesday as soon as Monsignor Bernardo raised his thumb and made a cross on my forehead with black ashes and reminded me that I was nothing but dust. For a teenager, thinking about dust was the furthest thing from my mind. But Mom and Nonna Galasso took the season of Lent very seriously, which meant that for the next forty days, they would be in a somber mood with endless trips to church where the monsignor recited penitential prayers while showering his flock with pungent smelling incense that left the congregation in a murky fog. To me those forty days meant only one thing—no sweets until Easter!*

*By the last week of Lent things started to look up as Mom and Nonna started making Easter specialties. Out came the lamb cake mold to make the almond-flavored cakes that were just like the ones displayed in the* pasticerria *(pastry shop) windows in Italy. Out came the big round tin (almost the size of a foot stool) used to make the* torta Pasqualina, *savory pastry pie that was filled with ham, cheese, eggs, and salame. Out came the pie pans for making* pastiera, *Neapolitan rice pie. And out came the baking sheets for forming* ciambelle, *those braided Easter breads with colorful eggs tucked into the dough. I loved the egg part because my job was to color them!*

*After forty days of such dinner fare as tuna casserole, baccalà, squid with spaghetti, and endless vegetable and cheese frittatas, I was definitely ready for some fun eating. And since we were a large extended family, Mom always took it upon herself to make lamb cakes for all her brothers and sisters and, of course, Monsignor Bernardo.*

*The week before Easter, Mom made Dad a long list of ingredients she would need from the store for all her baking. Flour, eggs, butter, almond extract, at least four bags of jelly beans (I will explain), and four pounds of coconut! I think she was obsessed with that lamb cake mold, and she dutifully made eight separate batters and filled that mold eight separate times!*

*What emerged from the oven was a sturdy flock—eight sitting lamb cakes huddled on cooling racks while tubs of confectioners' icing laced with almond extract were made. One by one we frosted those lambs; I liked to make squiggles with a pastry bag to simulate wool; other times I covered the lambs in snowy white* coconut "fur." Black jelly beans became eyes, a pink jelly bean became a mouth, and a rainbow colored row of them ran along the backs of each one. Purple ribbons around their necks were the finishing touch as they sat on green straw. The flock was ready for the big giveaway.

Dad and I delivered them to my aunts and uncles so they could have them for their table centerpieces. The monsignor always pinched me on the cheek when I delivered his.

After the deliveries, Dad stopped at Antoinette's homemade chocolate store to buy what he always bought for Easter, a two-foot high solid chocolate Kewpie doll that reminded me of the cartoon character, Betty Boop.

Dad was a shrewd shopper, always analyzing what was the best deal for the money. He examined chocolate rabbits, ducks, and chicks like a scientist, which of course, he was. So it made perfect sense when he said that there was no reason to pay good money for several hollow chocolate bunnies or chicks when one big solid one would go much further in terms of how many people could enjoy it! So Kewpie, who was as solid as they come, and wrapped in clear shiny cellophane, came home with us and stood tall on the dining room table, a pink bow atop her head.

Easter was finally here and dinner, a huge feast of roast lamb, spring peas, rosemary-scented potatoes, stuffed artichokes, and torta Pasqualina kept us at the dinner table for hours. How we had room for lamb cake, Neapolitan rice pie, and chocolate is still a mystery to me but the image of my father taking a meat mallet at the end of the meal, and smashing that darling Kewpie doll into edible chunks, is one of my fondest memories of Easters gone by.

# Fig and Grape Cake

## Torta di Fico e Uva

*Fresh figs are addictive eating for Italians; and make the best dessert. But when they are out of season, there are always dried figs to munch on or to add to desserts like this delicious country-style cake.*   ***Makes one 9-inch round cake***

**b**utter a 9 × 2-inch cake pan and line the bottom with a piece of parchment paper cut to fit. Butter the paper. Set aside.

Place the quartered figs in a bowl and toss with the orange liqueur or orange juice. Let stand 10 minutes.

Preheat the oven to 350°F.

Sift the flour, baking powder, baking soda, and salt into a bowl. Set aside.

In a separate bowl, whisk together the eggs, sugar, and olive oil. Fold in half the flour mixture until well blended. Add half the buttermilk and stir in. Add the remaining flour mixture and fold in, then stir in the remaining buttermilk.

Add the figs and their liquid and fold in well.

Pour the batter into the cake pan. Press the grapes into the batter.

Bake 45 minutes, or until the cake is nicely browned and a cake tester inserted into the center comes out clean.

Cool the cake on a cake rack until it reaches room temperature. Run a butter knife along the inside edges of the pan and invert the cake onto a cake plate.

Remove and discard the parchment paper. Serve the cake plain, or with a dollop of whipped cream or a sprinkling of confectioners' sugar.

**NOTE:** *If using whipped cream, pipe it out along the side of the cake and add a whole dried fig for garnish.*

**TIP:** *Not a fig lover? Substitute dried peaches, nectarines, or apricots.*

---

15 dried Calimyrna figs, stemmed and cut into quarters (1 cup quartered)

¼ cup orange liqueur or orange juice

2 cups cake flour

1½ teaspoons baking powder

½ teaspoon baking soda

⅛ teaspoon salt

4 medium eggs

½ cup sugar

⅓ cup extra-virgin olive oil

½ cup buttermilk

1 cup whole seedless red grapes

# Florentine Flat Cake

## Schiacciata alla Fiorentina

¾ **cup unbleached all-purpose flour**

¼ **teaspoon salt**

1 **teaspoon baking powder**

2 **large eggs**

½ **cup granulated sugar**

¼ **cup extra-virgin olive oil**

⅔ **cup whole milk**

**Zest of 2 oranges**

*Besides all the heirloom recipes from home, I am always on the lookout in my travels to Italy for new recipes like this easy-to-prepare schiacciata (flat cake) from Florence that has an interesting moist texture, and pleasant orange taste. As the name implies, this cake is only about a half inch high after it bakes. Cut it into squares, or rounds, or use cookie cutters for a more festive look.* **Makes one 11½ x 7½-inch cake to be cut into squares**

Preheat the oven to 325°F.

Lightly butter a 11½ × 7½-inch baking pan and set aside.

In a bowl, sift together the flour, salt, and baking powder. Set aside.

Beat the eggs and sugar together in another bowl with a handheld mixer until foamy and thick. On low speed, beat in the olive oil and milk. Stir in the orange zest.

On low speed, beat the flour mixture into the egg mixture until the batter is smooth. It will be the consistency of pancake batter.

Pour the mixture into the prepared pan and bake for 35 to 40 minutes, or until the cake springs back when touched in the center with your finger.

Transfer the pan to a wire rack to cool completely. When cool, turn the cake out onto a serving plate. Cut into squares, or other shapes.

This cake is delicious as is, but for a festive look, sprinkle the top completely with confectioners' sugar. Also try it accompanied with fresh fruit.

## Flour Power

Flour is a very complex thing. Use the wrong flour in a recipe and the results can be disastrous. There are many types of flour; in this book I have used King Arthur unbleached all-purpose flour, as well as King Arthur cake flour blend for many of the recipes. All-purpose flour has a higher-protein content; it is a hard wheat flour with enough gluten forming ability to allow for easy kneading of dough for bread and pasta.

Cake flour on the other hand would not be suitable for making bread or pasta because it is a lower-protein flour. For cakes and pastry, you want to avoid gluten development, which would make cake texture tough and pastry dough too hard. In some cases, high-protein flour can be used for cakes such as pound cakes, fruitcakes, or other dense type cakes. But for sponge cakes, chiffon cakes, and angel food cakes, where a tender crumb is the objective, use cake flour.

Keep in mind that in Italy, flours are measured by weight, not volume. To do this at home invest in a kitchen scale. But if you do not have a scale, then get into the habit of using the "sprinkle and sweep" method of measuring flour. To measure flour by the sprinkle and sweep method, lightly spoon the flour into a measuring cup with a spoon until the flour is over the rim of the measuring cup. Using a butter knife, sweep off the excess flour so that it is even with the rim. Now you have a true cup of flour, which can weigh anywhere from 3.5 to 4 ounces, depending on the type of flour.

Use dry measures (stainless steel and plastic) for measuring dry ingredients such as flour and sugar and use glass measures for measuring liquids. If you keep these simple rules in mind, then you will avoid using too much flour in a recipe and in the case of pasta or bread, you will find the dough a delight to work with.

As a rule I buy flour by the twenty-five pound bag because I go through it very quickly. If you find that a five-pound bag of flour lasts you forever then I suggest that you keep it in the refrigerator once it is opened to keep it fresh, and to avoid it becoming rancid. Flour can also be frozen; just remember to bring it to room temperature before you use it.

Following these few rules will ensure happy results in all you bake from cookies to cakes and bread and pasta.

# Fudgy Chocolate Cake with Walnuts and Cream Sauce

## Torta al Cioccolato con Panna e Noci

**CAKE**

2 cups walnut halves

8 tablespoons (1 stick) unsalted butter

3 ounces semisweet chocolate, broken into small pieces

3 large eggs

½ cup sugar

¼ teaspoon salt

Zest of 1 large orange

1 tablespoon plus 1 teaspoon vanilla extract or orange liqueur

**SAUCE**

3 tablespoons unsalted butter

2 tablespoons unbleached all-purpose flour

¾ cup heavy cream

3 tablespoons sugar

Pinch of salt

*For special occasions I turn to this wonderful fudgy and dense chocolate cake with a smooth and dreamy cream and walnut sauce. My inspiration for it comes from the city of Perugia (home of Perugina chocolate and Baci candy), where the annual chocolate festival, Eurochocolate, is held every year in October. Every conceivable chocolate fantasy is displayed from around the world.* **Makes one 9-inch round cake**

Preheat the oven to 325°F. Butter a 9 × 1½-inch round baking pan. Line the pan with parchment paper cut to fit the bottom of the pan and lightly butter the paper.

Place the walnuts in a medium sauté pan over low heat and stir them until they smell fragrant. Do not let them burn. Set aside to cool. Transfer 1⅓ cups of the cooled nuts to a food processor and process them until coarsely ground. Set aside.

Melt the butter in a bowl in the microwave or in a small saucepan. Stir in the chocolate and mix until smooth and well blended. Set aside.

Beat the eggs and sugar in a medium bowl with a handheld mixer until the mixture thickens. Stir in the salt, orange zest, and 1 tablespoon of the vanilla extract or orange liquor. Stir in the ground walnuts, then stir in the chocolate and pour the mixture into the prepared pan.

Bake the cake for 30 to 35 minutes, or until a cake tester inserted in the center comes out clean. Do not overbake. The cake should remain moist. Cool the cake in the pan for 30 minutes.

Run a dull knife along the inside edge of the pan to loosen the cake. Invert the cake onto a cooling rack. Discard the parchment paper. Invert the cake onto a plate.

To make the sauce, melt the butter in a saucepan and stir in the flour. Cook for 1 minute, until the paste is smooth and well blended. Slowly pour in the cream and stir in the sugar and salt. Cook the mixture over medium heat until the sauce is smooth and thickened. Remove the sauce from the heat and stir in the remaining ⅔ cup toasted walnuts and 1 teaspoon of vanilla extract or orange liqueur.

To serve, cut the cake into wedges and pour some of the sauce over the top.

# Mom's Chiffon Cake with Lemon Curd

*Popular in the fifties and sixties, a chiffon cake is delicious and light. There is no butter in this cake; it uses oil, and beaten egg whites and baking powder provide the leavening. It differs from a sponge cake in that a sponge cake uses oil and is butterfree but relies on egg yolks for fat. It usually needs no other embellishment, but for a special occasion I like to fill it with a lemon curd. To make the assembly easy, make the curd a couple of days ahead of time.* **Makes one 10-inch cake; 1¾ cups lemon curd**

**t**o make the lemon curd, combine the lemon or lime juice, zest, sugar, butter, and salt in the top of a double boiler. Cook, stirring constantly, over medium heat until the butter melts and the sugar no longer feels gritty in the bottom of the pan. Slowly pour in the eggs, stirring continually with a spoon or whisk, and cook until the mixture thickens and coats the back of a spoon. Transfer the curd to a small bowl. Cover and refrigerate for several hours or overnight.

Preheat the oven to 350°F.

To make the cake, mix together the flour, sugar, baking powder, and salt in a large bowl.

Make a well in the center of the dry ingredients and add the oil, egg yolks, water, vanilla extract or orange liqueur, and orange zest. Beat until smooth with a whisk or handheld mixer.

In a clean bowl, whip the whites with the cream of tartar until soft peaks form. Fold the beaten egg whites into the egg yolk mixture.

Pour the batter into a 10-inch ungreased tube pan. Bake for 55 minutes or until a cake tester inserted in the center of cake comes out clean. The cake should look golden brown and be firm to the touch.

Immediately remove cake from the oven and prop upside down placing the open funnel part of the tube pan over a wine bottle. This allows the cake to cool without collapsing. When cool to the touch, run a butter knife around the inside edges of the pan and remove the cake from the pan. Set aside on a wire rack.

## LEMON CURD

- ½ cup fresh lemon or lime juice (about 4 lemons or 6 large limes)
- 1 tablespoon grated lemon or lime zest
- 1 cup plus 2 tablespoons sugar
- 3 tablespoons unsalted butter, cut into bits
- ¼ teaspoon salt
- 4 large eggs, lightly beaten with a fork
- ½ cup heavy cream

## CAKE

- 2¼ cups sifted cake flour
- 1½ cups sugar
- 3 teaspoons baking powder
- 1 teaspoon salt
- ½ cup vegetable oil
- 5 eggs, separated
- ¾ cup water, at room temperature
- 1 tablespoon vanilla extract or orange liqueur

*(cont'd)*

**2 tablespoons grated orange zest**

**½ teaspoon cream of tartar**

**Confectioners' sugar for dusting**

When ready to fill the cake, whip the cream until it is stiff, then fold it into the lemon curd.

To fill the cake, split it horizontally into 2 layers using a serrated knife. Spread the curd between the layers.

Dust the top of the cake with confectioners' sugar and cut with a serrated knife to serve.

# White Lemon Cake

## Torta Bianca al Limone

*This unassuming, delicate white cake can be dressed up for a party with a fluffy frosting, or take on a country look with a simple glaze. It is also good with fresh fruits or ice cream. It was one of my mother's standby cakes for birthdays, holidays, and any other time a cake was called for.*   **Makes one 9-inch cake**

**P**reheat the oven to 350°F. Butter a 9 × 2-inch round cake pan. Line the bottom of the pan with a piece of parchment paper cut to fit and butter the paper. Set aside.

Using a handheld mixer, cream the butter with the sugar in a large bowl until light and well blended. Blend in the zest and juice. Set aside.

In another bowl, sift together the flour, salt, and baking powder. Add the dry ingredients to the butter mixture and beat in with the milk. The batter will be thick. Set aside.

In a clean bowl with clean beaters, beat the egg whites until soft peaks form; do not overbeat or they will be too dry and too hard to fold into the batter.

With a rubber spatula, fold the whites by thirds into the batter. Scrape the batter into the prepared pan.

Bake the cake for 50 minutes, or until it is golden brown and a cake tester comes out clean when inserted in the center.

Transfer the cake to a cake rack to cool. Meanwhile make a glaze. Mix the juice and sugar together in a medium bowl until smooth.

Remove the cake from the pan, and peel away and discard the parchment paper. Place the cake on a serving plate and spread the glaze over the cake.

### CAKE

- 15 tablespoons (1 stick plus 7 tablespoons) unsalted butter, softened
- 1¾ cup sugar
- Zest and juice of 1 large lemon
- 3¼ cups unbleached all-purpose flour
- ½ teaspoon salt
- 1½ teaspoons baking powder
- ¾ cup whole milk
- 6 large egg whites

### GLAZE

- Juice of 1 lemon
- ⅔ cup confectioners' sugar

# Vignola's Secret Chocolate Cake

## Torta Barozzi

Mention Torta Barozzi *in the town of Vignola, just outside of Modena, and the residents there will start to argue about what ingredients go into this sinfully delicious chocolate cake named after their native son, Giacomo (or Jacopo) Barozzi, a famous Renaissance architect credited with designing the spiral staircase among other accomplishments. Ironically he never finished the last step on the staircase. Pastry chef Eugenio Gollini created the Torta Barozzi in his Vignola* pasticceria *(pastry shop) in 1897 and named it in Barozzi's honor. The ingredients for this cake have been a well-kept secret all these years. I was very curious about them, and when I traveled to Modena, I was determined to find out what the secret ingredient was. This much I did know; this is a dense, flourless chocolate cake flavored with rum, coffee, and almonds and something else. After much research, I have to conclude that* aceto balsamico tradizionale *(the famous balsamic* condimento *of Modena) is the secret, and a very expensive, ingredient. Do not try and make this cake using balsamic vinegar from the grocery store; it is nowhere near the same thing. Nor do I expect you to buy a bottle of* aceto balsamico tradizionale di Modena. *Substitute a flavoring of your choosing if you do not have or want to purchase the real thing (just don't expect this cake to taste the same).*

*Some important points before you begin: use high-quality semisweet chocolate, beat the sugar and egg yolks very well, do not overbeat the egg whites, and most importantly, do not overbake the cake. It should remain moist and a bit "wet" when a cake tester is inserted into the center. This cake delivers every taste sensation of a moist, fudgy texture, punctuated with the crunchiness of the ground almonds, a meringue-like top, and the sweet and smooth taste of* aceto balsamico tradizionale.

**Makes one 9-inch cake; serves 8 to 10**

**C**oat a 9 × 2-inch springform pan with butter or nonstick cooking spray. Dust with cocoa, tapping out the excess. Place a sheet of parchment paper cut to fit in the bottom of the pan. Butter or spray the paper. Set the pan aside. Or, you can line the pan with a sheet of dampened parchment paper, allowing the excess to overhang the sides.

Preheat the oven to 350°F.

### CAKE

- 1 cup sliced almonds, toasted
- 7 tablespoons (1 stick less 1 tablespoon) unsalted butter
- 9 ounces bittersweet chocolate, cut into small pieces
- 4 large eggs, separated
- 1 cup sugar
- 2 tablespoons balsamic condimento (*aceto balsamico tradizionale di Modena*) or flavoring of your choice
- ¼ cup strong coffee

### TOPPING

- 1 tablespoon sweet ground cocoa (see Note)
- 2 tablespoons confectioners' sugar or almond-flavored confectioners' sugar

Grind the almonds to a powder in a food processor. Set aside.

Melt the butter and chocolate in a bowl set over simmering water. Do not let the bottom of the bowl touch the water.

In a bowl, beat the yolks and sugar until lemon colored and very fluffy; stir in almonds, chocolate mixture, balsamic condimento, and coffee. Set aside.

In a separate bowl with clean beaters, beat the egg whites until soft peaks form. Fold into chocolate mixture. Pour the mixture into prepared pan.

Bake the cake for 30 to 35 minutes, or until cake tester inserted in the center is slightly damp.

Remove pan from the oven and set on a wire rack. Cool completely. When cool, carefully run a butter knife along the inside edges of the pan and release the spring. Remove the pan sides.

Place the cake on a serving plate. Combine the cocoa and confectioners' sugar in a small sieve and dust the top of the cake.

Cut the cake into thin wedges to serve.

**NOTE:** *Ghiardelli makes a good sweet cocoa.*

# La Ca' dal Non

The town of Vignola, in the province of Modena, is an agricultural area with miles and miles of espalier pear, peaches, apple, and prune trees. It's most famous for moretta cherries, which were not in season when I had traveled there. I was there to film a segment with Mariangela Montanari, a young woman who has followed in her family's tradition of making the most famous product of the region, prized aceto balsamico tradizionale di Modena, balsamic vinegar.

"Look for a sign that reads: la ca' dal non," she had telephoned, and when I spotted it, it took some time for me to translate it from Italian dialect into English. It means "grandfather's house." Mariangela is the fourth generation of her family to make aceto balsamico tradizionale and manage the acetaia, the vinegar attic, a sacred place where it is kept and aged in a variety of wooden barrels. Her grandfather started the small production so the name made perfect sense, and she proudly explained that she received her own personal barrels of vinegar when she was a baby, because it was a tradition in years past for girls to receive them as part of their bridal dowry.

Traditional balsamic vinegar is one of the oldest products of Modena and Reggio Emilia, and can only be produced in those areas. Some culinary scholars believe that the Romans were the first to make it from cooked grape juice to which honey was added. They called it saba. The first documented proof of the famed elixir's production shows up in the eleventh century when the German emperor Henry II, traveling to Rome for his coronation, made a stop in Piacenza. Upon meeting Boniface the Marquis of Tuscany, he asked about special vinegar that he had heard of. It seems that royalty considered balsamic vinegar to have healing properties and it was often found on their tables. Back then it was called aceto vecchio, meaning old vinegar. The use of the word balsamico, meaning aromatic, started during the seventeenth century.

Many oral traditions surround this vinegar's history, and its fame spread far and wide in Italy. To make it, strict rules must be followed, and only Trebbiano and Lambrusco grapes from the area of Modena and Reggio Emilia can be used. The unfermented grape juice, or must, is cooked in stainless steel vats to around 190 degrees for about thirty-six hours. The juice is transferred into a series of wooden barrels of varying woods, including chestnut, oak, cherry, chestnut, ash, juniper, and mulberry. A minimum of three different types of wood must be used. The transformation to balsamic vinegar begins with alcoholic fermentation, then oxidation, and aging in the acetaia. During the long process, the liquid takes on a deep mahogany color and complex flavors. The vinegar must age a minimum of twelve years, although many are aged much longer. Makers like Mariangela do not have access to the vinegar once it leaves the barrel. It is sent directly from the factory to a consortium, a governing body that determines if the vinegar is worthy to be bottled and given the name aceto balsamico tradizionale. What the consortium is looking for is a good balance of visual density, color, flavor, clarity, smell, and acidic intensity. If the consortium gives its approval, the vinegar is put into specially designed bottles, sealed, and given a number. Then it is sent back to the factory where it was made and the maker's label is affixed.

I told Mariangela that there was much confusion in the States as to what is real balsamic vinegar. Supermarkets sell wine vinegar that has a snitch of balsamic vinegar added. These are referred to as commercial or industrial (industriale) and bear no resemblance to those in Modena and Reggio Emilia. Aceto balsamico tradizionale is a trademarked name and can only be used in reference to the consortium issued vinegars that have gone through rigorous steps of production and are deemed worthy enough to bear the name.

Besides the consortium approval and name, one can recognize the real McCoy by the shape of the squat bottle with a rectangular base for Modena and the more bulbous and longer necked one for Reggio Emilia. Modena's bottle label bears the words: Aceto Balsamico Tradizionale di Modena and Reggio Emilia's: Consorzio Produttori of Aceto Balsamico Tradizionale di Reggio Emilia. Reggio Emilia makes three grades: oro (gold) which is aged over twenty-five years, argento (silver) aged from twelve to twenty-five years, and aragosta (lobster) aged a minimum of twelve years. The gold label is the most expensive, followed by silver and then lobster.

Mariangela gave me soft slippers to cover my shoes before ascending into the acetaia to avoid contamination. I felt like I was going into a chapel. As soon as we began the climb up the ladder, I could detect that familiar sweet and sour smell of the vinegar. The attic was small, dark, and airy. Over each barrel's square opening is a small piece of cloth called a teglia, important to keep dust out and allow evaporation to occur.

*Finally it was time to sample this fine elixir that historically has sent kings searching and swooning. If made right, the taste is sweet and sour at the same time, the liquid has a syrupy texture, and a rich, shiny dark brown color. With a long, thin glass instrument that looked like a meat baster, Mariangela drew out a few precious drops for me to taste. It went down easy like a precious port and I savored every complex nuance of this amazing product. Don't think of using it to just dress a salad;* aceto balsamico *tradizionale is considered a* condimento, *a condiment, not vinegar as we think of it. A few drops over chips of Parmigiano-Reggiano cheese are a traditional way of enjoying it at the end of a meal. A few drops sprinkled on cooked meats brings a whole new taste dimension, and adding a drop or two to fruit salads gives them a savory sweetness and even underripe fruits such as strawberries get a great taste lift from a few drops. Forget hot fudge sauce over vanilla ice cream,* aceto balsamico tradizionale *is much better!*

*Mariangela told me that on June 24th, the feast of Saint John, a contest is held each year in Spilamberto, a town not far from Vignola, where the best balsamic vintages are judged. Prizes are given for the best ones. Making* aceto balsamico tradizionale *is serious business for Mariangela, and she should be proud of carrying on the tradition in* la ca' dal non.

# Fresh Plum Tart

## La Torta di Susina Fresca

### CRUST

2 cups unbleached all-purpose flour

¾ cup sugar

½ teaspoon salt

¼ teaspoon baking powder

8 tablespoons (1 stick) cold unsalted butter, cut into bits

### FILLING

6 to 8 large fresh red or purple plums, halved, pitted, and cut into ¼-inch-thick slices

Juice of 1 lemon

¼ cup coarse white sugar

½ teaspoon ground cinnamon

¼ teaspoon ground cloves

⅓ cup sliced almonds

2 large egg yolks

1 cup heavy cream

*One of Mom's summertime traditions was to pile us all in the car for a trip to nearby fruit orchards where we happily picked whatever fruits were in season. She was partial to plums and canned them for winter use, but also turned them into tart-sweet plum sauce for pouring over vanilla ice cream and this heavenly plum tart that I still make today. No one ever believes me when I say that this unconventional crust is one of the best you'll ever eat and there is no hassle with rolling out pastry dough.* **Makes one 9-inch tart**

Preheat the oven to 400°F. Butter a 9-inch, fluted tart pan with a removable bottom and set aside.

To make the crust, combine the flour, ½ cup of the sugar, the salt, and baking powder in a bowl. Cut in the butter with a pastry blender or fork until the mixture looks powdery.

Dump the mixture into the tart pan and pat it out evenly, making sure to fill in the fluted sides as well. Set aside.

Toss the plum slices with the lemon juice and the remaining ¼ cup sugar and arrange the slices on the crust in an overlapping pattern filling the entire surface.

Combine the coarse sugar, cinnamon, cloves, and almonds in a small bowl and sprinkle evenly over the top of the plums.

Place the tart on a rimmed baking sheet.

Bake the tart for 15 minutes.

Meanwhile, in a small bowl, whisk the egg yolks with the heavy cream. Slowly pour the mixture evenly over the top of the tart and bake 30 minutes longer, or until the top is golden brown. (You may have a little cream mixture left over.)

Remove the tart from the oven and cool on a wire rack for 10 minutes. Carefully remove the sides. Cut the tart into wedges and serve warm.

# Neapolitan Easter Pie

## Pastiera

### PASTRY DOUGH

2½ cups unbleached all-purpose flour

½ cup cake flour

1 teaspoon salt

⅔ cup sugar

10 tablespoons (1 stick plus 2 tablespoons) cold unsalted butter, cut into bits

1 extra-large egg plus 2 egg yolks, lightly beaten

5 to 6 tablespoons ice water

### FILLING

1 cup wheat berries, covered with cold water and soaked overnight

2 cups whole milk

One 3-inch-long piece of vanilla bean, split lengthwise

1 pound fresh whole-milk ricotta cheese

3 large eggs

2 tablespoons grated orange zest

1 cup sugar

1 tablespoon vanilla extract

*Pastiera means only one thing: classic Easter wheat pie from Naples, and making it was a tradition that was very important to Nonna Galasso. No Easter table was complete without several of them. Over the years, pastiera's ingredients have been tinkered with a lot. The wheat berries have given way to rice, the orange flower water to other flavorings, and the citron replaced with raisins.* **Makes one 9½-inch pie**

Spray a 9½-inch springform pan with nonstick cooking spray. Set aside.

To prepare the dough, mix the all-purpose and cake flours, salt, and sugar in a food processor or bowl. Add the butter to the flour mixture and pulse to blend if using a food processor, or use a pastry blender or fork to blend the ingredients by hand.

Add the eggs and pulse or mix them in by hand. Add just enough ice water to make a dough that is soft and not dry. Do not overmix the dough or it will be tough.

Gather the dough into a ball and wrap it tightly in plastic wrap. Chill the dough for 30 minutes.

To prepare the filling, drain the wheat berries in a colander and put them in a medium saucepan. Pour in the milk and, using a small paring knife, scrape the seeds from the split vanilla bean into the saucepan. Bring the mixture to a boil. Lower the heat to medium-low and continue cooking until the wheat berries absorb all the milk, about 10 minutes.

Transfer the wheat berries to a bowl. In another large bowl, beat together the ricotta cheese, eggs, zest, and sugar until smooth. Stir in the vanilla extract and cinnamon. Fold in the wheat berries and candied orange rind. Set the mixture aside.

Preheat the oven to 375°F.

Roll out two-thirds of the dough on a lightly floured surface into a 14-inch circle. Line the pan with the dough and trim the edges even with the top. Scrape the wheat berry filling into the pan.

Roll out the remaining one-third of the dough into a 12-inch square using a pastry cutter, cut the dough into ¾-inch wide, lengthwise strips. Place the strips about ½ inch apart over the filling to make a lattice top. Trim off the excess dough, making sure the edges are sealed. (Leftover dough can be re-rolled and cut with cookie cutters, sprinkled with cinnamon and sugar, and baked.)

Bake the pie on the middle rack of the oven for 40 to 50 minutes, or until the top is golden brown and a cake tester comes out clean when inserted into the center. Cool the pie on a rack, then carefully remove the sides of the pan and place the pie on a decorative serving plate. Cut into wedges to serve.

**TIP:** *Try soaking the wheat berries 2 days before.*

1½ teaspoons ground cinnamon

1 cup candied orange peel

# Glazed Strawberry Tart

## Torta di Fragole

**DOUGH**

½ cup sliced almonds

1¼ cups unbleached all-purpose flour

¼ teaspoon salt

¼ cup sugar

Grated zest of 1 lemon

7 tablespoons (1 stick less 1 tablespoon) unsalted butter, frozen and grated

1 whole egg plus 1 egg yolk, lightly beaten

½ teaspoon almond extract

2 tablespoons strawberry-rhubarb jam

**FILLING**

2 quarts ripe strawberries, stems hulled. 5 berries cut in pieces, the rest left whole

¾ cup sugar

2 tablespoons cornstarch

Juice of ½ lemon

*If you ever find yourself in the idyllic town of Nemi, in the Roman hills, during the* sagra delle fragole *(strawberry festival) you will be tempted to fly home and make this glazed strawberry tart. Nemi is known for its* fragoline di bosco *or wild strawberries that are small and indescribably delicious! The best advice I can give is to make this wonderful tart in season when strawberries are at their tastiest best.*   **Makes one 9 x 1-inch tart**

Preheat the oven to 425°F.

Whirl the almonds in a food processor until they are a fine consistency but leave a little texture.

Add the flour, salt, almond powder, sugar, and zest to the bowl of the processor and whirl until blended.

Add the butter and pulse several times; add the whole egg and egg yolk gradually through the feed tube until a ball of dough begins to form. Add the almond extract.

Gather up the dough, pat it into a disk, and wrap it tightly in plastic wrap. Refrigerate until cold but not hard, about 40 minutes.

Roll the dough out between two flour-dusted pieces of parchment paper to fit a 9 × 1-inch tart pan with a removable bottom. Trim off excess dough. Bake the tart shell for 8 to 10 minutes, or just until it begins to brown on the edges. Remove the shell from the oven and brush it with the jam. Set aside to cool completely.

When cool, arrange the whole berries in the shell to fill it completely. Set aside.

Place the cut-up berries in a small saucepan with 1 cup of water and bring to a boil. Lower the heat to medium and press on the berries with a wooden spoon to smash them. Strain them through a fine-mesh strainer set over a bowl. Set aside.

In the same saucepan, off the heat, combine the sugar and the cornstarch and mix well. Slowly add the strained juice and return the pan to the stovetop. Cook the mixture over medium heat until it begins to thicken.

Brush the berries with the glaze, making sure to coat each berry well and allow the excess glaze to drip down between the berries.

Refrigerate the tart for several hours. Cut into wedges and serve with a dollop of whipped cream.

# Upside-down Peach Tart

## Torta di Pesca Sottosopra

*This is a wonderful, moist, and easy-to-make tart from the Piedmont region of Italy. Crushed amaretti cookies give added flavor to both the batter and the crust.* **Makes one 9-inch round cake**

Preheat oven to 350°F. Butter a 9×2-inch deep round cake pan. Line the bottom with a circle of parchment paper cut to fit and butter the paper. Set aside.

To make the crust, in a food processor grind 8 amaretti cookies until they are crumbs and set aside. Add the remaining cookies to the food processor along with the sugar, almonds, and butter. Pulse until the nuts are finely ground. Press the mixture into the bottom of the prepared cake pan. Refrigerate for at least two hours.

To make the cake batter, sift the flour with the salt, baking power, and cinnamon into a bowl. Set aside.

In another bowl combine the ½ cup sugar and butter and beat well with a handheld mixer. Add the eggs, the dry ingredients, then the milk, orange zest, and extract one at a time, continuing to mix the batter well for 1 minute. Fold in the remaining amaretti cookie crumbs.

Arrange the peaches over the almond cookie crust in an overlapping design, leaving just a little space between the fruit and the sides of the pan. Pour the batter slowly over the peaches.

Bake the cake for 30 to 35 minutes, or until it begins to come away from the sides of the pan and is soft to the touch but golden in color.

Remove the cake from the oven and allow it to cool for 5 minutes. Unmold it onto a round serving platter. Carefully peel away and discard the parchment paper. Cut into wedges to serve.

This cake is best served warm with vanilla gelato or whipped cream.

### COOKIE CRUST

22 amaretti cookies

3 tablespoons sugar

½ cup sliced almonds

4 tablespoons (½ stick) unsalted butter, at room temperature

### CAKE

1½ cups unbleached all-purpose flour

¼ teaspoon salt

2 teaspoons baking powder

1 teaspoon ground cinnamon

¾ cup sugar

¼ cup (½ stick) unsalted butter, at room temperature

2 extra-large eggs

½ cup whole milk

Grated zest of 1 orange

1 tablespoon orange extract or liqueur

4 large peaches, blanched for 1 minute, peeled, pitted, and cut into ½-inch slices

# Pear and Pastry Cream Tart

## Torta di Pera con La Crema di Pasticerria

*Pears are a quintessential part of Italian desserts, and this recipe is a perfect example.*
***Makes one 9-inch tart; serves 6 to 8***

**DOUGH**

1½ cups unbleached all-purpose flour

½ teaspoon salt

⅓ cup sugar

6 tablespoons (¾ stick) frozen unsalted butter, cut into bits

1 large egg, slightly beaten

Ice water as needed

2 tablespoons orange marmalade

**PASTRY CREAM**

2 large egg yolks

⅔ cup sugar

Pinch of salt

2 tablespoons plus ½ teaspoon cornstarch

1 cup half-and-half

1 tablespoon vanilla extract

**TOPPING**

2 tablespoons unsalted butter, melted

2 to 3 large ripe Anjou, Bartlett, or Bosc pears, peeled,

To make the dough, combine the flour, salt, and sugar in a bowl or a food processor and mix or pulse the ingredients a couple of times.

Cut in the butter using a pastry blender, or if processing, pulse in the butter until it breaks up into small rice size bits. Do not overwork or the dough will be tough. Add the egg and pulse a couple of times. Add just enough water to form a ball of dough that starts to hold together.

Form the dough into a disk and wrap in plastic wrap. Refrigerate for 1 hour. Roll out the chilled dough between sheets of wax paper or parchment paper to a 10-inch diameter. Fit the dough into a 9 × 1-inch tart pan with a removable bottom. Trim the edges if necessary.

Cover the tart shell with plastic wrap and freeze for 30 minutes.

To make the filling, whisk the egg yolks in a small bowl until smooth.

In a medium saucepan off the heat, combine the sugar, salt, and cornstarch. Slowly whisk in the half-and-half.

Place the pan over medium heat and cook, whisking continuously, until the mixture begins to thicken, about 4 minutes. Transfer ½ cup of the mixture to the bowl with the egg yolks, whisking it in slowly to temper the eggs.

Return to the pan with the rest of the mixture and continue whisking over medium heat until thick. Remove the pan from the heat and stir in the vanilla extract.

Transfer the pastry cream to a bowl and place a buttered piece of plastic wrap directly on the surface of the pastry cream to prevent a skin from forming. Refrigerate the pastry cream at least a couple of hours or overnight.

Preheat the oven to 400°F.

To assemble the tart, using the tines of a fork, poke the tart shell here and there to prevent puffing when baking. Place a sheet of buttered aluminum foil over the tart shell and bake for 20 to 25 minutes.

Remove the foil and continue baking for about 5 minutes, or just until the tart shell is golden brown. Transfer the shell to a wire rack and brush the base of the tart with the marmalade. Cool completely.

Lower the oven temperature to 350°F.

Brush the melted butter on a baking sheet and add the pears in a single layer. Sprinkle the brown sugar over the pears and bake them for 5 to 8 minutes, or just until they take on a little color. Remove the pan from the oven and set aside.

Spread the pastry cream evenly over the base of the tart. Arrange the pear slices in a pleasing design over the top of the pastry cream.

Refrigerate the tart for at least 1 hour.

Whip the cream with the sugar until stiff. Fill a pastry bag with a star tip and pipe a border of whipped cream around the tart. To serve, using a sharp knife, cut the tart into wedges, place on individual plates, and scatter with the chocolate shavings.

cored, and cut into
¼-inch-thick slices

2 tablespoons coarse
brown sugar

1¼ cups heavy
whipping cream

3 tablespoons granu-
lated sugar

Dark chocolate
shavings

# Almond Paste Cookies

## Biscotti di Mandorle

1¾ cups whole shelled almonds

1½ cups granulated sugar

1½ tablespoons honey

1 teaspoon pure almond extract

4 large egg whites

1½ cups confectioners' sugar

*In my mother's notebooks are dozens of handwritten recipes for cookies of every variety. I love the notations alongside some of the recipes, such as a reminder to only use a certain baking product or a comment like "Dad liked these best and asked me to make some for his boss." With that comment, she was referring to this cookie, almond paste macaroons, which are dense and chewy.* **Makes one dozen**

Preheat the oven to 375°F.

Place the almonds and granulated sugar in a food processor and grind until the almonds are reduced to a powdery consistency. Transfer the mixture to a large bowl.

Stir in the honey and almond extract.

In a separate bowl, beat the egg whites with a fork just to break them up.

Pour half of the egg white mixture over the almond mixture and mix the ingredients with your hands until you have soft dough that holds together. If the dough seems dry, add a little bit more of the egg whites until the right consistency is obtained.

Sprinkle a work surface with half of the confectioners' sugar and, using your hands, roll the dough over the sugar into a log shape about 12 inches long.

Using a butter knife, lop off pieces of dough the size of a walnut shell and form each piece into a round ball. Place the balls about ½ inch apart on parchment paper–lined baking sheets.

Bake the cookies for 5 to 6 minutes. The cookies should not brown but remain pale with just a hint of browning around the edges. Do not overbake them; they will flatten as they bake.

Allow them to cool on the parchment paper; do not try to remove them immediately or they will crumble.

When cool, use a metal spatula to transfer them to a wire rack to cool.

# Little Hazelnut Cookies

## Biscottini di Nocciola

*These sweet little hazelnut cookies were one of the many that Mom made for the wedding cookie cake that graced the table when I got married. The texture is dry and biscuit-like and you will never be able to have just one.*  **Makes 2½ dozen cookies**

**P**reheat the oven to 350°F.

Line rimless baking sheets with parchment paper.

Cream the butter and sugar until light and fluffy. Beat in the flour, ground hazelnuts, and egg yolk until well combined.

Scoop out teaspoonfuls of the dough and shape with your hands to form small balls. Place them ½ inch apart on the lined baking sheets. Press a whole hazelnut into the center of each cookie.

Bake the cookies, one sheet at a time, for about 10 minutes, or until nicely browned.

Cool on the baking sheet for 5 minutes then transfer them to a wire rack to cool. Dust with confectioners' sugar.

**8 tablespoons (1 stick) unsalted butter, softened**

**¾ cup confectioners' sugar, sifted, plus extra for sprinkling on tops**

**1 cup unbleached all-purpose flour**

**¼ cup ground hazelnuts plus whole ones for inserting in cookie tops**

**1 egg yolk**

# Mom's Dried Cherry, Cranberry, and Pistachio Nut Shortbread Cookies

*Baking should not take all day. But quality should not be sacrificed, either. I think this crunchy, rich, and definitely addicting shortbread cookie from my mother's recipe box is a nice balance between time spent baking and delicious results.* **Makes about 4 dozen cookies**

1 cup shelled natural pistachio nuts

2¼ cups unbleached all-purpose flour

1 teaspoon salt

16 tablespoons (2 sticks) unsalted butter, at room temperature

⅔ cup sugar

2 teaspoons vanilla extract

½ cup dried cranberries

½ cup dried cherries

Preheat the oven to 350°F.

Line two baking sheets with parchment paper and set aside.

Spread the nuts on a baking sheet and toast them for about 5 minutes; watch closely so they do not burn. Cool the nuts, coarsely chop, and set aside.

In a medium bowl mix together the flour and salt and set aside.

In a stand mixer fitted with the paddle attachment, or with a handheld mixer, cream the butter and sugar until very smooth. Add the vanilla and beat for 1 minute. Add the cranberries, cherries, and nuts and combine on low speed. Slowly blend in the flour and salt.

Gather up the dough and transfer it to a large sheet of wax paper. Pat the dough into a rectangle roughly 4 inches wide and 18 inches long. Using the wax paper to help you, roll the dough into a log shape. Neaten the ends and place the wax paper-wrapped dough in the freezer for 10 minutes.

Lower the oven temperature to 325°F.

Remove the wax paper from the log and, using a sharp knife, slice the log into ¼-inch-thick rounds. (Or slice thicker rounds if you prefer.) Space the cookies about 1 inch apart on the lined baking sheets and bake for about 10 minutes. The cookies should not brown but remain pale with just a hint of browning around the edges.

Cool the cookies on wire racks and grab a cup of coffee, tea, or cold milk and enjoy this treat from Mom.

**TIP:** *Cookies like shortbread can be made ahead and frozen if well wrapped and sealed in tins, plastic containers, or plastic bags.*

# Little Orange-scented Madeleines

## Madeleinette Fior di Arancio

### GLAZE

1 cup confectioners' sugar

2 tablespoons orange, lemon, or lime juice

### BATTER

1¾ cups unbleached all-purpose flour

5 large eggs, separated

1 cup granulated sugar

1 tablespoon orange liqueur

10 tablespoons (1 stick plus 2 tablespoons) unsalted butter, melted and cooled

2 tablespoons grated orange zest

*Madeleines, those tender, dainty tea cakes shaped like a scallop shell, are said to be French in origin; after all they do have a French name. But they are also popular in places like Como and Torino so I snuck them in here. To make them you need a madeleine pan or two, found in cake making supply shops or online in bakeware catalogs.*
**Makes 4 dozen small madeleines**

butter and flour 2 madeleine molds and set aside or use a butter nonstick cooking spray.

Preheat the oven to 350°F.

Whisk together the confectioners' sugar and juice in a medium bowl until smooth. Cover and set aside.

Sift the flour into a bowl.

In another bowl, beat the egg yolks with the granulated sugar and orange liqueur until smooth; slowly beat in the butter and zest. Add the the sifted flour, a little at a time, over the batter and fold in.

In a clean bowl with clean beaters, beat the whites until soft peaks form. Fold the egg whites into the egg yolk mixture.

Refrigerate the batter at least 1 hour to make it easier to work with.

Fill madeleine molds two-thirds full with the batter. Bake for 12 to 15 minutes, or until lightly browned.

Remove the madeleines from the mold and transfer them to wire racks to cool. Refill the molds with the remaining batter and bake as above.

Dip the tops of each madeleine in the glaze and set on wire racks to dry.

# Mom's Date Nut Bars

## Biscotti di Datteri alla Mamma

½ cup plus 1½ tablespoons unbleached all-purpose flour

½ teaspoon baking powder

¼ teaspoon salt

2 large eggs, at room temperature

½ cup granulated sugar

1 tablespoon vanilla extract

2 cups diced dates (about 10 ounces)

1 cup toasted, chopped walnuts

Confectioners' sugar

*No holiday visit to Mom's was ever complete without her sending me home with a box of her famous date nut bars. Of all her confections, this was the one that everyone craved.* **Makes 24 bars**

Preheat the oven to 350°F.

Butter a 10-inch square pan and dust with flour, or line the pan with aluminum foil and butter it. Set aside.

Sift ½ cup of the flour with the baking powder and salt into a bowl.

In another bowl, beat the eggs until they are foamy. Gradually add the sugar and vanilla, beating until well blended. Fold in the flour mixture.

In a small bowl, toss the dates and nuts with the remaining 1½ tablespoons of the flour. This method will prevent the dates and nuts from sinking to the bottom of the pan while baking. Fold the date mixture into the batter.

Spread the batter evenly in the pan. Bake 20 to 25 minutes, or until golden brown on top and firm to the touch. Cool completely in the pan on a wire rack.

Cut into squares and sprinkle the tops with confectioners' sugar.

**CHEF'S SECRET:** *These bars can be made ahead and frozen without the confectioners' sugar for up to 3 months. Use baking spray to coat your knife to make it easier to dice the dates. They won't stick to the blade.*

# Dried Apricot Bars

## Biscotti di Albicocche Secche

*Memories of my mother preparing her sweet-tart dried apricot filling and then sand-wiching it between a lemon-scented dough leads me to the kitchen to carry on the tradition. These can be made ahead and frozen before glazing them. A combination of dried fruits can be substituted for the apricots.*   **Makes 36 bars**

To make the dough, in the bowl of a food processor or in a mixing bowl, combine the flour, salt, and confectioners' sugar and pulse or mix together. Add the butter and pulse or blend in with a pastry blender until the mixture resembles coarse cornmeal. Add the egg yolks, water, and lemon zest and pulse or mix with your hands until the dough comes together. If the dough seems dry, add a little more water. Wrap the dough in plastic wrap and refrigerate it for 1 hour.

Meanwhile, make the filling. Put the apricots in a saucepan, and add water just to cover. Bring to a boil, reduce the heat, and simmer until the apricots are soft, about 20 minutes. Drain the apricots and place them in a food processor. Add the granulated sugar and puree until smooth. Scrape the puree into a bowl and set aside.

Preheat the oven to 350°F. Butter a 15 × 11 × 1-inch baking pan. Divide the dough in half. Place each half between two sheets of lightly floured parchment paper. Roll over the parchment paper so each piece of dough is a 15 × 11-inch rect-angle. Carefully remove the top sheet of parchment paper and discard. Flip the dough over onto the baking sheet, remove the second sheet of parchment paper and discard. Press the dough down to even the edges.

Spread the filling evenly over the dough.

Remove and discard the parchment paper from the second piece of dough and carefully flip it over the filling. Pull the second sheet of parchment paper away from the dough and discard. Be sure to seal the edges.

Bake for about 30 minutes, or until the crust is golden brown. Remove the pan to a wire rack to cool slightly.

To make the glaze, in a small bowl, mix the confectioners' sugar and orange juice together until smooth. With a rubber spatula, spread the glaze evenly over the slightly warm crust. Let dry completely, then cut into bars.

**DOUGH**

3½ cups unbleached all-purpose flour

¼ teaspoon salt

¾ cup confectioners' sugar

14 tablespoons (1¾ sticks) unsalted cold butter, cut into small pieces

2 large egg yolks

¼ cup cold water, or more as necessary

1 tablespoon grated lemon zest

**APRICOT FILLING**

1 pound dried California apricots

½ cup granulated sugar

**GLAZE**

1½ cups confection-ers' sugar

3 tablespoons fresh orange juice

# Fat Tuesday Puffs

## Frittelle di Martedi Grasso

Scant ½ cup corn-
starch

1 cup unbleached
all-purpose flour

1 tablespoon baking
powder

⅓ cup granulated
sugar

1 teaspoon ground
cinnamon

¼ teaspoon ground
cloves

1¼ cups water

4 tablespoons (½
stick) unsalted
butter, at room
temperature

¼ teaspoon salt

1 teaspoon vanilla
extract

6 large eggs

2 Golden Delicious
apples, cored,
peeled, finely
diced

⅔ cup raisins

4 to 6 cups canola or
sunflower oil for
frying

Confectioners' sugar
for coating

*These ethereal little puffs of sweet dough filled with raisins and apples are a typical Venetian carnival food eaten on Martedi Grasso (Fat Tuesday), but they are good anytime. The technique for making the dough is similar to that for cream puffs. I suggest you call in the family, your friends, and neighbors to enjoy these as they are made, because they are at their best when eaten warm.* **Makes 7 to 8 dozen puffs**

In a bowl, sift together the cornstarch, flour, and baking powder.

In a small bowl, mix together the granulated sugar, cinnamon, and cloves and set aside.

Bring the water, butter, and salt to a boil in a saucepan. Remove from heat and vigorously stir in flour mixture.

Place saucepan with the flour mixture back on the heat and stir until the batter comes away from the sides. Remove from the heat; add sugar-spice mixture and the vanilla.

Add the eggs one at a time and stir vigorously to combine after each addition. Or use a handheld mixer. Add the apples and raisins.

Heat the oil in a deep fryer or heavy-bottomed, deep pot to 375°F.

Drop the batter by tablespoonfuls into the oil and fry until golden brown. Remove the puffs with a slotted spoon and drain them on paper towels.

When cool enough to handle but still warm, transfer the puffs a few at a time to a bag with confectioners' sugar. Close the bag and shake gently to coat the puffs in sugar. Serve warm.

# Golden Puffs

## Sfinge d'Oro

*These incredibly light-tasting golden puffs of sweet confection are so delicious that it is hard to stop at just one. These are best eaten warm, and lose their crispiness as they cool. Nevertheless they are addicting.*   **Makes 3 to 3½ dozen puffs**

1 cup water

1 tablespoon shortening, such as Crisco

1 cup unbleached all-purpose flour

½ teaspoon baking powder

2 teaspoons brandy

4 large eggs

Canola oil for frying

½ cup warm honey

Sugar sprinkles

**P**our the water into a large saucepan, add the shortening, and bring to a boil. Transfer the water mixture from the stovetop to the bowl of a stand mixer. Beat in the flour on medium speed until the mixture is lukewarm. On low speed, mix in the baking powder and brandy. Beat in the eggs, one at a time.

Heat 4 cups of the oil to 375°F in a deep fryer or heavy-bottomed, deep pot.

Drop heaping tablespoonfuls of the dough into the hot oil and fry until golden brown. Transfer the puffs to a warm platter. Drizzle the honey over them and sprinkle with the sugar. These are best eaten warm.

**Variation:** Instead of drizzling with honey, combine 2 teaspoons of ground cinnamon with 1 cup of granulated sugar in a clean paper bag. Close the bag and shake to blend the ingredients; as you fry the puffs transfer them to the bag and shake to coat in the cinnamon-sugar mixture.

## Noted

Mom had a huge kitchen, in fact, she had two. The very neat upstairs kitchen, where we all ate and welcomed guests, and the downstairs kitchen where all the messy work took place, like canning tomatoes and fruits and plucking chicken feathers.

The upstairs kitchen was also the meeting place for all the little Italian ladies who lived in the neighborhood that came to visit my grandmother. I can still rattle off their names because they came so often. There was Rita, Niesta, Gracie, Mrs. Condello, Mrs. Tigani, Mrs. Belurgi, Santina, Regina, and Mrs. Massanti to name a few. They came in their flowered aprons for coffee and to gossip about the non-Italians in the neighborhood. They often brought cookies, breads, cakes, and even pasta that they had made, sticking true to their Italian roots. My mother kept composition notebooks and jotted down the ingredients for the goodies they brought. Those notebooks are now one of my prized possessions and I often use them when I want to authenticate a recipe. One of my favorites is Mom's sfinge d'oro, fried golden puffs of dough that were drizzled with honey and sugar. I am sure this is one of those recipes from the old country. Sfinge means spongy and, for the life of me, I cannot figure out why these fried puffs are so named. Maybe because they are soft like a sponge. It all gets very confusing, especially when there are so many regional dialects. Some are fried and some are fried and filled with a pastry cream. Some are savory instead of sweet, made with anchovies and black pepper. One thing that is constant about sfinge-zeppole is that they are usually made for St. Joseph's Day on March 19th.

When I open those notebooks, I see Mom's very neat handwriting and it makes me feel closer to her. And when I re-create the recipes as she has written them, I feel like I am doing my part to keep the legacy of those sweet little Italian ladies alive. When I pass these notebooks on, I will have made my own notations in the hopes that tradition will live on.

# Powdered Sugar Strips

## Cenci

Cenci, *crisp fried and sugared strips of dough, go by many names including* frappe, crostoli, bugie, *and* gigi. *They are a typical street food, and Nonna Galasso always made them for* Martedi Grasso, *Fat Tuesday, the day before the start of Lent. Try eating just one.*   **Makes 6½ to 7 dozen strips**

⅓ cup whole milk

¼ cup granulated sugar

2 tablespoons unsalted butter, melted and cooled

2 large eggs

2 tablespoons rum, orange liqueur, or brandy

Grated zest of 2 large oranges or lemons

½ teaspoon salt

2 to 2½ cups unbleached all-purpose flour.

6 cups canola oil for frying

⅓ cup confectioners' sugar

**I**n a bowl, whisk together the milk, granulated sugar, butter, eggs, rum, zest, and salt. Stir in 2 cups of the flour and then, using your hands, form a smooth ball, adding only as much additional flour as necessary to make a nice pliant dough. (Or you can make the dough in a food processor.) Place the dough in a bowl, cover it with plastic wrap, and allow it to rest for 1 hour in the refrigerator.

Divide the dough into four pieces. Working with one at a time, roll out each piece with a rolling pin into a rectangle no more than ⅛ inch thick. Using a pastry wheel, cut irregular-shaped pieces about 5 inches long and 2 inches wide. Make a 1-inch slit in the center of each piece but do not cut through to the ends. Place the pieces on clean kitchen towels until all the dough is used.

Alternatively, roll out the dough with a pasta machine. Flatten the dough slightly with a rolling pin, then lightly dust it with flour and thin it in the machine using the roller section. I use the highest number on my machine, which is 7, because I like my cenci thin, but adjust the machine for the thickness you prefer. Cut into strips as described above.

Heat 6 cups of vegetable oil to 375°F in a deep fryer or in a heavy-bottomed, deep pot. (Test the temperature of the oil with a candy thermometer if using a pot.) Fry the cenci, a few at a time, until golden brown. Drain them on paper towels.

While still warm, place the cenci in a clean paper bag with the confectioners' sugar. Close the top of the bag and shake gently to coat. Enjoy!

## Festigiamo!

It would be hard to compete with the Italians when they throw a party. And nothing says party like carnevale, carnival. Now when we think of a carnival, the usual images of ferris wheels, cotton candy, and hordes of people eating sausage and pepper hoagies comes to mind. And these exist in Italy, too, but I'm talking about carnival as it exists in Venice, just before the beginning of the austere and dreaded fasting days of Lent. The word carnival means "meat go away," coming from the word carne (meat) and andare, to go. It seems appropriate considering that Lent is a fast period when meat cannot be eaten on Ash Wednesday, Fridays, and Good Friday.

Venice at any time of the year is one big party with its Grand Canal and palatial palazzii that seem to float on water and are viewed by fashionable beautiful people. Whenever I am there, I try to think how grand things must have been during its heyday of the Serenissima, which lasted over a thousand years until the end of the eighteenth century when the Republic went into decline.

One of my favorite things to do in Venice is to visit the many mask makers and costume shops in the campi (neighborhoods). Sometimes I just go in to look but one year, while strolling through the mask shops in Dorsoduro, I rented an entire outfit for a grand masked ball (un ballo in maschera) that I was invited to. I chose a crimson velvet floor-length robe, a crimson-plumed hat, and a traditional eighteenth century mask called a bauta, which was worn not only for carnevale but as an everyday accessory when you wanted to be incognito so that no one could guess your social status and it would let you be free to interact with others with no strings attached.

The ball was held in the splendid Palazzo Pisani Moretta and as we arrived by vaporetto, the palazzo looked spectacular, entirely lit by candlelight, and we could see strolling musicians in period costumes waiting for us inside. Masked waiters steered silver trays full of gorgeous Venetian glasses filled with Prosecco towards us. Suddenly, I was not me anymore, I was Venetian, a lady of high society who was escorted into the gold ballroom and seated on a red velvet chair at a round table for ten.

Everyone was in splendid costumes and masks; some very elaborate ones made me thank my lucky stars that I chose the half-face bauta mask which left my mouth area free; how some of these guests were going to eat dinner with full face masks eluded me.

We started with spinach tagliatellini with chunks of sole in a light sauce. Next came salmon with insalata russa (Russian salad). Then roasted quail with asparagus and mushrooms appeared. Tiramisù ended the meal, all the courses accompanied by the proper wines.

Dancing in the palazzo was done to period music, and I watched as accomplished professionals showed the rest of us the proper steps before we joined in. At the stroke of midnight, our vaporetti arrived to whisk us back to our hotels—like Cinderella, the ball, the costumes, the life of a high society Venetian in the eighteenth century was just a memory, but one for a lifetime.

# Nonna Saporito's Cannoli

## Cannoli alla Nonna Saporito

*The queen of all Sicilian desserts is definitely cannoli. Cannoli probably originally came from the Arabs, who influenced so much of Sicily's cooking. These crisp, flaky pastry dough cylinders are filled with sweetened sheep's milk ricotta cheese, nuts, citron, and bits of chocolate. I cherish Nonna Saporito's old recipe that originally called for sheep's milk ricotta cheese for the filling but when she came to America, it was impossible to find, so whole cow's milk ricotta was substituted instead. Whenever I make these, I use her old and very worn wooden forms, fashioned from a broom handle, but stainless steel forms are available in kitchenware stores.* **Makes 14 to 18 cannoli**

**t**o make the filling, whip the cheese in a bowl until smooth. Stir in the granulated sugar, cinnamon, and chocolate. Refrigerate, covered with plastic wrap, until ready to fill the cannoli shells.

To make the dough, place the flour in a bowl or food processor. Add the butter or lard and sugar and mix with a fork, or pulse, until the mixture resembles coarse meal. Slowly add the ¼ cup of wine and shape the mixture into a ball; add a little more wine if the dough appears too dry. It should be soft but not sticky. Knead the dough on a floured work surface until smooth, about 10 minutes. Wrap the dough in plastic wrap and refrigerate for 45 minutes.

Place the chilled dough on a floured work surface. Divide the dough in half. Work with 1 piece of dough at a time; keep the remaining dough refrigerated. Using a rolling pin or pasta machine set to the finest setting, roll the dough out to a very thin long rectangle about 14 inches long and 3 inches wide. Cut the dough into 3-inch squares. Place a cannoli form diagonally across one square. Roll the dough up around the form so the points meet in the center. Seal the points with a little water. Continue making cylinders until all the dough is used.

In an electric skillet (see Note), heat the vegetable oil to 375°F.

Fry the cannoli three or four at a time, turning them as they brown and blister, until golden brown on all sides. Drain them on brown paper or paper towels. When they are cool enough to handle, carefully slide the cannoli off the forms.

## FILLING

- 1½ cups whole-milk ricotta cheese, well drained
- 3 tablespoons granulated sugar
- 1½ teaspoons ground cinnamon
- 1½ cups coarsely chopped milk chocolate (4 to 5 small bars)
- ¼ cup pistachio nuts, coarsely chopped

## DOUGH

- 1 cup unbleached all-purpose flour
- 1 tablespoon unsalted butter or lard
- 1 tablespoon granulated sugar
- 4 to 5 tablespoons dry Marsala wine
- 2 cups vegetable oil
- Colored sprinkles
- Confectioners' sugar for sprinkling

To serve, use a long iced tea spoon or a pastry bag without a tip to fill the cannoli with the ricotta cheese mixture. Dip the ends into colored sprinkles, arrange them on a tray, and sprinkle confectioners' sugar over the tops. Serve at once.

**NOTE:** *If you prefer, you can fry the cannoli in a deep fryer. Be sure to fill the cannoli just before serving—any sooner will result in soggy shells.*

# Pugliesi Sweet Ravioli

## Calzoncelli di Ricotta

*I don't know how many versions of* calzoncelli *there were in the old neighborhood where I grew up, but these sweet ravioli from Puglia were my favorite. The best way to make them is to invest in a metal ravioli form that makes a dozen at a time.*  **Makes 7 to 8 dozen sweet ravioli**

**t**o make the dough, in a large bowl, mix together the granulated sugar, oil, egg yolks, and wine. Add just enough flour to make a soft but not sticky dough. Cover the dough with a clean kitchen towel and let it rest 30 minutes.

To make the filling mix all the filling ingredients together in another bowl and set aside.

Divide the dough into quarters. Working with one quarter at a time, roll each piece into a 5-inch-wide × 12-inch-long strip and place it over a ravioli form. Use the top of the form to make slight depressions in the dough. Fill each depression with 1 teaspoon of the filling; top with a second strip of dough and roll over it with a rolling pin to seal the edges. If the ravioli are not sealed well, they will come apart when fried. Shake out the ravioli and place them on clean kitchen towels in single layers.

Gather up the leftover strips of dough and re-roll to make more ravioli until all the filling has been used.

Heat the oil to 375°F in a deep fryer or heavy-bottomed, deep pot.

Fry the calzoncelli, a few at a time, until golden brown. Drain on paper towels. Sprinkle with confectioners' sugar while still warm. These are best eaten on the spot!

**DOUGH**

¼ cup granulated sugar

3 tablespoons extra-virgin olive oil

2 large egg yolks

¼ cup white wine

3 cups unbleached all-purpose flour

**FILLING**

One 15-ounce container whole-milk ricotta cheese, well drained

¾ cup granulated sugar

Zest of 1 large lemon

1 teaspoon ground cinnamon

Canola oil for frying

Confectioners' sugar for sprinkling

## Pizzelle alla Nonna Saporito

½ teaspoon anise seeds

⅓ cup heavy cream

1 cup plus 1 tablespoon unbleached all-purpose flour

¼ teaspoon salt

½ cup sugar

⅓ cup whole milk

1 large egg

½ teaspoon anise extract (or 1 tablespoon vanilla extract)

2½ tablespoons melted unsalted butter

*One of my most-treasured baking implements handed down by Nonna Saporito is her pizzelle iron. Pizzelle are thin wafer cookies that are popular at festivals. Each pizzelle is imprinted as it bakes with a design etched into the middle of the iron plate. I use Nonna's iron very infrequently because of the time involved but every once in a while I drag it out and make them using her recipe that I have tweaked just a bit by toasting the anise seeds for more depth of flavor. If you don't like the flavor of anise, use vanilla, rum, or almond extract. This recipe will work for any type of pizzelle maker.* **Makes 18 to 20 pizzelle**

Place the anise seeds in a small frying pan and toast them until fragrant. Watch carefully so they do not burn. Cool and transfer the seeds to a spice grinder and grind them to a powder or crush them by hand using a meat pounder or a can.

Combine all the ingredients in a large bowl and beat with a handheld mixer until smooth. Cover and refrigerate the mixture for 1 hour.

Preheat a pizzelle maker according to manufacturer's directions and when ready, spray with a nonstick, butter flavored cooking spray.

Place a heaping tablespoon of the batter in the center of each form. Close the top of the pizzelle maker and squeeze the handles for about 30 to 40 seconds. The pizzelles should be golden brown, not dark brown.

Using the edge of a small knife, carefully lift and peel each one out and place on a wire rack to cool and harden.

Repeat with the remaining batter, spraying the form occasionally if the batter starts to stick.

Cool the pizzelles completely before storing. Store in airtight tins or freeze in plastic containers for up to 3 months.

# Chocolate-Dipped Figs

## Fichi al Cioccolato

*Here is a classy dessert that you can make in no time, and it will fill that need to have something sweet and unusual.* **Makes 20 dipped figs**

**P**lace the figs in a glass bowl and pour the rum or orange liqueur over them. Cover with plastic wrap and let them soak overnight in the refrigerator.

The following day, drain the figs well and pat them dry.

Fill the bottom of a double boiler with water and bring to a simmer. Turn off the heat. Place the chocolate in the top of the double boiler and allow it to melt. Stir in the butter until the mixture is smooth and creamy.

Hold the stems of each fig and swirl them in the chocolate several times to completely coat them. Transfer them to a wire rack placed over a baking sheet to catch drips.

Chill the figs in the refrigerator until ready to serve, then bring them to room temperature.

**20 whole dried Calimyrna figs**

**2/3 cup rum or orange liqueur**

**2/3 pound (about 11 ounces) semisweet chocolate, chopped**

**4 tablespoons (1/2 stick) unsalted butter**

# acknowledgments

So many people had to put their faith in me when I began this book, and even though I have now written twelve cookbooks, it is always a brand-new adventure on a frequently traveled path. So I offer my most sincere thanks to my dear husband and best friend, Guy, who I can always count on to plant the many varieties of Italian vegetables that I will need to cook and write about and that are showcased on *Ciao Italia*. You have always being willing to listen and offer suggestions, and you are my number-one enthusiastic taste-tester. To Jane Dystel, one of the most passionate, caring literary agents that I am privileged to know. You are a stickler for excellence. Thank you for challenging and believing in me, for including me in your client list, and for your boundless energy and guidance in leading me in new directions. To my editor, Kathy Huck, for embracing me as one of your authors. It has been a pleasure to work with you. Thank you for your professionalism and patience. To creative directors Steve Snider and Michael Storrings, many thanks for all your thoughtful, gifted help in guiding the final look and presence of the book. To photographer Ben Fink, for the cover photo, thank you for letting me have fun! To associate publisher Matthew Baldacci, senior publicist Nadea Mina, and associate marketing manager Monica Katz, for your enthusiasm in promoting the book. To copyeditor Leah Stewart, for helping me put the manuscript in good order. Many thanks to book designer Kathryn Parise, for the refreshing layout. Kudos to John Hession, for the gorgeous food photography, and to food stylist Catrine Kelty, for showing off the recipes in clever and delicious-looking ways. Thank you to *Ciao Italia* PBS underwriters, King Arthur Flour and marketing director Tom Payne, and president Michael Bittel for always believing in the mission of *Ciao Italia*. To ACH Food Companies Inc. and Keith Dierberg, thank you for your support of the series, and to Lars Leight of Banfi Wines, for your continued support. To Rhode Island Public television and CEO David Piccerelli, for allowing us to film *Ciao Italia* in your studios. To Paul Lally, executive producer of the series, for your love, loyalty, and commitment to all things *Ciao Italia*. To Paolo Russo, for making possible our filming in Romagna. To The Dover Strategy Group, for tirelessly promoting my books through the Web site www.ciaoitalia.com, our blog, Facebook, *Huffington Post,* and in the press. To Anichini, for the loan of beautiful Italian linens for the photo shoot. Thank you to